Kenneth Rexroth
and James Laughlin

Kenneth Rexroth

AND

James Laughlin

/·/

SELECTED LETTERS

EDITED BY LEE BARTLETT

W · W · NORTON & COMPANY

NEW YORK   LONDON

Passages from *Excerpts from a Life* (Santa Barbara, Calif.: Conjunctions, 1981) reprinted with kind permission of Bradford Morrow, Literary Executor for the Kenneth Rexroth Trust.

Printed in the United States of America.

The text of this book is composed in
11.5/13 Bembo (Linotron 202),
with the display set in ITC Garamond Book Condensed.
Composition manufacturing by The Maple-Vail Book
Manufacturing Group.
Ornament by Deborah Pease.

First Edition

Library of Congress Cataloging-in-Publication Data

Rexroth, Kenneth, 1905–1982
[Correspondence. Selections]
Kenneth Rexroth and James Laughlin :
selected letters /
edited by Lee Bartlett.
p.   cm.
Includes bibliographical references (p.   ) and index.
1. Rexroth, Kenneth, 1905–1982—Correspondence.   2. Laughlin,
James, 1914–   —Correspondence.   3. Poets, American—20th century—
Correspondence.   4. Publishers and publishing—United States—
Correspondence.   5. Authors and publishers—United States—
History—20th century.   I. Bartlett, Lee, 1950–   .   II. Laughlin,
James, 1914–   Correspondence.   Selections.   1991.   III. Title.
PS3535.E923Z487   1991
811'.52—dc20
[B]   90–7443
ISBN 0-393-02939-5

W. W. Norton & Company, Inc.
500 Fifth Avenue, New York, N.Y. 10110
W. W. Norton & Company, Ltd.
10 Coptic Street, London WC1A 1PU

1 2 3 4 5 6 7 8 9 0

FOR BRADFORD MORROW

Why in the hell don't you write novels?
Your letters are a damn sight better than
Waugh and Huxley. Hell, just put it
down like it comes and get rich. You could
be the Stendhal of yr day. Hell yes!
　　　　　　　—JL to KR, January 1958

CONTENTS

INTRODUCTION

James Wright wrote of Kenneth Rexroth that he was "a great love poet during the most loveless of times," and indeed over forty years Rexroth wrote some of the most moving and durable American verse of our century. Yet there is more. After the appearance of his first volume of poetry in 1940, Rexroth published not only an additional nineteen collections of poems, but also scores of lively essays and reviews (many collected in his seven books of shorter prose), a study of modern American poetry and a history of communalism, an "autobiographical novel," a dozen books of translations from the Greek, Latin, Chinese, Japanese, and French, and a book of plays. In addition, he edited seminal collections of poetry by both D. H. Lawrence and young British poets, as well as books by O. V. de L.-Milosz, David Meltzer, and Kazuko Shiraishi. The great majority of these volumes were published by New Directions.

In his *An Autobiographical Novel,* Rexroth explains that there he has given us "a fairly straight-forward factual narrative" of the first twenty-one years of his life, the "tale of a boy's efforts to select and put in order the tools with which he would live his adulthood." (James Laughlin, his friend and publisher, describes the book as "only about half true," however; "as with the autobiographies of Ford Madox Ford, it ain't necessarily all so.") These tools included a quick intelligence and a facility with languages, a respect for his "caste responsibility" for the Populist tradition (with an intense early interest in Debsian socialism and various other progressive movements), and a truly impressive literacy ("an omnivorous appetite for reading things in sets and subjects," including the *oeuvres* of novelists such as James, Dostoevsky, Conrad, London, works by Spencer, Lyell, Darwin, Chekhov, Mendel, Faraday, and books by myriad other scientists, philosophers, archeologists, and poets), all nurtured during a rather idyllic childhood by highly literate and politically aware parents. Shortly after Rexroth's death in 1982, Laughlin would recall:

Kenneth was a marvellous man. He had Pound's extraordinary vitality, his love of books, had done an incredible amount of reading. He had a photographic memory. I remember seeing him in his San Francisco apartment lying in the bathtub after lunch for a couple of hours with a reading board across the tub, reading one of his light-reading favorites, Joseph Needham's *History of Chinese Science and Medicine*. The pages would turn almost without a pause; everything would go into his computer.[1]

Rexroth was born on December 22, 1905, in South Bend, Indiana. His ancestors were a ragtag crew, "German revolutionaries of '48, Abolitionists, suffragists, squaws and Indian traders, octoroons and itinerant horse dealers, farmers in broad hats, full beards, and frogged coats, hard-drinking small town speculators."[2] His father was the pharmacist son of a Socialist plumber, and the friend of James Whitcomb Riley, Eugene Field, and Theodore Dreiser; his mother (whose own father had known Eugene Debs) attended college for a time, attempted a career in business before her marriage, and was an "extreme feminist." Rexroth's early years were spent in Elkhart, Indiana, where he was raised with an emphasis on self-discovery and self-awareness rather than learning by rote. His mother functioned as his teacher in a "one-teacher, one-student school-room with blackboard, desk, pictures, bookshelves, and cases of what are now called educational toys," and in the evenings she continued his education with long tales from Greek myth and the world's folklore. On weekends and holidays, Rexroth went on fishing and camping trips with his father to Michigan, Wisconsin, and Canada. He recalled that "the period just before the First War witnessed the last flowering of Western European family structure,"[3] and for him his childhood seems to have been certainly a golden age.

However, in 1912 Rexroth's mother contracted tuberculosis. The family took a brief tour through Europe, then on their return they moved to Michigan. There Rexroth's father, depressed over sudden failure in a new business and worried about his wife's condition, began drinking heavily. The family moved again in 1915, this time to Chicago, where Rexroth enhanced his education by "listening to the birth of jazz at the Clef Club or Schiler's café, or wandering wide-eyed through the Armory Show behind" his "gesticulating parents." But his mother's health worsened, and she died less than a year later; by 1918, Rexroth's father's alcoholism had destroyed him, and after his death Rexroth was sent by his paternal grandmother to live with an aunt on the South Side of Chicago.

There he decided to become a writer and artist, and for a time attended the Chicago Art Institute. Soon, however, this formal education gave way to the "Washington Park Bug Club." Here until midnight could be heard passionate exponents of every variety of human lunacy. There were Anarchist-Single-Taxers, British-Israelites, self-anointed archbishops of the American Catholic Church, Druids, Anthroposophists, and geologists who had proven the world was flat or that the surface of the earth was inside of a hollow sphere. . . . Besides, struggling for a hearing was the whole body of orthodox heterodoxy—Socialists, communists (still with a small "c"), IWWs, De Leonites, Single-Taxers.[4]

According to *An Autobiographical Novel,* during these years he read widely; he hung out with musicians; he worked at many different jobs, and began to paint; for a time he was involved with the Wobblies.

Eventually, he began traveling around the United States, hitchhiking, then in 1926 worked his way to Europe and back on a ship. After sampling Buenos Aires, Mexico City, and Oaxaca, Rexroth returned to Chicago and a few months later married Andrée Dutcher. Following a honeymoon in Seattle, the couple settled in San Francisco. "One provincial culture is much like another, and San Francisco, in those days, was better than most. . . . It is the only city in the United States which was not settled overland by the westward-spreading puritan tradition, or by the Walter Scott, fake-cavalier tradition of the South. It had been settled, mostly, in spite of all the romances of the overland migration, by gamblers, prostitutes, rascals and fortune seekers who came across the Isthmus and around the Horn. They had their faults, but they were not influenced by Cotton Mather." Rexroth would remain on the West Coast for the rest of his life, as "it was pretty apparent that we had found the ideal environment for ourselves. . . . We decided to stay and grow up with the town."[5]

During the thirties Rexroth wrote, painted, and

worked intensely in Leftist politics. He served as the primary organizer for the San Francisco John Reed Club, for example, wrote for the labor newspaper *Waterfront Worker,* and helped found *Partisan Review* and *Anvil.* His first book, *In What Hour,* appeared in 1940, and in the same year Andrée (who suffered from epilepsy) died. The following year he married Marie Cass, a nurse, and during the war the poet, who had registered as a conscientious objector, worked as an orderly in a psychiatric ward. In the late forties, Rexroth became the "presiding figure" of the first San Francisco Renaissance, championing the work of younger West Coast writers such as William Everson and Robert Duncan. Further, he was a primary force in the founding of an anarchist group called the "Libertarian Circle"; as he recalled in *Excerpts from a Life:*

We had the largest meetings of any radical or pseudo-radical group in San Francisco. The place was always crowded and when the topic was sex and anarchy you couldn't get in the doors. People were standing on one another's shoulders. . . . There was no aspect of Anarchist history or theory that was not presented by a qualified person and then thrown open to spontaneous discussion. . . . Our objective was to refound the radical movement after its destruction by the Bolsheviks and to rethink all the basic principles, i.e., in other words to subject to searching criticism all the ideologists from Marx to Malatesta. In addition to meetings of the Libertarian Circle, we had weekly poetry readings. At the dances we always had the best local jazz groups. . . . This was the foundation of the San Francisco Renaissance and of the specifically San Francisco intellectual climate which was about as unlike that of New York as could be conceived.[6]

In 1948, Rexroth and Marie divorced, and following his travel through Europe on a Guggenheim Fellowship he married Marthe Larsen. The fifties saw the birth of two daughters, Mary and Katherine, and the publication of scores of books, articles, reviews, and poems. Rexroth remained fairly active politically, but most of his public energies went into supporting the burgeoning San Francisco literary scene, and his Potrero Hill house became a center for literary activity. He had a weekly literary program on KPFA, co-founded the San Francisco Poetry Center (with Ruth Witt-Diamant, Robert Duncan, and Madeline Gleason), and continued to suppport the work of not only Duncan and Everson, but Gary Snyder, Allen Ginsberg, Lawrence Ferlinghetti, and many others, helping them with readings and avenues of publication. As William Everson recalled of this period, Rexroth "touched the nerve of the future and more than any other voice in the movement called it into being. Though others picked up his mantle and received the plaudits, it remains true that today we enjoy the freedom of expression and lifestyle we actually possess largely because he convinced us that it was not only desirable but possible, and inspired us to make it be."[7]

In 1961 Marthe and Rexroth divorced, and in 1966 he married Carol Tinker; the couple moved to Montecito, near Santa Barbara, where the poet lived until his death. During the sixties and seventies he won numerous awards for his work, including a grant from the National Academy of Arts and Letters, the William Carlos Williams Award from *Contact* magazine, Rockefeller and Akademische Austauschdienst awards. He taught first at San Francisco State College, then beginning in 1968 at the University of California at Santa Barbara. At his death in June 1982 at the age of seventy-six, the poet had published over fifty books of poetry, essays, translations, plays, and anthologies, and was at work on the second volume of his autobiography.

Writing an assessment a few months later, Eliot
Weinberger argued that "Rexroth at his death was
among the best known and least read of American
poets. It is a sad distinction he shares, not coinciden-
tally, with the poet he most resembles, Hugh
MacDiarmid. . . . Nevertheless, there is no question
that American literary history will have to be rewrit-
ten to accommodate Rexroth, that postwar American poetry is the 'Rexroth Era' as much (and as little)
as the earlier decades are the 'Pound Era.' "[8]

"For over a generation," Rexroth wrote in his
American Poetry in the Twentieth Century, "modern
literature has owed more to James Laughlin, publisher of New Directions, than to any other single
person. All through the years when the avant-garde
was not supposed to exist, he went bravely on, publishing them—everybody—from all languages—for
many years at considerable financial loss. This is the
kind of patronage that counts. It meant nothing for
Otto Kahn to give Hart Crane a check for $1000.
Laughlin worked day after day, often till far into the
night, himself, and hard, to publish writers who often
were far less good than himself, year after year, for
little thanks. He is an excellent and original poet,
and might have been writing his own poems. If he
lived in a civilized country his chest would be covered with medals and his wall with honorary doc-
torates."[9]
Laughlin was born in 1914, making him nine years
Rexroth's junior, though as is apparent in the correspondence they considered themselves contemporaries. While attending Choate in the early 1930s, he
studied under Dudley Fitts, who introduced him to
the work of such modern and as yet uncanonized
writers as Ezra Pound, T. S. Eliot, and Gertrude
Stein. Following a year at Harvard (where Laughlin

worked on the *Harvard Advocate*), Fitts arranged for him to go to Rapallo, Italy, to study with Pound at his "Ezuversity." According to Laughlin, this was "a marvellous educational institution where there were no tuition fees whatever and you were allowed to play tennis or go swimming with the professor if the weather was good. I was in this glorious institution, off and on, for about half a year. Classes took place mostly at meals or at tea time, or when we were walking in the hills. The class was simply Pound's continuous and fascinating monologue."[10]

Laughlin spent part of his time with Pound trying to write poems, producing work which the older poet found lacking. When it came time for Laughlin to return to the United States, he and his mentor "had a serious discussion about what they now call career planning." Pound bluntly told the young man that he would never make it as a writer. He felt that because Laughlin "wasn't smart enough" to get away with "assassernating" Henry Seidel Canby, editor of *The Saturday Review,* he should become a publisher. According to Laughlin,

I thought to myself that if I couldn't be a writer, maybe as a publisher I could hang around with writers and have a good time, so it was agreed that I would become a publisher. I asked him how I'd find writers and he said, "Don't worry, I'll take care of that. I have lots of friends who don't have publishers. . . ." So I went back to Harvard, which made my family very proud of me; they supported the publishing venture, and in fact kept it up for 25 years because for the first 25 years I never made any money.[11]

And Pound arranged for his friends (including William Carlos Williams, e.e. cummings, Marianne Moore, and Louis Zukofsky) to contribute work to help get New Directions (which Pound liked to call "Nude Erections") off the ground.

While the surviving correspondence between Rexroth and Laughlin begins with the first letter collected here, dated June 15, 1937, in fact the two men both corresponded and eventually met much earlier in the decade. According to Rexroth, "In the early thirties Ezra Pound wrote me a letter and said that Gorham Munson was starting what Westbrook Pegler called a 'butcher paper magazine' with a Social Credit bias. The literary editor was a brilliant young Harvard student, a graduate of one of the most fashionable prep schools in the country. I was very skeptical about this, but I sent them some poems, which they published, and I got some very nice letters from James Laughlin IV." The following year, 1933, Rexroth continues,

we were living on Westmoreland Street, on Potrero Hill, and the doorbell rang and a man who looked like he was six foot twelve in height was standing in the doorway with a shy look on his face. I said, "Gee, you must be Jim Laughlin. Come on in." So he came in, and I said, "Where are you staying?" And he said, "The Fairmont." I told him he could stay with us. So he stayed at our house and many, many, many years later he told me very wistfully, while we were talking about Western ways, "do you know you were the first person to spontaneously call me 'Jim'?" He stayed with us and I showed him San Francisco.[12]

For the next fifty years the two would develop a very close friendship which was far more personal than the usual author-publisher relationship. Rexroth and Laughlin shared a common passion, for instance, for getting away from the city into the backcountry, and through the years they would take many backpacking trips together into the Sierras. Laughlin was an extremely proficient skier, an activity Rexroth enjoyed, and, as Rexroth remembered, "he would drop in almost every year and we'd go up in the mountains together. Of course, I spent the summertime in the mountains anyway, so I knew good places to go, easy places to get to for basecamps and good ski slopes."[13] According to Laughlin, Rexroth "was a great outdoorsman and a fine rockclimber, even if he did not always keep the rope on me taut and I had a few bad moments. He taught me all that I know about climbing."[14] Further, while Rexroth suggested a number of new writers to Laughlin (including Christopher Isherwood, William Everson, Gary Snyder, and Denise Levertov), for his part Laughlin kept Rexroth's books in print even when sales were very slow and often helped him out of financial difficulties.

Of course, as these letters indicate, this friendship was hardly without a certain ongoing tension. Like Pound, Rexroth was paradoxically both a very generous and an extremely difficult individual. As William Everson suggested two years before Rexroth's death, "His faults are the excesses of his virtues, and he quarrels with his friends as readily as he clobbers his enemies,"[15] and certainly he had serious fallings out with any number of younger writers he supported, including Everson, Robert Duncan, and Allen Ginsberg. The pattern with Laughlin seemed to be fairly predictable—Rexroth would flood New Directions with manuscripts (his own and others), suggestions for anthologies and translations, ideas for the *New Directions* annuals, and schemes for new publishing ventures. Laughlin would be traveling, or working on other projects, and very soon Rexroth would lose patience and rail. Further, especially during the late forties and fifties, Rexroth became extremely defensive of his status as a westerner, and repeatedly chided Laughlin for his relationship with such writers as Delmore Schwartz. (In 1981, Rexroth would tell Bradford Morrow, "The establishment has always been symbolized to me by the image of

Mary McCarthy holding a flaming copy of *The Partisan Review* in the middle of New York harbor.")[16] Upon not finding his name in the advertising for Laughlin's New Directions retrospective anthology *Spearhead,* for example, Rexroth stormed in a letter of June 11, 1948 (letter 49):

I am certainly as important as nincompoops like John Berryman and Randall Jarrell. The trouble is—you are ashamed of me. Why dont you mention Goodman and Patchen as well? The readers of *Retort* are certainly not interested in has-beens of *Paris America* or in the storm-troopers of the *P[artisan]* & *K[enyon] Review*. I have mentioned this to you before. I have had about enough. In fact I am perfectly sore. You are completely under the domination of the NYC cocktail academic set.

Generally, Laughlin would let these attacks go without comment, though on occasion he too would lose his temper: "You act like a child with your thousand confused suggestions . . . I don't know whether to consider you my best friend any longer, or whether to think of you as another of the many who tried to get a ride on the gravy train" (letter 45, March 8, 1948). Still, these storms were somehow weathered for five decades.

Laughlin's preface to *New Directions* 15 (1955) articulated the publisher's agenda. "The theory was simply this":

Literature, a whole culture in fact, goes dead when there is no experiment, no reaching out, no counter-attack on accepted values. Even if the experiment is a failure, it must exist as a force and be given a showing place. And not completely to satisfy anybody was also intentional. There was to be no one cult and no one canon. From the first, space was saved for writers whose work the editor personally did not like but which was vouched for by people whose judgement he respected. . . . Schwartz and Patchen, whose adherents generally despise each other's taste, are

side by side; the diffuse Henry Miller keeps company with
the strict John Berryman, and Tennessee Williams makes
his poetry out of the emotions, while John Wheelwright
made his out of the mind.[17]

Thus, while New Directions authors range from the
avant-garde to the more measured, generally Laughlin
has looked for work which "makes the bell ring."
Working for Gertrude Stein "one summer when I
was young," he remembers, "and she talked about
good books making 'the bell ring.' I listen for the
bell when I start on a manuscript from a new
writer."[18]

Obviously, Rexroth was one of New Directions'
authors who made the bell ring most loudly for
Laughlin. Through the years, his poetry especially
offered a kind of microcosm for the breadth of New
Directions writing, ranging from the severe inno-
vation of "A Prolegomenon to a Theodicy" to such
neo-romantic and elegiac work as the shorter lyrics
collected in *The Signature of All Things*. Save for his
first book, *In What Hour* (published by Macmillan in
1940) and *The Art of Worldly Wisdom* (published by
Decker in 1949), Laughlin published all of Rexroth's
major collections of poetry, as well as many of his
prose books, volumes of translations, and editions.
Rexroth's work appeared more frequently than almost
any other writer in the *New Directions* annuals. As
the poet summed up to Bradford Morrow in 1981,
"I wouldn't have had a career without Laughlin, and
I look on Laughlin as, I suppose, my best friend, and
always a good comrade. I have always thought of
him not as a person to whom I was related literally,
but to whom I was related personally. I just write
him abusive letters about literature," he concluded,
grinning, "saying why does he publish such shit in
New Directions."[19]

NOTES

1. James Laughlin, "For the Record: On New Directions and Others," *American Poetry*, 1,3 (Spring 1984), 56.

2. Kenneth Rexroth, *An Autobiographical Novel* (Garden City, N.Y.: Doubleday & Company, 1966), vii.

3. *Ibid.*, 31.

4. *Ibid.*, 105–06.

5. *Ibid.*, 367.

6. Kenneth Rexroth, *Excerpts from a Life*, ed. by Bradford Morrow (Santa Barbara, Calif.: A Conjunctions Book, 1981), 58.

7. William Everson, "Rexroth: Shaker and Maker," *For Rexroth* (*The Ark*, 14, 1980), 26.

8. Eliot Weinberger, *Works on Paper* (New York: New Directions, 1986), 116–17.

9. Kenneth Rexroth, *American Poetry in the Twentieth Century* (New York, 1971), 126.

10. Laughlin, "For the Record," 48.

11. *Ibid.*, 49.

12. Bradford Morrow, "An Interview with Kenneth Rexroth," *Conjunctions,* 1 (Winter 1981–82), 49.

13. *Ibid.*, 50.

14. Laughlin, "For the Record," 55–56.

15. Everson, "Rexroth," 25.

16. Morrow, "An Interview," 53.

17. James Laughlin, Preface, *New Directions in Prose and Poetry*, 15 (1955).

18. *Ibid.*

19. Morrow, "An Interview," 67.

NOTES ON THE TEXT

The letters gathered here have been selected from the surviving correspondence between Kenneth Rexroth and James Laughlin, a collection of approximately 350 letters and cards written between 1937 and Rexroth's death in 1982. The text is drawn from both originals and carbons housed in the files of the New Directions Archive at Mr. Laughlin's office in Norfolk, Connecticut. While many of the letters are reproduced entire, many others are not; in the main, the attempt has been to give as accurate a reflection as possible of the myriad facets and concerns of an important literary friendship. At Mr. Laughlin's request, the focus is on Kenneth Rexroth, with a few of Mr. Laughlin's many letters included to provide greater focus.

Headings: Each letter is preceded by a headnote which gives its number in the present edition, its form, and the number of its pages. The letters are a mix of holograph and typescript, indicated in the headings by ALS (autographed letter signed), TLS (typed letter signed), and PCS (postcard signed). About half the correspondence is undated; probable dates derived from postmarks of original mailing envelopes (many have been lost) and internal evidence are included in brackets, along with city of origin.

Text: We have attempted to produce as readable a text as possible, though without making any substantive alterations. Neither Rexroth nor Laughlin wrote with Ezra Pound's quirkiness of punctuation and spelling, for example, and thus obvious errors have been silently corrected. Sometimes we have supplied proper nouns or proper names in brackets for clarification. Paragraphs are retained as in the originals. The deletion of a passage of any substance (either because the material is simply redundant or due to questions of libel) is indicated by ellipses.

Annotations: Annotations follow many letters, keyed to a name or phrase in the text. In these notes we have tried to explain cryptic or obscure references where possible, as well as to identify literary references and essential bits of history and biography. Often, where either Rexroth or Laughlin has commented on a particular author or book, we have quoted from their works. Recurrent sources are abbreviated as follows: Rexroth—*AN (An Autobiographical Novel); APTC (American Poetry in the Twentieth Century); BB (Bird in the Bush); NBP (The New British Poets: An Anthology); SFP* (KR's interview in *The San Francisco Poets); WOTW (The World Outside the Window).* Laughlin—*AP* ("For the Record: On New Directions and Others," *American Poetry,* 3,1); *PR* ("Interview with James Laughlin," *Paris Review,* 89, 90); *Conjunctions* ("A Festschrift in Honor of James Laughlin," *Conjunctions: I*); and *ND (New Directions in Poetry and Prose* annuals). Full citations are included in the Selected Bibliography.

Acknowledgments first to James Laughlin, who suggested this project to me. He answered numerous queries with patience and good cheer, and with his wife Ann offered me a week of their legendary hospitality (as well as a few rounds of golf) in Norfolk. Like everyone with an interest in modern writing, I owe him a debt impossible to repay.

Bradford Morrow, Kenneth Rexroth's editor and literary executor, and Ruth Pokras, trustee of the Rexroth Trust, kindly gave permission for the publication of Rexroth's letters, as well as permission to quote from the poet's works. This book is dedicated to Brad Morrow in recognition of his many years of unselfish and diligent effort to bring important Rexroth work either back into print or into print for the first time, as well as his service to the larger community of letters as founding editor of *Conjunctions*.

Further, I have drawn on personal reminiscences of Rexroth from William Everson, Robert Duncan, and Nathaniel Tarn. I have greatly benefited from Morgan Gibson's, Don Gutierrez's, Linda Hamalian's, and John Tritica's work on Rexroth, and have made use of James Hartzell and Richard Zumwinkle's early *Kenneth Rexroth: A Checklist of His Published Writings,* as well as Shirley Cox's *A Personal Name Index to New Directions.* I would like to thank Hobson Wildenthal, Dean of Arts and Sciences, and Paul Risser, Vice-President for Research, of the University of New Mexico for a grant which allowed the completion of this volume. My colleague at the University of New Mexico, Hugh Witemeyer, established the format of the series in which this book is a part with his edition of the William Carlos Williams/JL correspondence. Finally, thanks to Amy Cherry at Norton, whose editorial suggestions were of great help.

LETTERS

1. TLS-1

June 15, 1937
Norfolk, Conn.

DEAR REXROTH,

In spite of your last letter saying that you are going up into the Sierras before my arrival I still hope that you will break a toenail or something and will be still in San Francisco when I get there. . . .

It's fine that Macmillans are interested in you. This surprises me. Or perhaps you've written some poems very different from the ones you sent me.

About doing a separate book. It is hard to say. It will depend on how I make out with these ones. If these pay their way I'll go on to others. If not I'll concentrate on the annual anthologies and put all my energy into that. I'll know more about the possibilities of a book in the fall. I'm delighted that you're to have one with such a good house.

And thanks for arranging for the reviews in the *[San Francisco] Chronicle.* I'll be looking forward to them. You have done a great deal and I hope I can make it up to you somehow.

Have fun in the mountains, if I don't see you. I was up there for a month this winter, skiing. I started in from Soda Springs and went all the hell over the place around there. I dare say you'll be going further south though. Damn fine country. Nothing like the mountains. I expect to see some good ones in New Zealand.

Yours
LAUGHLIN

/ · /

Macmillans: Macmillan published KR's first collection of poems, *In What Hour,* in 1940.

the annual anthologies: The first number of *New Directions in Prose and Poetry,* an annual anthology, appeared in 1936 in hardback and paper editions, while its editor JL was a sophomore at Harvard. According to his preface to *ND* 1, the annual's original intention was as much broadly political as it was aesthetic: "I believe then, that experimental writing has a real social value, apart from any other. For however my contributors may see themselves I see them as agents of social reform as well as artists." By *ND* 7 (1942), JL was arguing that the primary aim of the series had been to offer a collection "of writing that lies outside the commercial and conventional spheres—the work of writers who are attempting to go in directions, which if they are not 'new' (for so little is ever really new), are certainly different from those commonly being followed by the average writer. As usual I have tried to make an impartial exhibition gallery where any competent artist can get a showing, no matter who his friends are or what his tendencies may be. This book does not attempt to preach or judge which direction is the right one. . . . The final value of many of the things we have published is not so much in what they are in themselves as in what they will lead to in the work of other writers who may develop what is here begun." KR's first contribution to the annuals appeared in *ND* 2 (1937), the poems "Easy Lessons in Geophagy" and "Organon"; as one of *ND*'s most frequent contributors, his poetry, plays, and translations subsequently appeared in another dozen numbers. JL dedicated *ND* 8 (1944) to KR.

these ones: ND's first book was Montague O'Reilly's (Wayne Andrews) *Pianos of Sympathy,* a sixteen-page pamphlet, published in 1936. By the date of this letter, JL had published Dudley Fitts's *Poems 1929–1936,* Robert McAlmon's *Not Alone Lost,* and William Carlos Williams's *White Mule* (with a postscript by JL); already committed for 1938 publication were Edouard Dujardin's early stream-of-consciousness novel *We'll to the Woods No More* (trans. from the French by Stuart Gilbert, with notes by JL), Dudley Fitts's *One Hundred Poems from the Palatine Anthology* (the Greek anthology in English paraphrase), Charles Henri Ford's *The Garden of Disorder & Other Poems* (with an introduction by W. C. Williams), JL's story about his days in Paris *The River,* Merrill Moore's *Sonnets from New Directions* (with a preface by W. C. Williams), Ezra Pound's *Culture* (in cooperation with Faber & Faber; later, *Guide to Kulcher*), W. C. Williams's *Life Along the Passaic River* and *The Complete Collected Poems,* and Yvor Winters's *Maule's Curse.* ND would not publish a collection by KR until *The Phoenix and the Tortoise* in 1944.

up there skiing: JL, an ardent skier in his youth, wrote numerous articles on European ski areas and skiing competitions for American magazines in the forties. His *Skiing East and West,* with photographs by Helene Fischer, was published by Hastings House (New York) in 1946. In his *PR* interview, JL admits, "I think you have to bear in mind the skiing mania. It's been a big part of my life. I was crazy about skiing and did a lot of it." The Laughlin family is the majority stockholder in a ski resort in Alta, Utah, which JL helped manage: "I saw the ski resort, apart from the pleasure of skiing, as an opportunity to make a little money to support the publishing." Ezra Pound once sent JL a pc about his "mania": "ARE YOU DOING ANYTHING? Of course, if you spend ¾s of your time sliding down ice cream cones on a tin tea-tray. If you can't be bothered with detail, why t'hell don't you get Stan Nott [London publisher of EP's "Money" pamphlets] who could run it. Then you could scratch yr arse on Pike's Peak to your 'earts content." In 1937 JL was a member of a collegiate ski team which raced in New Zealand and Australia.

2. ALS-2

October 21, 1939
San Francisco

DEAR JIM LAUGHLIN,

Forgive me for not answering your note sooner. No excuse. However, I do fear that I can furnish you no new address. This is not a monster metropolis—I guess I have made all the friends I am going to. Not to speak of those I have lost since the Nazis . . . who doubtless are now on tenterhooks awaiting my confession of complicity in the Tokyo earthquake or the Reichstag fire.

Life may not be precisely glamorous nowadays—

but it certainly has an evil glitter. I wonder how you are taking it all—like the rest of us—I suppose. Slightly numb, but trying desperately to do something. I hope *ND* is not so far put to bed that you can't insert a piece on the war. I for one would be glad to forgo my contribution if you could still turn it into an antiwar number. As far as that goes I have poems on that subject I could send you.

We have organized a group of writers, artists, professionals, calling itself the Randolph Bourne Council, dedicated to a principled socialist opposition to war and to the furtherance of a bona fide Socialist alliance of all groups not pledged to questionable commitments. I will send you our statement when we get it off next week.

How far away the mountains seem. Even more so when one is in them these days. I have been doing a lot of climbing this fall—every piton I drive in is like a fond kiss at the station as the troop train pulls out. Still, good climbing technique should be handy in and around Leavenworth. Unfortunately, I am not good enough with my flutterkick to ever get away from Alcatraz. Marie [Cass] and I have talked seriously of going to Bolivia, where we want to go anyway—but I am afraid I am too deep in this thing to take a powder. I would let down too many people, if nothing else.

Still monkeying around with the capitalist class trying to get my book published. I get some wonderful bites—a strike every time—usually get the critter out of the water—but he always gets away on the bank. I guess I need a landing net. I don't know the right people. When are you going to loosen up and offer to publish me?

. . . Don't misunderstand us. We have no delusions about this legislative fight. But popular pressure for the embargo will mobilize and set in motion a tremendous mass against the War Deal.

So—Happy Days are Here Again.

Faithfully
KENNETH

/ · /

I hope ND: KR's contribution to *ND* IV (1939) was "Value in the Mountains."

Randolph Bourne Council: Randolph Bourne (1886–1918) was an American social critic and pacifist whose close friends included Van Wyck Brooks and John Reed. According to KR's *SFP* interview, "All during [the 1930s] we always had poetry readings and discussions and then during the war we set up a thing called the Randolph Bourne Council in which we gathered up the radical intellectuals in town that were not Stalinist. We tried to gather the Trotskyites, which was hopeless. Immediately after the war we simply organized an open and above-board Anarchist Circle." In addition, the Fall 1939 issue of the *Partisan Review* carried a statement by the League for Cultural Freedom and Socialism calling for American neutrality in the European conflict; drafted by *PR* editor Dwight Macdonald, it was signed by both KR and JL, as well as William Carlos Williams, Delmore Schwartz, Kay Boyle, Weldon Kees, Katherine Anne Porter, and others.

a lot of climbing: Like JL, KR was a hiking and camping enthusiast. In his review of KR's *The Phoenix and the Tortoise* in 1945, William Carlos Williams wrote: "Rexroth, so I am told, is a mountain climber of no mean distinction who will go up a rock-face unlikely to be attempted by most professionals. He climbs apparently out of some mystic purpose—as another might become a Trappist monk." Earlier in the 1930s, KR had written a 234-page manual for the WPA, *Camping in the Western Mountains,* which remains unpublished.

Marie: Marie Cass, KR's second wife. KR had married his first wife, Andrée Dutcher, in 1927; like the poet she was an artist and political activist, and KR was devoted to her (see, for example, his poems "In Memory of Andrée Rexroth" and "Andrée Rexroth," as well as chapter 37 of *An Autobiographical Novel*). According to *AN,* "We agreed about everything. We had read all the same books, and seen all the same pictures, and liked the same music. . . . We started painting together on the same picture without conflict, like one person." While Andrée didn't write poetry, "as soon as a page or two of a first draft was done we'd go over it together." Andrée suffered from epilepsy, however, and eventually the condition worsened. In *Excerpts from a Life*, KR describes how, "As time went on, she ceased almost entirely to paint, slept a great deal, and devoted her time to the Communist Party work. Then she began to develop what the psychiatrists call 'fugue.' " She began to suddenly disappear, entering into semi-amnesiac periods in which she would become sexually involved with other men. In time, recognizing that after more than a decade he had come to the "end of a true marital relationship that had been for so long as idyllic as any human relationship of any kind I have ever experienced," KR and Andrée separated, and it was at that point that the poet "began to quietly separate [himself] from all organizations dominated by the Communist Party." While working to help organize a nurses' union, KR met a nurse named Marie Cass, "a handsome, stately woman with bright red hair. . . . The first night I drove her home, I kissed her passionately. She drew away and said, 'I am not a sixteen-year-old who enjoys necking in a small coupé. It's a warm night and there's a lovely cemetery two blocks away at the end of the street.' So began many years of happiness" *(Excerpts)*. She and KR married in late 1940, following the death of Andrée in October, and later divorced in 1948; a number of KR's books from the forties are dedicated to Marie, including his long poem *The Phoenix and the Tortoise*. According to JL, "Marie was a *great* person. More than just a nurse. She had executive ability and became a supervisor in the S.F. Health Service. She was of Hungarian extraction. Tell, red-haired, very graceful. Had a lovely voice and used to sing around the house. KR treated her very badly, though her income was what kept the marriage afloat. He made her divorce because she couldn't have children. Psychically, even after the separation, he relied on her constantly. She got cancer and when she knew it was incurable took pills and died. She was the rock in his life" (JL letter to the editor).

3. TLS-1

5 III [19]41

[San Francisco]

DEAR JAMES LAUGHLIN,

These are a "new direction" for me, anyway. The more I think on't, the more I feel that contemporary verse has got itself into a rhetorical impasse of the most inextricable character. At least, with [T. S.] Eliot and the [W. H.] Auden group, rhetorical incantation is "coercive"; with most of the US

younger poets, it's just incantation, going nowhere.
Tertullian imitating Elizabeth Coatsworth. I dont like
it, and my verse, not consciously to the extent of
being programmatic about it, but definitely, tends
to go towards a rational "immediacy of utterance."
I feel so much contemporary work is misconceived.
The struggle begun by Baudelaire was toward san-
ity, it was an attempt to reinstate the will, the intellect, not the reverse. Rimbaud is powerful because
of his intellect, promethean will, and his "hallucina-
tions" are weapons against a will-less, irrational, truly
hallucinated society. After all, bonafide hallucina-
tions are remarkably alike, to the point of tedium, as
a glance at any collection of case histories or surrealist lyrics will demonstrate. Maybe these elegies are
Ovidian, but I think the realm beyond the wall DH
Lawrence battered for so long was a world far more
like Catullus than like Mr. [Lawrence] Durrell. Did
you ever read DHL's "None of That"? It pretty
effectively answers his "admirers," particularly the
nasty women who write memoirs of him. Be that as
it may, I for one stand for the reinstatement of the
rational intellect, the conscious will, the erect
penis. . . .

Skiing? We took a long trip late last year, camped
on the snow for 14 days the first hitch, 10 the second. Made several nice climbs and gave the iceaxe
some work for a change. (The Sierras are mostly
rockclimbs in the summer.) Terribly poor this year
but I hope to make a trip along the Sierra summit
from Carson Pass to Senora or Tioga Pass sometime
this month.

Thanks for the present of Bill [Williams]'s new
poems. What would we do without him? I have given
away my last copy of [Williams's] *White Mule*. I am
anxious to see [Malcolm] Cowley's poems, there is
a fine poet, damn near destroyed by the City Club.

Moral, avoid the *New Republic.* Is Bob McAlmon
dead? I cant locate him. If he is, I think Bill should
do a collection of his work; it would be criminal to
allow him to vanish. He really knew what it was
about, it is a pity he was so dissolute, erratic. Did
you see [Yvor] Winters' *Collected Poems?* Shame on
you for not publishing it yourself. His troubled career
is another indictment of US literary politics. Not that
I am accusing you of playing politics, you are one of
the very few who don't, but you cant be expected
to do all the work which should be done by dozens
of others. . . .

faithfully
KENNETH

/ · /

"new direction": Several carbon typescript sheets were attached, headed
"Selections from The Phoenix and the Tortoise, a collection of elegies."

Eliot: T. S. Eliot (1888–1965), American poet, playwright, critic, and
editor. While Eliot never published a volume with ND or appeared in
the *ND* annuals, he contributed poems to the "New Directions" section of *New Democracy* and wrote an important introduction to Djuna
Barnes's *Nightwood;* edited and introduced *The Literary Essays of Ezra
Pound;* and contributed an essay to Peter Russell's *An Examination of
Ezra Pound,* all published by ND. KR: "Eliot was the representative
poet of the time, for the same reason that Shakespeare and Pound were
of theirs. He articulated the mind of an epoch in words that seemed its
most natural expression. . . . Eliot is certainly the most personal poet
of the classic American Modernists" *(APTC).*

the Auden group: W. H. Auden (1907–1973), British poet, playwright,
essayist. According to KR, the "Auden circle" also included poets Stephen Spender, C. Day-Lewis, and Louis MacNeice; from this group
he chose to include work only by Spender (the sole one to have "made
a transition into the new period") in his *New British Poets* anthology,
published by ND in 1949. In the introduction to *NBP,* KR argued:
"Looking back, it seems today that the Auden circle was more a mer-
chandizing cooperative than a literary school. . . . His influence in
England is slight." KR's "A Letter to Wystan Hugh Auden" (one of
his only rhymed poems), advising WHA that he would be better off

"making wild salads out of bracken shoots, / Or weaving violets in an endless chain," appeared in the *New Masses* in 1937. According to Robert Duncan's *Conjunctions* interview, KR "talked a lot about how well he got along with Auden, something I didn't know. Kenneth liked the self-civilizing Auden but us kids were all for the savage Kenneth!" WHA never published a volume with ND, though *ND* 27 and 28 (1973–74) included translations of the Swedish poet Henry Martinson by WHA and Leif Sjoberg.

Elizabeth Coatsworth: (1893–1986), American poet, novelist, and author of children's books, including *Fox Footprints, Night and the Cat,* and *Summer Green.*

Baudelaire: Charles Baudelaire (1821–1867), French poet, critic. ND published a number of the writer's works in translation, as well as Jean-Paul Sartre's critical study, *Baudelaire.*

Rimbaud: Arthur Rimbaud (1854–1891), French poet. ND published Delmore Schwartz's translation of *A Season in Hell* in 1939, and Henry Miller's study of the poet, *The Time of the Assassins,* in 1956. In a 1957 review, "Rimbaud as Capitalist Adventurer," KR argues that while the poet is "an innovator in syntax, the first thoroughly radical revealer of the poetic metalogic which is the universal characteristic of twentieth-century verse . . . the whole Rimbaudian gospel is open to question" *(BB).*

D. H. Lawrence: David Herbert Lawrence (1885–1930), British poet, novelist. ND would reprint Lawrence's *The Man Who Died* in 1947, as well as publish KR's edition of Lawrence's *Selected Poems.* KR's Introduction to the *Selected Poems,* entitled "Poetry, Regeneration, and D. H. Lawrence," remains one of his liveliest and most influential prose pieces.

Catullus: Gaius Valerius Catullus (c. 84–54 B.C.), Roman poet. In the mid-1960s, KR would write a series of brief essays on a variety of authors and books for *The Saturday Review,* including a piece on Catullus in which he argues that the poet is great because "he speaks with accents of emotional liberty. It also makes him possibly untranslatable." The first sixty of these essays were collected into *Classics Revisited* (ND, 1968), the second twenty-eight (including "Catullus") into "More Classics Revisited" as part of *The Elastic Retort* (Seabury, 1973).

Durrell: Lawrence Durrell (1912–1990), British novelist, poet, travel writer. JL was the first to publish Durrell in the United States, using his work in *ND* 4 and 5; KR included selections by the writer in *NBP.* Between 1957 and 1960, KR wrote three reviews of Durrell's poetry and fiction, collected as "Lawrence Durrell" in *Assays.*

Bill's new poems: William Carlos Williams (1883–1963), American poet, novelist, essayist, physician. His *The Broken Span* appeared in the first group of ND's Poet of the Month series in January 1941. Introduced to WCW by Ezra Pound, JL would become the writer's first comme. cial publisher in 1936, with the publication of WCW's "How to Write in *ND* 1. KR first came to Williams's attention much earlier, with ¿ letter to the editors of *Blues* in the fall of 1929 (KR's first prose publication; his first published poems had appeared earlier in the year in the first issue of *Blues,* Charles Henri Ford and Parker Tyler's journal out of Mississippi, of which Williams was a contributing editor). In his "Letter from San Francisco," the twenty-four-year-old KR had chided Williams for a confused and inadequate response to the "neoclassic-neothomist-neodostoyefsky philosophy" of Yvor Winters. Writing to Ford in 1929, Williams admitted that "Rexroth is one of my favorites, though I like his present effort less than some others. . . . He has something, that boy. And he is quite right in jumping me for my lack of lucidity and my statements which did not help." On a hitchhiking tour across the country, KR appeared at WCW's door in Rutherford, New Jersey, on May 3, 1931; Williams reported to a friend that he liked the young man, though found him "somewhat bitten by the prevalent Anglo-Catholicism drift."

Work by both KR and WCW appeared in Louis Zukofsky's *An "Objectivists" Anthology* (1932), and WCW thought highly enough of the young poet's effort to single it out in a review as "a poetry of conviction," quoting at length from two poems. WCW published an extended review of KR's first ND volume in 1945, praising the work as "strong meat and drink written in a verse clear as water," and in the 1950s positively reviewed KR's work in the *New York Times Book Review* and *Poetry.* For his part, writing on WCW's fiction and drama in 1961, KR argued that the physician was "not only the finest poet writing in America, the master of those (of us, all of us) who know. He is also a consummate master of prose"; his work is "amongst the most precious possessions of the twentieth century in any language" *(With Eye & Ear).* KR's "A Public Letter for William Carlos Williams' Seventy-fifth Birthday" is collected in *Assays,* while selections from WCW and KR (along with Denise Levertov) comprise *Penguin Modern Poets* 9 (1967). In *Excerpts,* KR remembers, "One day I met Parker Tyler walking down Sixth Avenue, three feet above the ground. 'You look very elated,' I said. 'Oh Kenneth,' he said, 'I just got a letter from Bill Williams, saying my Granite Butterfly is as great as Dante.' 'Calm down,' I said. 'He's told me I'm as great as Homer or Shakespeare.' "

see Cowley's poems: Malcolm Cowley (1898–1989), American poet, editor, and critic. In 1941, ND published Cowley's book of verse, *The Dry Season.* KR's poetry and letters appeared frequently in the *New Republic* during Cowley's tenure as literary editor.

Bob McAlmon: Robert McAlmon (1896–1956), expatriate American poet and fiction writer, director of the Contact Publishing Company. KR: "[McAlmon] started out as perhaps the best of the ultimate generation of Populist poets. . . . A comparison of McAlmon's narrative poems with the self-conscious farmer poetry of Robert Frost or the cowgirl

tragedies of Robinson Jeffers is an elementary lesson in literary dis-
crimination. He, like Laura Riding, is a great lost poet" *(APTC)*. KR's
1969 review "McAlmon and the Lost Generation" is collected in *With
Eye & Ear*.

Winters' Collected Poems: Poems, published in 1940 by Gyroscope Press.
(Arthur) Yvor Winters (1900–1968), American poet, critic, editor; from
1927 to 1966 a member of the Department of English at Stanford. ND
published a number of Winters's books, including *Maule's Curse: Seven
Studies in the History of American Obscurantism* (1938), *The Anatomy of
Nonsense* (1943), *The Giant Weapon* (1943), and *Edwin Arlington Robinson* (1946), as well as the anthology *Twelve Poets of the Pacific* (1937).
According to KR, "Yvor Winters is a very considerable poet indeed.
. . . He was the true exile, the true aliene. Years must have gone by
where nobody knew what he was talking about except his wife, or his
echoing students. He became cranky and cantankerous and is responsible for some of the most wrong-headed and eccentric criticism ever
written" *(APTC)*. In his "Reflections on KR" *(Sagetrieb,* 2, 3), Thomas
Parkinson points out that while KR disliked Winters's criticism, he
"typed out the early and inaccessible poetry of Winters from library
copies and had the poems bound in a folder." Reviewing *An "Objectivists" Anthology* in 1933, Winters argues that of the younger contributors, "Mr. Rexroth, the best of a bad lot, employs a method of
construction similar" to T. S. Eliot's structureless "psychic impres-
sionism . . . but his thought is less original and appears ill-digested."
KR's "The Place" is dedicated to Winters. (See also letter 4, note on
Crane.)

4. ALS-2   [April 1941]
                                          [San Francisco]

DEAR JIM,

   Ah, moeurs contemporains! Ah, my former disciples! Poor [Malcolm] Cowley, I knew him well.
Just a boy from the Amish Mts. with his head filled
with scrapple. And now, war being waged, it is
beginning to go sour. What do you suppose moved
him to do that number? Last year, reviewing [Louis]
Aragon, he said, "The less said about La Rime en
1940, the better." I thought he was being very civilized—now I guess he thought it was moderne . . .

I suspect the wear and tear is just too much for both Louis and Malcolm. At least the former has good reasons—he has been worn and torn more than goes on chez City Club (or has he? Which is worse—a *N[ew] R[epubic]* luncheon, or the blitz?) and the verse of the last two books of Aragon is just eccentric, but still good—like the Occleve-Lydgate experiments of the Fugitives (if they had written good verse). Of course the appendix on prosody in Fraser & Squire is one of those things never read by most, like the instructions for finding the date of Easter in the Book of Common Prayer, maybe he just ran across it and rush[ed] naked around the Croton Reservoir screaming JE TROUVAIS—I hope he rests easier these troubled midnights. Even snottty old [Paul] Valéry, writing to impress the high school French teachers in Tallahassee and Saigon—o well, what's the use. One of the nice things about the art of measuring the beautiful words is that almost nobody knows anything about it anymore, so that somebody who does it is in the enviable position of a craftsman who really has a trade secret—not a common thing nowadays, with these unions and all. The thing about French prosody, as Valéry has said so well, is that most of its rules are purely conventional and have very little to do with the actual sound and rhythm of the verse (all languages, of course, actually have stress accent, tonic accent, sonorous quantity, breath quantity, volume changes), therefore—1) it is hard to observe all the rules—which keeps the fools away. 2) attention is kept at maximum concentration, because almost every line must be reworked. 3) the system comes from society's traditions, not the poet's head, which shears off the excessive intimacies which are a blight on the French mind anyway—e.g. the famous and hackneyed comparison of Baudelaire & Racine—what crap Baudelaire would have written if he had used his own resources for discipline! 4) finally—the French verse is free verse—the liberty to vary the actual phonetic values within the Alexandrine is unlimited and the adherence to conventional pattern makes something new each time. An analogy: Schoenbergian music all sounds alike, confused, shapeless, and insufferably sentimental. Modern "white" diatonic music, whether Stravinsky's last symphony or [Ralph] Vaughan-Williams, is clean, clear and pointed. The means are neatly proportionate to the effects, and effect balance. Therefore something is said-achieved. Now actually, modern instruments are based on the equal tempered piano. The twelve-tone system of Schoenberg is really phonetically far sounder than the Pythagorean system of the diatonic scale (unless one is writing for Russian choirs or string ensembles with unspoiled ears). In fact, due to the rule that small variations of vibration rate are less pleasant than large—the Pythagorean scale, on the modern piano, is always out of tune and definitely about as cacophonous as it can well be. The twelve-tone scale is the natural harmonic system of the piano. . . .

The reason [Yvor] Winters is wrong is that English prosody is not purely conventional. It takes one aspect of phonetic order and raises it to a position of such importance that it distorts and renders less accessible all the other values. Also—it is not constant, but subject to very definite historical development, and due to the iambic nature of the language, a development confined within very narrow limits. (I think Swinburne demonstrated once for all that trochaic rhythms and anapests and dactyls are simply not English.) Therefore, rhymed iambs today tend to sound anachronistic if definitely patterned, and shapeless if not. Winters points out that the false importance given to things Greek, qua Greek, in HD is sentimentality. How about Barnabe Googe, qua Googe? In Winters this doesn't work out this way. 1) Winters doesnt sound like Googe. 2) he doesnt because he cant. It is obvious from reading things like the "Manzanita" that he is still in the Chicago Renascence and thinks making it rhyme is very very hard. As long as it is hard, the poet works; if he works, he probably writes good verse—assuming he has talent in the first place. Contemporary taste in metrics is incredibly debased. [Archibald] MacLeish, [Hart] Crane, REF Larsson, [W. H.] Auden, etc. etc. are supposed to be metrists of great merit. Actually, of course, they hypnotize themselves with very simple rhythms, hit the typewriter and let the words fall where they may. This is not strictly true of WHA [Auden] who is always trying to get at a conscious control of his medium—he has just never been able to keep quiet long enough. Maybe Gerald Heard?

I am shocked at [Robert Penn] Warren. I think his work extremely derivative. And derivative from very bad exemplars. MacLeish, T. S. E[liot] at his worst, the Middle English experiments of the Fugitives above mentioned, [Allen] Tate (!), Auden. (Once in a great while [Laura] Riding, though it may come thru Auden, or thru the Fugitives as a group.) It is like the newspapers, as this sort of stuff goes by in periodicals, it is individually rather impressive, en masse it is anything but . . .

Contemporary poem, serial number 98735214305254475303

Nobody has seen the baby
Since we left him playing by the vacuum cleaner.
Why does the postman always scream
When he delivers your letters?
Why do I always dream of gloves?
Whose are the teeth I am hearing
Always, nightly, gnawing beneath

The cellar floor? Are they false? Are
They real? Have they survived the skull?
When we were at St. Tropez, we
Made love in the water, you cut
Your foot on a sea urchin, on
That small, fecund, sensitive beast.
The water of that sea is full of eyes.
What is it that comes at night when
We are talking? What is it stands
There shrouded in the radio music?
What is it hides in the romaine lettuce?
What whispers in the salad?
I take off my shoes and look at them and
There is nobody in them, when
I have my shoes on they are busy and occupied.
Unfortunately I have run out of paper.

[appended in holograph:]
 I get tired of nonsense about Original Sin by ama-
teur Origens. Original Sin is the statement of the
Socratic Dilemma. When man is confronted with a
rationally realized good he does not infallibly choose
it. In fact—on the whole—men tend to choose a lesser
immediate good for a greater final good and apologize for it-by calling it the choice of the lesser evil.
The choice of an evil—greater or lesser—of course is
not a choice. Politics is the art of circumventing the
freedom of the will. "War is the health of the State."
 All that is in "The Phoenix and Tortoise," but it
is hardly news. . . .

> Love and kisses to all
> KENNETH

/ · /

books of Aragon: Louis Aragon (1897–1982), French poet and novelist,
published *Le crève-coeur* in 1941. *ND* 5 (1940) included selections from
Aragon, translated by Charles Henri Ford, Hubert Creekmore, and
Clara Cohn.

Fugitives: In "The Influence of French Poetry on American" *(Assays),* KR writes that the Fugitives were: "a little coterie of political reactionaries, under the leadership of their English professor, John Crowe Ransom . . . fugitives from modernism, liberalism, humanitarianism, socialism, interracialism, and all other cusswords of the reactionaries." In his 1969 *SFP* interview, KR recalled: "Once I pinned the name 'Pillowcase Head Dress School of Literature' on Red [Robert Penn] Warren, Allen Tate, and John Crowe Ransom, it stuck! You have no idea the domination of these people. They are afraid of me, because they have never dominated me."

Valéry: Paul Valéry (1897–1945), French poet, philosopher. In 1950, ND published Valéry's *Selected Writings.* In "Disengagement: The Art of the Beat Generation" *(The Alternative Society),* KR argues that "no avant-garde American poet accepts the I. A. Richards–Valéry thesis that a poem is an end in itself, an anonymous machine for providing esthetic experiences. All believe in poetry as communication."

Winters is wrong: KR is reacting here to Yvor Winters's *Primitivism and Decadence: A Study of American Experimental Poetry,* which had been published in 1937. Of H.D. (see note below) in particular, Winters had written that because in her work "the relationship between the feeling and the Greek landscape has no comprehensible source and is very strong, one must call it sentimental." In "The Influence of French Poetry on American" *(Assays),* KR writes of Winters that "he wrote a long attack on H.D. which was his own farewell to Imagism. . . . Now this essay has an odd note about it of never quite comprehending H.D. and of somehow missing the whole point of her work."

H.D.: Hilda Doolittle (1886–1961), American poet, novelist. KR: "Her metric is something else—like Whitman's, a unique, purely personal discovery. There is nothing in European literature at all like it. . . . No one before or since had ever more perfectly mastered strophic verse" *(APTC).* Much of KR's "The Poet as Translator" *(Assays)* is an appreciation of her work. ND would eventually publish a number of H.D.'s books, including *Helen in Egypt, Hermetic Definitions, Trilogy,* a *Collected Poems 1912–1944,* and a *Selected Poems.*

Barnabe Googe: British poet (1540–1594). In *APTC,* KR writes of Yvor Winters: "He changed the style of his verse to a stark neo-classicism of his own invention, which he always insisted owed much to, of all people, the late Tudor writer of doggerel, Barnabe Googe."

MacLeish: Archibald MacLeish (1892–1982), American poet, Librarian of Congress (1939–44). His "The Soundtrack & Picture Form: A New Direction" appeared in *ND 3* (1938).

Crane: Hart Crane (1889–1932), American poet. In "Why Is American Poetry So Culturally Deprived?" *(The Alternative Society),* KR writes: "Hart Crane's *The Bridge* failed precisely because of its total lack of intellectual content. . . . His intoxication with his own rhetoric defeats his gospel." KR's *Excerpts* recalls, "Of all his American contemporaries, the poet Yvor Winters admired most was Hart Crane, and he was in continuous correspondence with him." At one point Crane wrote Winters that he was traveling west to see him. "Winters' family home was in Pasadena, and he was au tremblant, agog with excitement about meeting America's greatest poet, whose work he had given a mystical, religious interpretation which it did not merit. . . . Andrée and I knew that he was in for a nasty shock and we tried to prepare him. I told him that Crane was a homosexual and, not only that, a rather flagrant one, and when he got drunk, violently abusive to everyone within reach. And Andrée backed me up. We had been asked for dinner; instead, we were asked to leave. Two weeks later, Janet [Lewis Winters] called us up and said Winters was sorry he had been so angry and asked us down once more for dinner. After the amenities—no apology—I said: 'Well Arthur, how was Hart?' Winters was seated at his desk by the window and he looked out with a face straight off Mount Rushmore and tapped his fingers on the desk. 'He's nothing but a vagrant,' he said. And there was no more talk of Crane in that house."

Larsson: Raymond Ellsworth Larsson, American poet. JL published his poem, "The Last Visit to Mallarmé," in *ND* 13 (1951); KR considered him to be the finest Catholic poet of his day. KR's "Okeanos and the Golden Sickle" is dedicated to Larsson.

Gerald Heard: (1889–1971), British essayist, philosopher. In the late thirties he left England for America to settle permanently in Southern California.

Warren: Robert Penn Warren (1905–1989), American poet, novelist, and critic. ND published his chapbook, *Eleven Poems on the Same Theme,* in 1942. KR was fond of using his nickname, "Red."

Tate: Allen Tate (1899–1979), American poet and critic. Tate contributed a brief essay to *ND* 7's "Homage to Ford Madox Ford" in 1942. One of KR's *bêtes noires*.

Riding: Laura (Riding) Jackson (1901–), American poet and novelist, who in 1940 "renounced poetry" in favor of the study of linguistics. In *APTC*, KR would write of Riding that she "is the greatest lost poet in American literature. W. H. Auden once called her the only living philosophical poet. . . . Prosody is to poetic rhythm as written music is to jazz. The discoveries of Laura Riding's subtle ear escape analysis. . . . Laura Riding's criticism published under her own name alone is amongst the best ever written by an American. . . . [She] has meant more to me than any other American poet, and in the years since her retirement she has been a woman much missed. I think the history of the last thirty years of American poetry would have been different had she been around."

Contemporary poem: previously unpublished.

"The Phoenix and Tortoise": KR's long poem which would be featured in *ND* 8 in 1944, and published by ND as a separate volume later in the year.

5. ALS-3

[June, 1941]
[Norfolk]

DEAR KENNETH,

. . . At one point you say, "Don't stop writing—that's a lot of b.s." But then, at another: "Sure I will publish the poems if I can—why did you think I wrote them?" Ain't it the truth—any art is most like sex in that it presupposes a response. Because in my case that response has for a long time been prodigiously lacking, I've been at the point of concluding that for years I've just been kidding myself—and that therefore the only rational thing to do is secede from the whole thankless effort. Looks like it's out of the question for me to get my work published (at least by any publisher I'd want); so the incentive to go on writing just ain't. This doesn't mean, though, that I'm going to hurl my typewriter out into the cruel night. . . .

Did you read of Virginia Woolf's suicide?

As ever
JIM

/ · /

Virginia Woolf's suicide: Virginia Woolf (1882–1941), British novelist, essayist, and publisher, committed suicide on March 28, 1941. ND published David Daiches's critical study of the writer the following year.

6. ALS-1   2 October [19]41
                                            [San Francisco]

DEAR JIM,

A letter from Mr. [Charles] Finney in Tucson. It seems he is the author of *The Circus of Dr. Lao,* a Jurgenesque number which adds up to little, and *Past the End of the Pavement,* which got good reviews, but, he says, no sales whatever. Anyway, I fear he is what grandma calls common, and will not come to much. To continue with your contributors, I called on [Charles] Snider. He is certainly done up in the Original Package bearing the signature (I guess) Arthur Rimbaud, I suppose that is the original signature, so many have crowded their names on the label since, you cant make out what is inside the bottle. . . . As you know full well, or should, I dont like this kind of poetry, I think it sentimental and melodramatic, but, of its kind, this is the genuine article. I couldn't say if it is better than Dylan Thomas, but it *doesnt* occupy some misty region betwixt Allen Tate and A[ndré] Breton, and, conversely, it makes gents like James Vergillius Cunningham really stink, or conversely again, Rbt. Horan. I.E. I think Snider the real thing, if you like that kind of thing.

I left Podesta's geologist's pick. I think in the station wagon. It is a handforged one and he will have kittens if it is lost. If you find it, put it in the car when you come to Cal. . . .

Finished Arthur [Winters]'s book, and it depresses me that you arent taking his new one. *Maule's Curse* is certainly a good one. Although I was impressed by the contrast between Phil Rahv's essay on Hawthorne and Winters'. Somebody should really sneak up behind Arthur some night in an alley and say

"Titty!" Just who *are* you going to publish in 1942? The Memoirs of Gordon Wren?

[Robert] McAlmon is now in LA. If he is still recovering from TB, I imagine he will stop recovering, in association with H[enry] Miller and H[ilaire] Hiler. Breton is in LA too, maybe you can use him to flush Sonny. (no double entendre).

See you soon, and see if you can locate that damn pick. Love and kisses from Mrishka.

Faithfully
KENNETH

/ · /

Mr. Finney in Tucson: Charles G. Finney, whose *Circus of Dr. Lao* was published in 1935.

I called on Snider: Charles Snider's work is included in JL's "A Little Anthology of Contemporary Poetry" in *ND* 1941; according to the contributors' notes, "Snider lives in San Francisco and is active in left-wing politics there."

Dylan Thomas: (1914–1953), Welsh poet and short story writer. In 1939, ND became Thomas's exclusive American publisher with the publication of *The World I Breathe,* a collection of stories and poems. KR on Thomas: "If Auden dominated the recent past, Dylan Thomas dominates the present. There can be no question but that he is the most influential young poet writing in England today. . . . He takes you by the neck and rubs your nose in it. He hits you across the face with a reeking, bloody heart, a heart full of worms and needles and black blood and thorns, a werewolf heart. . . . Thomas' impact was not just literary, it was in a special sense social, a cultural coup d'état" *(NBP).* KR's poem "Thou Shalt Not Kill" is an elegy for Thomas.

André Breton: (1896–1966), French poet, leader of the Surrealist movement. *ND* 5 (1940) contained a 100-page anthology of Surrealist writing edited by Nicolas Calas; Breton was represented by thirteen selections, including "White Gloves: From 'Les Champ Magné-tiques,' " translated by JL and Clara Cohn. KR's "Fundamental Disagreement with Two Contemporaries" is dedicated to Breton and Tristan Tzara.

James Vergillius Cunningham: J. V. Cunningham (1911–1985), American poet and critic, studied with Yvor Winters at Stanford; his work is included in Winters's *Twelve Poets of the Pacific* (ND, 1937).

Horan: Robert Horan (1922–), American poet; his *A Beginning,* with a foreword by W. H. Auden, was published in the Yale Series of Younger Poets in 1948.

Arthur's book: Yvor Winters's *Maule's Curse: Seven Studies in the History of American Obscurantism* had been published by ND in 1938.

Philip Rahv: American editor, critic (1908–1973); co-founding editor of the *Partisan Review.* His essay on Hawthorne was "The Dark Lady of Salem," *PR* 8 (1941). In his introduction to *BB,* KR writes, "Just try saying: Mark Twain is a better writer than Henry James . . . Kierke-gaard is dull and silly. No adult can take Dostoevsky seriously . . . *Finnegans Wake* is an embarrassing failure. . . . Just say anything like that and see how far you get with Phil Rahv." ND published Rahv's *Image and Idea,* a collection of essays.

Gordon Wren: JL's friend, the American Olympic ski jumper.

Hiler: Hilaire Hiler (1898–1966), American artist. A close friend of Henry Miller's in Paris in the 1930s and California in the 1940s, he gave Miller painting lessons and introduced him to W. C. Williams. ND published a collection of essays, *Why Abstract?,* by Hiler, Miller, and William Saroyan in 1945. In his *The Air-Conditioned Nightmare,* also published by ND in 1945, Henry Miller devotes a chapter to "Hiler and His Murals."

Podesta: Probably KR's climbing companion Frank Trieste.

Mrishka: Marie Rexroth.

7. TLS-2

Dec. 28th [19]41
[San Francisco]

DEAR JIM,

. . . San Francisco is in a state of psychological siege; contrary to opinion in NY, the West Coast, with the exception, for some reason, of Seattle, has always dreaded a Japanese war, and, behind its blus-tering chauvinism and race prejudice, has a very healthy respect for the Japanese navy. In the last weeks the city has prepared itself for a large scale air raid. Everybody realizes that there will be only one, the city will burn up. This isn't propaganda either. . . . A few pursuit planes loaded with incendiaries will finish SF. A large section of the public still thinks it isn't going to happen, but I know of no responsible person who doesn't expect it to happen pretty quick. Also, they tell me *Time* raked up Homer Lea last week. I have no idea whether many people in California have ever read him, but his ideas seem to be commonly held, possibly with some slight optimism, ie, "We will defeat the Japs, but the tide will turn when they try to operate between the Sierras and the Rockies." People seem to take an invasion attempt for granted, and expect our yellow brothers to wage a war of literal extermination against California. I sometimes wonder if this isn't guilt. The prejudice against orientals in California has always sickened me. Maybe the constituents of Senator Johnson realize they are being called to a terrible accounting for the Oriental Exclusion Act. On the whole, I am inclined to agree with Matsuoka's statement of some months back, "If war is permitted to break out between the US and Japan, it will mean the complete extinction of modern civilization, of which, in spite of the American Oriental Exclusion Act, Japan considers herself a member." Let's hope that, a thousand years hence, Bantu historians will be able to preserve a scientific calm when they come to the story of these times. Maybe they'll make a better job of it, but it is certainly appalling to see the entire Northern Hemisphere destroy itself as effectively as if it were sawn off at the equator and hurled into the sun.

Americans, even well informed ones, seem to be blissfully ignorant of what is going on in the world. The stories brought back from France, including unoccupied France, and Poland, and Spain, are real horrors. Camps in which a thousand men live in holes in the ground, covered with straw, which they must vacate when it rains. What do they do then? They must stand in the rain. The excellent possibility is that most of the infants and children of France will die in the next year or two. 30 to 40 children buried a day in one small town in Vichy France. Warsaw a city of shell-shocked neurotics. The efficiency of the German bombardment has resulted in a very "embarrassing problem." An immense city whose people are all "mental cases" most of them incapable of performing their ordinary duties. Spain, in which the typhus epidemic was born, you know is destroying the rich, or once rich, as well as the poor. When you remember that Spain, Poland and France are agriculturally self-sustaining and the first two even export foodstuffs, well, people just simply no longer have any will to live. When seed grains are distributed, the people eat them up. Nowadays, when I go into a Safeway Store with its overburdened shelves they mean only one thing to me: loot—which half the world is struggling to get at. . . .

Is it really true that you plan to publish nothing but the Complete Delmore Schwartz from here on?

Faithfully
KENNETH

/ · /

the Oriental Exclusion Act. The Immigration Act of 1924 (also called the Japanese Exclusion Act and the National Origins Act). The Act distinguished between non-quota (Western Hemisphere) and quota (Eastern Hemisphere) immigrants. Non-quota immigrants were allowed an unlimited number of visas; quota immigrants were not. At this time foreign-born Japanese, Chinese, and Korean immigrants were not allowed to apply for U.S. citizenship. As visas were limited to 2 percent of the U.S. citizens residing in the continental United States as of the Census of 1890, the Act was obviously discriminatory against Asians.

the Complete Delmore Schwartz: a reference to ND's publication of Delmore Schwartz's *Shenandoah,* a verse play, in November. Schwartz (1913–1966), American poet, short story writer, and essayist, first corresponded with JL in July 1937, submitting work for the *ND* annual, declaring that "the enclosed pieces are the kind of work you want for your anthology," which JL accepted for *ND* 2. In 1938, ND published Schwartz's *In Dreams Begin Responsibilities,* and Schwartz's translation of Rimbaud's *Une Saison en Enfer* the following year, part of a contract to publish his first five books. Eventually JL and Schwartz became close friends, and the publisher often helped the poet (through advances and editorial work) out of financial difficulties.

According to JL's *PR* interview, "Delmore was one of the great talkers, particularly as a parodist. He was a marvellous mimic and fantasist and confabulator. . . . He was very helpful in reading scripts. He had excellent taste." Unfortunately, Schwartz suffered from severe paranoia (aggravated by heavy use of alcohol and, especially, amphetamines), and by the end of his life was comparing JL to Adolf Hitler, accusing him of "triumphs of duplicity," and (according to the James Atlas biography) telling friends that "the whole of New Directions was based upon a complicated evasion of income tax." While KR didn't overtly quarrel with Schwartz, as an editor of *Partisan Review* Schwartz was another of KR's primary literary *bêtes noires*. In his 1958 lecture at the Library of Congress, Schwartz referred to KR's "San Francisco Howlers," arguing that they were "engaged in an imaginary rebellion . . . Mr. Rexroth does not recognize the difference between the Red Army and the *Kenyon Review* critics, between Nikita Khrushchev and John Crowe Ransom." In *APTC,* KR returned the favor, making only passing reference to Schwartz, calling him a member of the "Reactionary Generation": "Schwartz, Elizabeth Bishop, Jean Garrigue, Robert Penn Warren—what characterizes these people is their narrowness, their lack of broad contact, or even interests, in anything but a narrow range of contemporary English and American poetry, Baroque English poetry, and their complication without complexity . . . crippled by frivolity and hypocrisy."

8. TLS-1

21 I [19]42

[San Francisco]

DEAR JIM,

Aint war awful? My pretty epigrams were due in the *P[artisan] R[eview]* this month, but since I thot them a trifle too flip, considering the awfulness of the present situation in the minds of most of 200,000,000 people, I asked Dwight [Macdonald] not to print them, there are things one just shouldn't be facetious about. But he also omitted the more sober ones that were agin the war. Maybe it's just as well. I wonder if anybody will print my Phoenix and Tortoise poem. I think it is going to be harder to get anything through this thing to the distant human beings on the far side of it than ever it was to get Sappho through the Byzantine monks. Every time I look ahead the coming darkness looks darker and the ice age icier. O well, as they used to say in the days of Athelstan and the Danes, "That passed away, so will this."

The business about the ski troops sounds incredible. What about all this literature sent out to Mtneering clubs and Ski clubs, etc.? I understood the Army was combing the draftees for skilled skiers and climbers, and falling over backward to encourage people to enlist. Many Sierra Club people are joining. . . .

Now that you have become part of the war, how about some of your ill gotten lucre for the A[merican] F[riends] S[ervice] C[ommittee]? (Don't send it to me.) If your conscience can't object, it might at least feel remorseful. . . . When you come to SF I will have a nice little Japanese girl for you, a regular little Lady Murasaki. "She is a Catholic," so I know she will be safe in your hands.

Faithfully
KENNETH

/ · /

Dwight: Dwight Macdonald (1906–1982) from the late 1930s served as an editor of the *Partisan Review*, until in 1944 he broke from the journal over political differences and founded *Politics*. KR: "I was corresponding with Simone Weil, Camus, before the *Partisan Review* ever heard of them! Later they were turned up for New York by Dwight and Nancy Macdonald" *(SFP)*. The *Partisan Review* started as an organ of the Communist John Reed Writers' Club under the title *Partisan Review and Anvil* in February 1934, "from the womb of the depression crying for a proletarian literature and a socialist America"; as Western organizer for the John Reed Club (though not a member of the CP), KR was fond of pointing out that he was one of those responsible for founding the journal, and in 1936 published a poem in its third issue. Eventually, the magazine broke with the John Reed Club, regrouping under the editorship of William Phillips, Philip Rahv, Macdonald, Mary McCarthy, F. W. Dupee, and George Morris as the *Partisan Review*.

KR contributed poems to the early issues, but after Macdonald's departure came to regard the journal (as it began progressively to feature more university poets and critics, especially those associated with New Criticism) as the official organ of "the self-styled New York Establishment." For example, Norman Podhoretz's extremely influential attack on a number of the younger writers KR supported, "The Know-Nothing Bohemians," appeared in *PR* in 1956. In his *SFP* interview, KR would point out that "since most of the people, except the southern agrarians, had been onetime Stalinists, they just took over all the techniques of Stalinism . . . you know, hatchet reviews and logrolling and wire-pulling and controls of foundations and academic jobs and so forth. . . . They had the thing absolutely by the balls, just like the Commies had had it just before them. If you got in the *Partisan Review* you could put up your little pattie and get a job on any English faculty in the USA. We fought these people continuously" *(SFP)*.

Sappho: (c. 620–565 B.C.), Greek poet. In "The Poet as Translator" *(Assays)*, KR gives a number of translations of Sappho's "Apple Orchard," including his own, which offered "one of the memorable experiences of my life, just because of the completeness of projection into the experience of that great dead Greek woman."

part of the war: JL's bad back (injured in a ski race) kept him out of the Army. He supervised a ski school for the Army at his resort in Alta, Utah, which trained paratroopers to ski. Supposedly, they were to parachute down on dams in northern Italy to blow them up; actually, they were shot down over Sicily by American anti-aircraft fire.

Lady Murasaki: Murasaki Shikibu (c. 979–1031), Japanese poet and novelist. In "The Art of Literature" *(WOTW)*, KR argues that the *Tale of Genji* by Murasaki Shikibu "has sometimes been considered by obtuse critics as no more than a satire on the sexual promiscuity of the Heian court. In fact, it is a profoundly philosophical, religious, and mystical novel."

9. **TLS-1**   25 July [19]42
                                          [San Francisco]

DEAR JIM,

Congratulations on being still in the land of the living. . . .

During the evacuation we did a lot of work with the Japanese. Since then I have done some in re library and art service for the camps, and Marie [Rexroth] donated her vacation as Public Health Nurse for Tanforan, the concentration camp nearest SF. We decided that it would be impossible to work for the Resettlement Camps without becoming morally involved in the procedure, so we abandoned that idea. There is no chance of working with one Quaker camp, if it ever opens. They have their own people, and they are also very chary of anybody who looks like a radical pacifist. I suppose you know from "the folks in Penn" that the Friends are having one of their good old quakerly dogfights about the war, socialism, the state, and like issues. . . .

I had an art exhibit at the museyroom here. Well enough received. I wish I could get my pictures on to Chicago and NY. The asst. curator thinks he may be able to do that little thing for me eventually. I have been very busy with the long poem, the Phoenix and the Tortoise, very philosophical and all. . . . Do you publish ND just to make the works of James the Four shine by contrast? You and [Sanders] Russell were much the best in the number, which gave me a headache. [Robert] Symmes is out here now, as I guess you know, certainly a fetching boy. Little as I fancy that milieux, their stuff, that group I mean, is about as lively as anything being written by youngsters now.

Of course there is a large amount of pacifist, [Gerald] Heardian sort of verse accumulating here and in England against a dam of "voluntary censorship." You might gain a species of kudos by featuring it in *ND* 42. But to me it is no end muggy, and I guess it is going to take more than the current commotion to produce the surgical poetry of the late TE Hulme's fancy. After all, Sappho did live at the *beginning*, Sidonius at the *end*, of classical civilization. . . .

Faithfully
KENNETH

/ · /

an art exhibit: KR had attended the Chicago Art Institute for a time as a teenager, and throughout his life continued to paint and draw, as well as write essays on art and artists for *ARTnews*, the *Nation*, and other journals.

You and Russell: ND 1941's "A Little Anthology of Contemporary Poetry," with work by JL and Sanders Russell, as well as Josephine Miles, Charles Henri Ford, John Berryman, and fifteen other poets. With Robert [Symmes] Duncan and Virginia Admiral, Sanders edited the literary journals *Ritual* and the *Experimental Review*.

Symmes: American poet Robert Duncan (1919–1988), who until 1941 published under the name Robert E. Symmes. Although in the September 1941 issue of *Experimental Review* in a review of *ND* 5 Duncan attacked JL as "bad intentioned, long winded and irresponsible . . . an undergraduate book reviewer," ND eventually published a number of Duncan's books, beginning with *Bending the Bow* in 1968. In his "San Francisco Letter" (*Evergreen Review,* 1, 2, 1957, later quoted on the jacket of *The Opening of the Field,* Duncan's first major press book), KR wrote: "Of all the San Francisco group Robert Duncan is the most easily recognizable as a member of the international avant garde. Mallarmé or Gertrude Stein, Joyce or Reverdy, there is a certain underlying homogeneity of idiom, and this idiom is, by and large, Duncan's . . . the theme is consistently the mind and body of love."

The two poets' first contact came when Duncan wrote KR asking for work for the *Experimental Review;* later, after they began spending time together in San Francisco, Duncan wrote Pauline Kael, "We have, here, become rabid Rexroth devotees—for the man himself I mean. He has a truly amazing quantity of knowledge. We learned only this last week that he reads the *Encyclopaedia Britannica* from cover to cover yearly. . . . That is coupled with a high-style in the Johnsonian tradition, a never ceasing to delight and astonishing gift for burlesque, a caustic and an affectionate wit" (Fass, *Young Robert Duncan*).

According to Duncan's *Conjunctions* interview, Rexroth continuously tried to get JL to publish the younger poet (and was responsible for Duncan's first appearance in an *ND* annual with the reprinting of "Heavenly City, Earthly City" in *ND* 10, 1948): "But Laughlin is actually independent. Kenneth was most important to him because he felt that Kenneth opened up so much of what made it lively all over again for him to print."

TE Hulme: Thomas Ernest Hulme (1883–1917), British poet, essayist. His four published poems were appended to Ezra Pound's *Personae*.

10. TLS-1   [Fall 1942]
                                               [San Francisco]

DEAR JIM,

. . . Was called on by R[obert] Duncan-Symmes, an engaging creature, but have yet to meet Aurora Bligh. Bob says, "She called herself Aurora because she likes to stay up all night, and she called herself Bligh after Captain Bligh." It's getting so you have to wear a board in your britches when you go out in doubledome society. Just think, I have lived through Sex, Sophistication, Thomism, Humanism, Stalinism, Trotskyism, Homosexualism, and now Sadomasochism. Those intellectuals, always up to something. . . .

Faithfully
KENNETH

/ · /

Aurora Bligh: American poet and artist Mary Fabilli (1914–); her prose piece, "The History of the Secret Guardian," appeared in *ND* 8 (1944).

11. TLS-1

November 9 [1942]
Norfolk

DEAR KENNETH,

Glad to hear that things appear to be working out the way you want them. I was afraid they had you. Think how RUGGED you will get chopping trees down. Hell you'll be able to knock out any of [Robert] McAlmon's teeth that Hemingway has left—not to mention you might get up that cliff up there at the needles that we kept sliding down that day.

As Henry Miller says, always cheery and bright or JUST TRY to find the silver lining.

Yes, I definitely want to use some of your new poem in the next ND. So let me see as much as you can finish when you go, and I'll pick out a good chunk.

Re the verse of your sick-green period. I have no doubt it is much better than almost any other effort of the period barring billyums and Zuk the zucker, but I don't think I want to go back for it. As to printers to print it for you . . . Anaïs Nin wants to do some printing. Her setting is better than [James] Decker's but her ink control bad. Unlike the squid which she is said to resemble in bed, as printer she cannot make it flow.

I'm afraid [Charles] Snider is dead or buried in some jail. Not a peep out of him in months and he knew I wanted to print him. too bad. An original. . . .

J

/ · /

Hemingway: Ernest Hemingway (1899–1961), American novelist. Hemingway contributed a brief piece to Peter Russell's *An Examination of Ezra Pound,* published by ND in 1950, and an introduction to Elio

Vitorini's novel *In Sicily*. In his 1963 essay "The Institutionalization of Revolt, The Domestication of Dissent," KR would write: "Hemingway was certainly a thoroughly conventional personality—anyone who could sit still for five minutes in Harry's Bar . . . is indisputably a square. His tough guy code was bluster and bullying, he was the model and idol of a generation of junior executives, especially the type of Yale man or *Time* editor, but he had talent and a certain tragic feeling" *(WOTW)*.

the next ND: KR's "The Phoenix and the Tortoise" (titled "The Phoenix and the Turtle" on the contents page) appeared in *ND* 8 (1944).

Henry Miller: (1891–1987), American novelist. ND published a number of titles by Miller, including *The Cosmological Eye, The Air-Conditioned Nightmare,* and *The Time of the Assassins*. JL: "*Tropic of Cancer* is a marvellous book. Did I tell you how I got to know about Henry? One day I was having lunch with Ezra [Pound] in 1935 in Rapallo, and he threw a paperback across the table. 'Waall, Jas, here's a dirty book that's pretty good.' I wrote to Henry and we got into a correspondence" *(PR)*. In a 1935 letter to Lawrence Durrell, Miller offered to introduce Durrell to JL, "an enterprising young man at Harvard . . . Laughlin is the chap who tried to reprint my *Aller Retour New York* (under the title 'Glittering Pie'). He had the first ten pages published in the *Harvard Advocate,* and then the Boston police descended upon the paper, destroyed the existent copies and locked the editorial staff up overnight, threatening them with a severe jail sentence. Mine wasn't the only offending contribution. Seems a story by Laughlin himself was also responsible for the mess. Anyway, it's all blown over sweetly and the boys have promised to behave. . . . He's a good egg. And he has connections!"
 In "The Influence of French Poetry on American" *(Assays)*, KR wrote: "Miller, of course, is another writer so American he is completely assimilable to French culture and stands at ease in the small company of Restif, Céline, and Sar Peladan"; "The Reality of Henry Miller" prefaced Miller's *Nights of Love and Laughter,* a 1955 pocketbook. In 1957, Miller would review two of KR's ND volumes in the *San Francisco Chronicle,* arguing that "his work is probably more widely known throughout the world than that of any other poet barring Ezra Pound. . . . He is, in effect, the poets' ambassador from Heaven sent."

billyums and Zuk the zucker: W. C. Williams and Louis Zukofsky. Zukofsky (1904–1978, American poet) published KR's "Prolegomenon to a Theodicy," "Fundamental Disagreement with Two Contemporaries," and "The Place for Yvor Winters" in his *An "Objectivists" Anthology* in 1932, marking KR's first anthology appearance. Zukofsky was a close friend of Ezra Pound and W. C. Williams; though he published no volume with ND, his "Mantis" appeared in the first *ND* annual, a substantial selection from his long poem *A* in *ND* 3, and a selection from the in-progress prose work, *Bottom: On Shakespeare,* in *ND* 14. KR's "The Sufficient" is dedicated to Zukofsky.

Anaïs Nin: In volume 5 of her *Diary* (Winter 1954–55), Nin writes of KR: "I broke with The Living Theatre after seeing a play by Kenneth Rexroth, and another short piece by Gertrude Stein. I wrote a letter and asked that my name be removed from the list of sponsors." Her press, which published its first books in 1942, was called Gemor. According to KR's *Conjunctions* interview, "One of the most extraordinary things is that these silly neo-feminists that have been created by television personalities and editors of magazines have made a heroine of this woman, who suffered to the hundredth degree from the feminine form of what they call macho. What I would call *cunto.* How anybody could be a feminist and stand her is beyond me. Anaïs Nin used to call me up when she lived in San Francisco, and invite me to come over to dinner. And I'd say, no baby, you're not gonna get me in that diary!" W. C. Williams's essay on Nin, "Men . . . Have No Tenderness," appeared in *ND* 7.

Decker's: James A. Decker would publish KR's *The Art of Worldly Wisdom* in 1949.

12. TLS-2

[Summer 1943]
[San Francisco]

DEAR JIM,

. . . Those who have taken my position in life are as of date either in jail, concentration camps, dead, or in just my fix, and that their number is legion and their favorite sport is writing the immensely wealthy James IV and asking him for "advances" on the radioactive Baedekers to the Isles of Langherhans that they are all busy trying to write. You know, nobody has any notion of the coffin of circumstance that walls in somebody like [Kenneth] Patchen or [Henry] Miller or myself or dozens of others. . . .

I dont know which is worse, the news that Marie [Rexroth] has gone forever, or that she has gone over to the Enemy. I am so stupefied at the thought that her years with me have meant so little that she could do such a thing. Still, Nicola Sacco's son Dante is a scissorbill storekeep in Boston, has changed his name, and denies that he is the son of his father. Basically, I suppose, she has never understood my ideas, or had any real belief in the importance of my writing. Let alone painting. I dont believe today she thinks I can paint—it's just one of Kenneth's hobbies. The funny thing is, it always seems to happen—Fanny Brawn[e] or whoever. Only Blake and Cowper ever got the kind of wives poets should have, and Blake's was illiterate, and Cowper's wasnt his wife. That of course is the reason I have been so bitter about the book the *P[hoenix]* & *T[ortoise]* and would never [have] actually tried to publish it if you hadn't taken it. Just think—I closed that mss. at Xmas 1942—in January she had run away. The poems have a pretty bitter taste—I don't like to read them, and I dread seeing them in print. The point d'appui of my whole life concept is the Sacrament of Marriage. I cant understand it. . . .

c̄ love
KENNETH

Mon coeur mis à nu

Musique
De l'esclavage
Des femmes du monde
Des filles
Des Magistrats
Des sacraments
L'homme de lettres est l'ennemi du monde.
Des bureaucrates

Dans l'amour, comme dans presque toutes les affaires humaines, l'entente cordiale est le résultat d'un mal-entendu. Ce malentendu c'est le plaisir. L'homme crie: O mon ange. La femme roucoule: Maman!

Maman! Et ces deux imbéciles sont si perdues qu'ils pensent de concert.—Le gouffre infranchissable, qui fait l'incommunicabilité reste infranchi.

It's all there bud!

/ · /

Patchen: Kenneth Patchen (1911–1972), American poet and artist. JL first published Patchen's work in *ND* 3 and 4, followed by *First Will & Testament* (1939), remaining the writer's primary publisher throughout his life. During 1938–39, Patchen and his wife Miriam lived in Norfolk, Connecticut, working for ND. In her memoir of this period *(Conjunctions),* Miriam Patchen recalled: "We worked solidly. Kenneth covered all orders which came in, took care of bookkeeping, press material, some correspondence. Anything which needed an editorial opinion was immediately sent on to JL . . . Kenneth had nothing to do with the editorial work. However, it is due to the strength of Kenneth's feeling that ND published Dylan Thomas. . . . He did the same thing with our beloved Louis Céline and Henry Miller. . . . Kenneth discovered that the only photograph in Laughlin's room was that of— Kenneth Patchen! That surprise remained an unspoken secret to anyone but me. . . . JL would suddenly appear in Norfolk, work like a demon on book design, write letters, chat with Kenneth, then, batches of work finished, grab an axe and go into the woods to chop trees for firewood." In "Kenneth Patchen, Naturalist of the Public Nightmare" *(Bird),* KR would write that Patchen's poems "are amongst the very few poems of their kind, written by an American, which can compete confidently in the international arena of contemporary 'comparative literature . . .' Patchen has become the laureate of the doomed youth of the Third World War."

Nicola Sacco: Nicola Sacco (1891–1927) and Bartolomeo Vanzetti (1888– 1927), Italian anarchists executed in the United States in 1927. KR closes his *AN* with, "During the third week of our stay in San Francisco, Sacco and Vanzetti were executed. A great cleaver cut through all the intellectual life in America. The world in which Andrée and I had grown up came forever to an end. One book of my life was closed and it was time to begin another."

Blake: William Blake (1757–1827), British visionary poet, engraver. In "The Institutionalization of Revolt, The Domestication of Dissent" *(WOTW),* KR would write, "The Romantic credo may have presented the artist, and especially the poet, as prophet, as the permanent, irreconcilable critic of society. There is almost no evidence to support this claim. Prophets, like madmen and albinos, arise in all walks of life. Actually a personality like Blake is much more likely to be found among self-educated skilled mechanics than among intellectuals, and of course this is what Blake really was, a professional engraver who lived by the sweat of his brow, almost the only self-supporting artist or poet of the entire Romantic tradition."

13. TLS-2   [Fall 1943]
                                               [San Francisco]

DEAR JIM,

. . . I suppose my last letter sounded pretty bitter. Certainly I hope Marie [Rexroth] returns—tho I dont expect it. But there is no question that I must get over my dependence on her—financially because it is warping her terribly—emotionally? . . . After all, my main object in life is to get my work done. The news about Kenny Patchen is very depressing. I have always thot that crik in his back psychogenic, can't he get it bugged out of him? His work has really gone slowly sour since 1st Will & Testament. No society has ever treated its worst criminals like this one treats its artists. I dont wonder the Kierkegaard Beat Me Mama Boys like [Arthur] Koestler and friends are so popular. This world is not only destroying its caste of humanists, but it is torturing them to death on a life-long basis, like having your bowels twisted out onto a drum, hour after hour, year after year, till at last you holler Uncle and Vyshinsky rests his case. Six hundred years BC there must have been a sunspot. A conspiracy started c̄ Buddha and Kung Fu-tse and Thales—humanist culture began—essentially an occult secret society of the good will. By hook or crook it has perpetuated itself to the present. At last it has been found out. It set out to redeem the state—it succeeded in educating the state to the point where it was able to realize the threat to its organized irresponsibility. If the Parthenon was the symbol of Athens, the Moscow trials are the symbol of this society. Soon we will all be gone, and the world will sink back into purely impersonal, irresponsible social forms—"anonymous and communal," the formic order of Egypt and Babylon. The idea that culture in the humanist sense—the system of values that have prevailed in Europe since Homer—is something that comes natural to the human race is nonsense. For six thousand years civilized life was as impersonal as the Pyramids or Lenin's tomb, and uncivilized life for maybe a million years before that. What I stand for is a fugitive aberration in the life history of the species. The trouble is that we have irritated the world with poetry and armed it with explosives—the future Assyrians will unquestionably destroy the race, and the planet along with it most likely. You know, it is notions like this, that never leave my mind, that make me such a difficult person for the gals to live with. I envy no one the job of being my wife, mistress or lover—or even friend for that matter. . . .

Marie has always fed the dog. I am having one hell of a time making her eat.

c̄ Love
Kenneth

/ · /

that crik: The "crick" in Kenneth Patchen's back was the result of his attempt to separate the locked bumpers of two cars involved in an accident. First thought to be arthritis, later the problem was diagnosed as a slipped disc. In 1959, Patchen experienced a "surgical mishap," and spent most of the last decade of his life bedridden and in severe pain.

14. TLS-2   [Spring 1944]
                                        [Norfolk]

DEAR KENNETH,

Thanks for the proofs . . . I'm glad you liked the dedication. I feel it is deserved. It isn't there entirely because I happen to like you, screwball that you are. In my opinion you are one of the leading men of letters of this republic. I doubt that this view will be widely espoused in our lifetimes, but any little thing I can do to register that fact I shall. . . .

Why don't you stop asking me WHO IS Svevo and go get the book at the library and READ it. Italo Svevo: CONFESSIONS OF ZENO. It's the most wonderful thing I've come onto in years. He was a pal of Joyce's in Trieste. A business man. Worth all of [Robert] McAlmon, [Mary] Butts and that gang combined. Page after page of miraculous revelation of how the mind actually functions in life as is. [Edouard] Roditi is rediscovering him in the next *P[artisan] R[eview]* so you better hurry to get something into *Circle* before, so they won't say you copied *PR*.

Sending you Merton and Melville.

Will write [Harry] Duncan at Cummington to send you the [W. C. Williams] *Wedge*. . . .

I disapprove of the idea of your publishing your early stuff. I don't have a clear recollection of it but I seem to recall it was obscure. It will just snarl up your "new" reputation. Forget it. Or print for private circulation only. . . .

I never did reach the Rosa Luxemburg letters. Do you have them? Have you the [Randolph] Bourne stuff? I can't get at nothing here. Can the SF library produce [Christopher] Isherwood's LAST (or

RETURN OF) MR NORRIS? I badly want to read that too. . . .

                                                    Be good
                                                    J

                            / · /

the proofs: JL's second book of poems, *Some Natural Things,* published by ND in 1945.

Italo Svevo: (1861–1928), Italian novelist, playwright, critic. ND reprinted the 1930 Knopf edition of Svevo's *The Confessions of Zeno* in 1947. Svevo's *As a Man Grows Older* was published in 1949 by ND as a joint production with Putnam's, London.

Joyce: James Joyce (1882–1941), Irish novelist. ND had imported *Our Exagmination Round His Factification for Incamination of Work in Progress* (a symposium on Joyce by Samuel Beckett, W. C. Williams, and others, published by Sylvia Beach's Shakespeare and Company, Paris), in 1939. This was followed in 1944 with Joyce's *Stephen Hero* (the first draft of *A Portrait of the Artist as a Young Man*), and in 1945 with Joyce's play *Exiles* (first published in the U.S. in 1918). In his *Conjunctions* interview, KR called Joyce a "man of insufferable conceit. . . . Unlike Gertrude Stein, his syntactical and technical devices are unusable. Anyway, I, for one, simply cannot take seriously a man who insisted that only Italian be spoken at his dinner table in the very week that a new glory was born in a Dublin post office."

Butts: Mary Butts (1892–1937), British novelist. Her 1925 *Ashe of Rings* included scenes of witchcraft, incest, adultery, and spiritualism.

Roditi: Edouard Roditi (1910–), American poet, journalist, linguist. ND published his *Oscar Wilde* in 1947, *Poems 1928–1948* in 1949, and *The Delights of Turkey* in 1977. Roditi's first work appeared with KR's in Charles Henri Ford's *Blues* in 1929. Roditi's essay on Italo Svevo was included in ND's 1949 edition of Svevo's *As a Man Grows Older.*

something into Circle: In 1944, KR published essays on Robert McAlmon and Mina Loy in George Leite's *Circle;* see note, letter 21.

Merton and Melville: In 1944, ND published Herman Melville's *Selected Poems* (edited with an introduction by F. O. Matthiessen); Thomas Merton's first book, *Thirty Poems.*

the Wedge: Dedicated to Louis Zukofsky, W. C. Williams's *The Wedge* was published in a limited edition by the Cummington Press in 1944. According to Williams's *I Wanted to Write a Poem,* "I have always been proud of this book. The Introduction, written in the most forthright prose, is an explanation of my poetic creed at that time. . . . Jim Laughlin said he couldn't get any paper—it was war time. There were two young men [Harry Duncan and Paul Williams] living in Cummington, Massachusetts, running the Cummington Press. They were interested in publishing small volumes of poetry. They were very poor . . . We met and they decided to do the book for me."

Rosa Luxemburg: (1871–1919), German Socialist activist. In "Simone Weil" *(Assays)*, KR wrote of Luxemburg: "She had a tenacious orthodoxy: she was perfectly confident of the sufficiency of Marxism as an answer, though she was more humane about it than Lenin. She had a warm, purely human love of people—physically, their smell and touch and comradeship."

Isherwood: Christopher Isherwood (1904–1986), British novelist. ND would publish an American edition of Christopher Isherwood's novel *The Last of Mr. Norris* (along with *Goodbye to Berlin*) as *The Berlin Stories* in 1945. KR: "[Isherwood was] very polished and at the same time witty and ironic. And he never made an international cause of his disabilities. I told Laughlin once, if you want to know the intellectual climate of Weimar Germany there are two books you can pick up by Christopher Isherwood: they are *it*" *(Conjunctions)*.

15. TLS-2   [December 1944]
                                         [San Francisco]

DEAR JIM,

. . . H[enry] M[iller] showed up yesterday. I like him very much. He is a much more professionalized person than I had been given to understand. I told him he looked more like Yvor Winters than Wambly Bald. Lepska [Miller] is a really ideal little girl. Well read, intelligent, obedient, extremely young, very hot looking. Like all Slavs, she gives off a sort of muffed and booted aroma of Venus in Furs—but there were no loud noises from the bedroom last night—but they were tired, or maybe they do it with hatpins. [Harry] Ro[skolen]ko and his girl used to sound like Mercedes the Queen of the Great Cats, except there were no pistol shots. Actually—Lepska has a gaze of turquoise innocence. I dont see any reason why we shdnt get along with Miller. Strange as it may seem to you, in the recesses of my vast erudition I know much more about this Neo-Brahmin stuff than even [Gerald] Heard, let alone Miller. The thing that annoys me about them is not what they are talking about, but the fact that they know so little about it—Heard has always reminded me of the articles on the Wonders of Science in the Hearst Sunday Supplement. . . . A vulgar man. Miller is not vulgar—he is definitely NOT trying to mislead anyone. . . .

Now look, Jim, you have got to stop all this late anal stuff—most people dont take the attitude "Mistah Laughlin he sick"—and it makes you hard to be friends with. . . . When the publisher of *New Directions* talks about sloppy business methods I just feel tired. You watch out—the next step is radio messages thru the bedsprings, next sexual intercourse by Frequency Modulation, after that—chaos. Loosen up—the world isnt out to do you in—or if it is, no more than anybody else. I think a week's strict regimen of lighting cigars with $10 bills would do you a lot of good. . . .

I cant tell you how pleased I am you are writing again. And how impressive your poems are. What you need is to take Maggie [Laughlin] and the little ones to some quiet far away place and sit and write for about a year—the future is losing by your distractions. . . . It is so god damned much better than the current mumble.

I got a letter from Ted Weiss saying he didnt think he shd print a poem in favor of Y[vor] A[rthur] Winters. So I wrote him a nice little lecture on how he was a bad boy. A funny little constipated note from Arthur Himself—addressed, of all things, "Dear Kenneth." I almost fainted. I have always been, "My dear Mr. Rexroth" chez the wintry Winters. I was immeasurably touched. He sure is ignorant—he says I would be quite a poet if I didn't write free verse and even poor old Babbitt Estaban knows it aint free verse. . . .

KENNETH

/ · /

Wambly Bald: An American newspaperman who worked for the Paris edition of the *Chicago Tribune* and in 1931 wrote a column on Henry Miller, the first publicity the writer received.

Lepska: Janina Martha Lepska Miller. She and Henry Miller had just arrived in San Francisco to spend a week with KR following their marriage.

Roko: Harry Roskolenko (1907–1980; also spelled Roskolenkier), American poet.

Maggie: Margaret Laughlin, JL's first wife. KR: JL "met a Salt Lake girl, Margaret whom I've always liked very much, whom he married. And Laughlin and Margaret did all the work for New Directions in the barn of Meadow House. In my opinion, ND would be a far better publishing house if it was still operating on that basis" *(Conjunctions).*

Ted Weiss: Theodore Weiss (1919–), editor of *The Quarterly Review of Literature,* which published KR's "A Homestead Called Damascus" in 1957. The "poem in favor of YA Winters" was "The Giant Weapon," published in *QRL* in 1945 as "February 1944."

16. TLS-3   December 9 [1944]
                                              [Alta, Utah]

DEAR KENNETH,

I bitterly and personally resent your attack on my New York office. They have done everything and more than could be expected for your book. We literally bombarded the San Francisco stores with propaganda about your book, beginning six weeks ago

. . . I put more work into the promotion of your book than I have done on any other book in years and I bitterly resent your allegation that we did not do our best for it. I wrote over forty personal letters to critics and important figures in the poetry world. . . .

On the whole I don't worry about the book. Marjorie Farber is said to be reviewing it for the TIMES. If she is favorable we will sell out the edition. But it is a pity that the San Francisco stores have to continue being impossible in their attitude toward poetry.

Turning to other matters: the question of [Harry] Roskolenko. I have not answered his wire and I will not see him because I have never forgiven him for swindling me six years ago. At that time he ordered books under five or six false names and addresses, not paying for them and then selling them around the Village for cash. We caught up with him because he used the same typewriter for each order and it had a defective key. When confronted he sent me a preposterous letter stating that it was his duty to communist culture to exploit a capitalist publisher in this way and "get the books into circulation." . . .

If he wrote a good poem that I liked I would not hesitate to praise it. I have never expected good poets to be good Xtians, good liberals or anything else, but I certainly don't mix with out and out thieves. . . .

I note what you say about stressing the pussy to sell P&T. We'll do that if necessary. I don't really like to, however, as I don't think that is the best part of the book. Several of the people who have written in, who have otherwise liked the stuff, censure the poem about fucking in the beeloud glade or whatever. I still think that is a frightfully embarrassing poem. There are ways and ways of talking about fucking in poetry and that, in my opinion, does not get away with it. . . .

Do you want to come up here this winter and tour around a bit and work on cabins? I am very behind with my work and would not be able to recreate much with you. And you would have to avoid getting pickled and antagonizing the conventional guests . . . but there are a hell of a lot of books here you could read. . . .

love
JIM

[TPC ENCLOSED]
POSTSCRIPT—

Oh shit. Life is too short to malinger grievances. Tell Roskolenko to come along and ski if he wants to but I won't do business with him. It will do my hubric ego good to stomach a few past wrongs.

J

/ · /

your book: The Phoenix and the Tortoise, KR's first ND volume, which won the California Literature Silver Medal Award for book design, contained the title poem (a philosophical reverie), a selection of lyrics, elegies, and satires, as well as a section of translations and imitations. W. C. Williams reviewed the volume for *The Quarterly Review of Literature* in 1945.

stressing the pussy: Earlier, KR had advised JL that in the marketing of *Phoenix,* he should "drop the philosophy and push the pussy."

17. ALS-6   [December 1944]
                               [San Francisco]

DEAR JIM,

What's all this about "attacks" on your New York Office? I just told you what dealers told me. It so happens that the book began to show up right after that . . . I knew you were doing more than any "capitalist publisher" would ever dream of doing. As for the first two poems in the 2nd section—you always liked them until you have been had at by your perpetually disappointed vice presidential candidate on the Parnassus Ticket. Somebody showed me a review of his in the *Nation* of ND c̄ a snide reference to me. Why on earth does he dislike me so? Worse— he has made the *Partisan Review* completely unreadable which is a pity—it was a good magazine as long as Dwight [Macdonald] was on it. . . .

I have never forgotten how Buddy [Oppen] deliberately tried to do me as much literary damage as he could. He told Ezra [Pound] I was a "passed" Jew & a communist. Two or three years later—he then a Stalinist—told folks in NY I was a Pro-Nazi Trotskyite. The Oppens are crazy. If you care to, you can put on your tombstone "The only rich man Rexroth ever liked." Knowing that world—how can you blame the [Harry] Rosko[lenko]s if without knowing you they thought you are just another Buddy Oppen? I am sure nobody thinks so anymore. . . .

Surely you understand that the poem that embarrasses you is a deliberate bit of defiance of literary fashion amongst other things. The *Chronicle* reviewer is one of the editors of their weekly newsmagazines & the least Stalinist person available. . . . It is the best to be hoped for out of Red San Francisco, where the Jewish millionairesses and the whores of the kept press snub me on the street because I am a counter revolutionary. . . .

KENNETH

/ · /

vice presidential candidate: Delmore Schwartz. Schwartz reviewed *ND* 8, "Delights and Defects of Experiment," for the *Nation* (October 21, 1944): "Mr. Laughlin, an old one at eating his cake and denouncing it too, denounces imperialism in his preface, which is good fun because it illustrates how inexpensive righteous sentiments are, and he invokes the necessity of experimentalism as a literary method, which, in the abstract, one can no more object to than one can object to blank verse or piano-playing, in the abstract. Most of these authors try hard to be experimental, and they show very well how predictable experimental writing can be."

Buddy: George Oppen (1908–1987), American poet. Following the publication of his first book by the Objectivist Press in 1934, Oppen stopped writing poetry for twenty-five years. In 1962, ND published his second book, *The Materials,* then *This in Which* (1965), *Of Being Numerous* (1968), and *Collected Poems* (1975). In *Excerpts,* KR calls Oppen "one of the best of my contemporaries." Winner of the 1969 Pulitzer Prize.

Ezra Pound: (1885–1972), American poet, essayist, translator. It was Pound who suggested JL begin ND, which remained Pound's principal publisher, following the 1938 release of *Culture* (later, *Guide to Kulchur*). According to JL, "At the time we started he was being published by Farrar and Rinehart, a distinguished old firm, but they made an odd mistake—how could they have known?—of sending him at Christmastime a copy of his latest book bound in leather. His judgement of this, quite unjustified, was 'They must be crooks.' I have no idea what his rationalization was. So he took his work away from them and gave it to me" *(PR).* JL's various essays and talks on Pound are collected in *Pound as Wuz* (Greywolf Press, 1988), and in *PR* he reiterated that Pound and KR were his greatest influences in developing ND's list.

In *APTC,* KR wrote of Pound that he "was fond of comparing himself to Lenin, writing angry letters from abroad. . . . He deliberately set out to teach the simplest elements, the basic foundations of culture, how to read and how to write. . . . Pound's verse was better than anybody else's at that moment and opened up new prosodic regions for poets who would come after him. . . . Pound's Chinese translations and his Nōh plays made Far Eastern literature meaningful in the context of modern society." KR had a number of strong objections to both Pound's political and his aesthetic theories. JL believes this was because "he considered Pound a fascist and Kenneth was an anarchist" *(PR);* Robert Duncan, however, argues that "in Parker Tyler's anthology, there is some indication that Pound objected to Rexroth. So Rexroth's objection to Pound was not just that Pound was a fascist, but that Pound had not appreciated him" *(Conjunctions* 4).

18. TLS-1

[December 1944]
[San Francisco]

DEAR JIM,

"I'm sorry I was cross" as they say. I dont know why I should start taking my frustration out on you. You know Jim, I guess I am beginning to get a little snakey. I have sunk into an absolute abysm of bitterness. The fact that I do not seem to be able to ever become even selfsupporting, let alone capable of supporting a wife and home and children, is beginning to destroy me, as it has, apparently, destroyed my marriage. Marie [Rexroth] has run away again—partly because she is sure I am sleeping with June [Oppen]—which just happens not to be true—but I think mostly because it has become literally impossible for her to keep our household functioning on her salary. It is just absurd that a person as smart and talented and whatnot as I am should be unable to feed himself. I have worked terribly hard, and done good, permanent work—and I have passed the turn of my life and I am a beggar with no more recognition than the slightest poetaster. Nothing in this life or any other is more important to me than my marriage—yet it is constantly falling to pieces—and is probably gone for good this time. I think of Ezra [Pound], who has always been better fixed in every way than me, growing diseased with bitterness—and it terrifies me. Why in the name of god did I ever choose such a profession? It horrifies me to think that behind what I really believe is some of the best love poetry of the 20th century lies vast expanses of jealous recrimination and bickering about money. I dont care how great the accomplishment is—it isnt worth that price. I shouldnt take all this out on you. I know you have troubles enough of your own. But

I have never had very many friends—and now those I had here are either gone or I have quarreled with them out of my own spleen and disorder. I have got to have somebody to talk to. Least of all am I appealing to you for "help." There isn't any help. I dont see anything to do about it. I shouldn't write you all this. This started out to be simply a letter of apology for my own bad manners. I despise people who publicize their own private troubles—but I have just got beyond the bearing point.

> with love
> KENNETH

19. TLS-2

[January 1945]
[San Francisco]

DEAR JIM,

. . . I have been reading last night [John] McTeggart and [D. T.] Suzuki in tandem—I dont think there is much question but what McT is essentially a mixture of Zen, Shingon and Kegon Buddhist; it makes fascinating reading. To think that he was at Cambridge at the height of the New Utilitarianism. You wdnt read 3 pages of the *Nature of Existence,* but you wd like it in his essays where he says better worship a crocodile which is at least sentient than the state.

[appended in holograph:]

Lots of love & give my regards to everybody in NY and start thinking about going up in the Sierras this summer.

> c̄ Love
> KENNETH

/ · /

a mixture of Zen: John McTeggart's *The Nature of Existence* had appeared in 1921. Through books like *Essays in Buddhism, Manuel of Zen Buddhism,* and *Zen and Japanese Culture,* D. T. Suzuki became one of the leading exponents of Zen Buddhism in English, especially on the West Coast. Suzuki's dialogue with Thomas Merton on the relationship between Buddhism and Christianity, "Wisdom in Emptiness," was published by JL in *ND* 17 (1961). While KR believed as did the mathematician Kurt Gödel that "a self-contained system is a contradiction in terms" (he would use the quote as an epigram for his 1965 volume, *Gödel's Proof: New Poems*), according to Robert Duncan *(Conjunctions 4),* "Kenneth thought deeply about the inner relation. He professed to be an Anglo-Catholic who also thought that Buddhism was the deeper reality, which is of course quite possible because Buddhism doesn't exclude having Christian beliefs." In his autobiography *In My Own Way,* the philosopher Alan Watts (who was a friend of both KR and Suzuki) would later write of the poet, "Try the idea of taking T. S. Eliot and pushing him all the way over into Mahayana Buddhism without taking away his fascination with Christian mysticism, and season it all with a spirit of intense, if cynical, social concern."

  KR's own preface to *The Signature of All Things* refers readers to the "better statements" of his "religious anarchism" in the work of Suzuki, along with Chuang Tze, Lao Tzu, and others. Further, in *SFP,* he would explain that "the West Coast is close to the Orient. It's the next thing out there. There are a large number of orientals living on the West Coast. San Francisco is an international city and it has living contact with the Orient. It also has an internal oriental life. Once a week you can go to see a Buddhist baseball game if you want to. There are Buddhist temples all over the place. To a New Yorker this is all ridiculous, the Orient means dimestore incense burners. It is very unreal."

20. TLS-2

[February 1945]
[San Francisco]

DEAR JIM,

  The [Robert] Graves is OK but he has no trouble getting printed. Why shd you do him when his regular publishers will if he annoys them enough? If you want an import, once more I recommend DOROTHY WELLESLEY—THE LOST PLANET. I think, while we are on the subject of Graves, that Laura Riding, who

hasn't been heard from in several years, needs publication much more. And what about Mina Loy? If
you dont like her work, you are mistaken in your
judgement. You could do worse than print the
English of the Sorley Maclean *Dain De Eimhir* that
you gave me. He is by far his own best translator;
and he is the best of the lot; tho a selected Hugh
MacDiarmid is badly needed in the US—I thought
that Macmillan announced it years ago—1940 I
think—but it never came out. . . .

I cant get over Dudley Fitts. Tell him I think I met
his local padre years ago—I think he is a Holy Cross
Associate—or else I served Mass for him at St. Luke's
Trinity, a favorite stopover for visiting anglocath-
olics in NY. Did I ever tell you that Rolfe Humphries is one of them too? O, we're really [a] brood.

Arent people funny? Neither Bob [McAlmon] nor
Mina Loy ever wrote and thanked me for the articles
I did on them. And I have never neglected to thank
even the most paltry newspaper reviewer of my own
stuff.

The P[hoenix] & *T[ortoise]* seems to be selling out
in SF. . . .

I think I will do a number on the Millionaire poets
for *Circle*—beginning—the possession of wealth is
both a privative and positive evil. [Walter Conrad]
Arensberg, [Harry] Crosby, [Winifred] Bryher,
[Nancy] Cunard, [Walter] Lowenfels, [George]
Oppen—can you name anymore? You won't be in
it dear, so don't get upset—but I hope you profit by
their example —not to say that you very conspicu-
ously haven't. That Jamesian clause means you *have*
so profited. In fact—if you weren't always slipping
over into paltry anal retentive mechanisms—I wd say
that you were pretty close to being saintly in your
devotion to your responsibilities. God knows, it must

be a terribly difficult life to live. I wdnt want it, for all its conspicuous amenities. Though I shdnt mind the spiritual satisfaction of its achievements. . . .

Did you ever read Hardy's *Two on a Tower*? It is his best novel and one of the Greek Myths. I think it is better than most of Lawrence. It didnt hurt and parch Hardy the way it did Lawrence. It just gnarled him, and gnarled is better than parched.

The faction in the Cal. [Berkeley] Eng. Dept. put thumbs down on my giving a reading there. . . .

I notice a lot of interest on the part of the local comrats in me lately. I expect I will have trouble with my draft board soon. The FBI once told me— the people who are making you trouble are, without exception, known Communists.

A conscientious objector named Weber was just sentenced to hang at Camp Roberts. There but for the grace of God. If you see Dwight [Macdonald], tell him to get on his horse about it. I am mad at him. He knows I am penniless, and yet he stopped sending me his magazine. Of course, his support of the Stalinists in Greece has finished him as a serious person—what moral frivolity!

> c̄ love from me and mine which now in-
> cludes a cat (named Mary)
> KENNETH

/ · /

Graves: Robert Graves (1895–1985), British poet, novelist, translator, essayist. In "The Poet as Translator" *(Assays)*, KR wrote of Graves's translation of the *Iliad, The Anger of Achilles*: "The recent hair-raising performance of Robert Graves both violates the text and fails to trans-late anything resembling Homer. This is not Homer for the readers of *Punch;* it is the invasion of the text of Homer by the text of *Punch* . . . an unpleasant eccentric eccentricity." The reference to a Graves MS is probably *Poems 1938–1945*, which was published the following year by another publisher.

Dorothy Wellesley: (1889–1956), British poet, editor of the Hogarth Living Poets series (for Virginia and Leonard Woolf's Hogarth Press). W. B. Yeats included a substantial number of her poems in his 1936 *Oxford Book of Modern Verse;* his *Letters on Poetry* were written to Wellesley, Duchess of Wellington.

Mina Loy: (1882–1966), British-born American poet, associated with the writers whose work appeared regularly in Alfred Kreymborg's magazine *Others* (including W. C. Williams and H.D.); her "Hot Cross Bum" appeared in *ND* 12 (1950). In the *Conjunctions* interview, KR argues that "Mina Loy and Laura Riding are the two long-lost major writers of the heroic age of American modernism. Both are utterly original and both are capable of the most profound thought." Loy's posthumous *The Last Lunar Baedeker* is dedicated to KR.

Sorley Maclean: (1911–), Gaelic poet, one of the leading figures of the modern Scottish Renaissance. KR includes work by Maclean in his *NBP:* "If other people can write poetry like this in Gaelic, there is no question but what it will again be a living language."

Hugh MacDiarmid: (1892–1978), Gaelic poet, critic, and a founder of the National Party of Scotland; pseud. of Christopher Murray Grieve. Expelled from the Communist Party in 1938 (which he rejoined in 1956). MacDiarmid's "The Divided Bird" had appeared in *ND* 6 (1941), and KR includes selections from his work in *NBP:* "He is unquestionably one of the most important writers in the British Isles, and a genuine world figure, but he is also a deliberate eccentric. . . . In many ways he resembles Ezra Pound."

Dudley Fitts: (1903–1968), American poet, classicist, translator, and critic. Fitts was JL's teacher at Choate, and a number of his poems had appeared in the first *ND* annual in 1936. His *Poems* (1937) was one of ND's first volumes, followed by *One Hundred Poems from the Palatine [Greek] Anthology* (1938) and *Poems from the Greek Anthology* (1956). In his *PR* interview, JL recalled: "Fitts was a very inspiring composition teacher; he got me writing prose. It was largely through him that I became editor of the Choate literary magazine. He was my introduction to modern poetry. He gave me Pound and Eliot to read. . . . [Fitts] who had been corresponding with Pound for a number of years, gave me a letter of introduction to him."

Rolfe Humphries: (1894–1969), American poet and translator. Humphries had given a mixed review of KR's first book in the *New Republic* (August 12, 1940), praising KR's imagery, finding fault with his "abstract thought."

Neither Bob: KR's "Les Lauriers sont coupés" (an essay on Robert McAlmon) and "Les Lauriers sont coupés, No. 2" (on Mina Loy) had appeared in *Circle* in 1944.

Arensberg: Walter Conrad Arensberg (1878–1954), American writer and art collector, financial backer of Alfred Kreymborg's *Others.*

Harry Crosby: (1897–1929), American poet, nephew of banker J. P. Morgan; with his wife Caresse, founded the Black Sun Press, whose many books published between 1925 and 1936 included D. H. Lawrence's *The Escaped Cock,* Hart Crane's *The Bridge,* and Ezra Pound's *Imaginary Letters.*

Winifred Bryher: (1894–1982), British novelist and poet, daughter of Sir John Ellerman, one of England's richest men; married to Robert McAlmon, who with funds from Ellerman established the Contact Publishing Company, which between 1922 and 1931 published W. C. Williams's *Spring and All,* Gertrude Stein's *The Making of Americans,* H. D.'s *Palimpsest,* and many other books.

Nancy Cunard: (1896–1965), British writer, heiress; between 1928 and 1931, her Hours Press published Samuel Beckett's first book, *Whoroscope,* as well as Ezra Pound's *A Draft of XXX Cantos* and Laura Riding's *Twenty Poems Less.*

Walter Lowenfels: (1897–1976), American writer, whose family fortune grew out of the butter business; Cunard's Hours Press published his *Apollinaire.*

You won't: JL's family fortune derived from a major Pittsburgh steel company founded by his Irish grandfather and a Welsh iron puddler in the nineteenth century. As JL recalled, "I adored my father, who was a marvellous man, very unlike a businessman. In fact, he wasn't a businessman. He stopped working in the steel mills when he was forty. . . . If I asked him for money, he'd say, 'Are you going to publish some more of those books that I can't understand?' And I'd say, 'Yes.' And he'd give it to me" *(PR).* According to KR, however, in the early days New Directions was financed by JL's aunt Leila Laughlin Carlisle, who also provided an office for ND in a converted stable on her estate in Connecticut *(Conjunctions).* By the mid-fifties, the publishing company had become self-sustaining.

known Communists: While KR described himself as "sort of the outdoor organizer for the John Reed Club" in San Francisco, and in fact served as San Francisco delegate to the first National Conference of the John Reed Clubs in May of 1932 (where Maxim Gorky, John Dos Passos, and Langston Hughes were nominated as honorary members of the presidium), he was never a member of the Communist Party, though he did apply. According to *SFP,* "Very few of these people were orthodox Commies because the basic tradition on the West Coast was IWW. The attitude was really an anarchistic attitude, and for many years I treasured—to flaunt in the face of the FBI, if they ever bothered me—an application to the CP that had written across it, 'Comrade Rexroth is a very valuable comrade, but he is entirely too much of an anarchist to be good party material.' It was signed by Earl Browder, the general secretary of the Party." Further, in *Conjunctions,* KR tells of visiting "the angel of the [Objectivist] group on his yacht in San

Francisco Bay. He wrote [Louis] Zukofsky that he could not support any book publication by me, because I was a self-evident Communist. In a few years he had made a complete about-face and then wanted to have nothing to do with me because I was a 'decadent-formalist-Trotskyite-Japanese-and-German agent'—the standard term, really one long, compound word, for anyone who had read the works of Marx and was not a member of the Communist Party." According to JL, "The angel of the Objectivist Press was George Oppen's father, who had a beautiful sailing yacht on SF Bay. The name was originally Oppenheimer and the money came from canneries. One of KR's myths was that most of the rich Jews in SF were Stalinists. Not so, of course. KR chased after George's sister June, a real beauty. She told me that he liked to drink champagne out of her slippers" (JL letter to the editor).

21. TLS-1   3 [19]45
                                          [San Francisco]

DEAR JIM,

I am annoyed. Be a good fellow and answer a letter now & again. . . .

Muriel Rukeyser seems to have dropped us. It came out that she was angling to get me to window dress her course at the Commy school. I refused politely and never saw her again. For which I am glad—the International Set has a definitely disturbing effect on me. The things they say and do make me so damned mad that I cant eat my supper.

All indications are that George Leite has gone over to the Top of the Mark unit of the Communist Political Association. It is only to be expected. He is completely without ethics, principles or morals, and they will feed him cocktails and give him small sums to print them and their friends. There is nobody else out here to do it. I certainly am never invited out, as they say. The great trouble with the [Henry] Miller outfit is their antinomianism—the characteristic sin of all irresponsible mysticism. The thing they dont realize is that the primary channel of spiritual realization is prayer, and prayer is the highest form of responsibility. People who are so unworldly that they have no regard for the truth or other people's property are, according to the best authorities, Devil worshippers. I used to think Henry was tarred with the same brush, but since I have met him, I doubt it. It seems to me that he is simply careless and inarticulate, and encourages vices in others simply because he himself is too innocent to be aware of them. The trouble with this Mene Tekel Upharsin school of current letters—[Aldous] Huxley, [Gerald] Heard, [W. H.] Auden, [Henry] Miller, [W. Somerset] Maugham (what an assortment a passing fashion brings forth, huh?)—is that they have no real understanding of evil. They can never make up their minds and waver between dualism, and complete denial of the existence of evil. This is the old, old story—first century Gnosticism was gnawing the same dilemma. I am afraid I am incurably orthodox. . . .

Now be a good boy, keep out of mischief, and write.

c̄ love
KENNETH

/ · /

Muriel Rukeyser: (1913–1980), American poet. Rukeyser won the Yale Younger Poets Prize for her first book, *Theory of Flight,* in 1935, when she was only twenty-one. ND published her *Elegies* in 1949, *Selected Poems* in 1963. At the time of this letter, Rukeyser was teaching a poetry writing workshop at the California Labor School; during this period she introduced KR to the painter Morris Graves and established a close and long-term friendship with Robert Duncan. In 1958, KR published an important review of Rukeyser's *Body of Waking* in the *New York Times Book Review;* later, in his foreword to Louis Kertesz's *The Poetic Vision of Muriel Rukeyser* (1980), KR would write: "Muriel Rukeyser is the best poet of her exact generation. . . . Purely as a thinker, she is certainly more profound than anyone else in her generation. It's just that her thoughts were not their thoughts. She is one of the most important writers of the Left of her time. . . . She never gave it all up to join the Anglican Church or edit a magazine for the CIA. . . . She is a poet of liberty, civil liberty, woman's liberty, and all other liberties that so many people think they themselves just invented in the last ten years." In another 1945 letter (not included here), KR writes JL, "Muriel Rukeyser is out here, giving a course for the Stalinist School. My, how she's grown. She has definitely become what the gels who handle it commercially characterize as a lot of mama. We had dinner c̄ her at [Jean] Varda's the other night. She seemed very wrought up about the P[hoenix] & T[ortoise], and almost came up my left nostril. Dunt leff, but her own recent book is the best she has written. She, like all of us, is definitely dropping the class struggle for the ass struggle, which is all to the good. Where the poems have any specificity they arent bad— and the specific lines—like "arched like the torso of love"—arouse in me the desire to give it to her any way she'd like it, as they say chez Harlem. But most of it is awfully vague—current argot of the etiolates. Not as bad as Geo. Barker, tho. You know, one reason for the emergence of the cunt and tit school in the present crisis in the soul of Western Man is that you cant go wrong."

George Leite: Editor of *Circle,* the most important literary journal to appear in the Bay Area during this period, published in Berkeley. *Circle*'s first number appeared in 1944, and it ran for ten issues. Its focus was literary, though it was both pacifist and anarchist as well; its credo: "When a technique becomes a school, death of creation is the result. Eclecticism is the only approach to Art in which there is no death. *Circle* is completely eclectic." Contributors included KR, William Everson, Robert Duncan, Henry Miller, W. C. Williams, Thomas Parkinson, and Anaïs Nin. KR designed the cover for issue 3.

Huxley: Aldous Huxley (1894–1963), British novelist whose interest in mysticism, parapsychology, and pacifism (as well as his failing vision) led him to emigrate to Southern California in 1937.

W. Somerset Maugham: (1874–1965), British novelist and playwright, who in his 1938 autobiography said that he was "in the very first row of second-raters."

22. TLS-1   [March 1945]
                                               [San Francisco]

DEAR JIM,

    . . . Isn't it awful? As the whole filthy body of dying Europe is being laid bare, it is apparent, what

I have said for years, that the world is in the grip of a pandemic of sadomasochism of a horrible náture and of terrifying proportions. Can it be isolated, and will it? I doubt it. A very large section of the human race seems to have become permanently and incurably mentally diseased. I imagine this is what happened in the Jurassic. As a species decays it always goes through the same maneuvers—the overbred sow eats her farrow, the poets and millionairesses of Proust devour each other in copulation. So doubtless did the dinosaurs as the climate urged. . . .

[Yvor] Winters and I gave papers at a thing called the American Society for Aesthetics last Saturday. Jesus Christ, what people! The recipe seems to be . . . extract taste and remove wit, add one tweed suit, one Phi Beta Kappa key, stir thoroughly with a blunt object, stuff balls with flour and half-bake. And poor Winters believes the university is replacing the monastery as the focus of responsibility! I call it Devil worship. I think Max Bodenheim when young had the right idea, "Ladies and Gentlemen, just to show you how I appreciate your intelligent interest, I am going to shit on the podium."

Love
K R

/ · /

Proust: Marcel Proust: (1871–1922), French novelist, essayist, critic. KR's reference is to Proust's seven-part *Remembrance of Things Past*.

Winters and I: In *Excerpts,* KR recalls that when Yvor Winters was up for tenure review at Stanford, "rumors went about that he would be dropped. Many people at U.C. Berkeley were anxious to get him. So, as an exploratory move, he was invited to give a talk before the Aesthetics Society, along with myself. I haven't the faintest memory of what my talk was about, but his was an acerbic criticism of a poem of Gerard Manley Hopkins. Unfortunately, he didn't have the faintest idea of what the poem was about."

Max Bodenheim: Maxwell Bodenheim (1892–1954), American poet and novelist. A member of Walter Arensberg and Alfred Kreymborg's *Others* group, and an influence on W. C. Williams. In *SFP,* KR recalls: "When I was a young kid in my teens, I ran a place in Chicago, with a couple of girls, called the Green Mask . . . Maxwell Bodenheim (who couldn't write for sour owlshit) and Langston Hughes and myself used to do poetry and jazz with a Chicago group, the Austin High Gang."

23. TLS-2

May 16 [1945]
[Norfolk]

DEAR KENNETH,

I too am sad to miss the Sierra trip, but life seems to hem in more and more. I don't think we'll even get close to Jackson as the children are always sick or the nurse is sick or there is some reason to stay home and fuss.

But don't be downhearted, there will be better times later on.

The symbol of my life is shutting endless doors so that there won't be a draft. And we go to lots of movies too. I am trying real hard to be a good husband and father. I do this on account of WH Auden says this is an important thing to do. . . .

Why don't you become a professional analyst? It's work like any other kind of work and if you are good at it—as I judge you are—why then not make something out of it. I don't get the subtle point. Merrill Moore in Boston has a girl who helps him and she makes a good living out of it. She isn't an MD or anything, just a girl with a flair for drawing them out, and I don't mean out of their pants either. Henry Miller did it for a while too.

What shall I include in the 10th anniversary retrospective anthology that comes out in [19]46? Do you like SPEARHEAD for a name for it???? I shall print 3500 of it (as against the usual 1500) and advertise it widely. In these times it will sell. I thought of the whole "P[hoenix] and T[ortoise]." OK? There'll only be about 15 people in it—really solid stuff.

When I get back East in June I mean to go down to Washington to see Ezra [Pound]—if they let him have visitors—and see what can be done for him. I suppose he will have to stand trial but I believe it would be possible to prove—from his letters, conversations and broadcasts—that he has been intermittently out of his head for the past ten years. Of course this is terribly insulting to him but I don't see any other way to keep him from being hung. I am going to try to get him out of his contracts with those moribund bastards who bought up the remains of Horace Liveright so that I can get out a cheap selected edition of his stuff. I'll also re-issue the *Cantos* in one volume and perhaps a selection of his best essays. How good is the *Spirit of Romance?* . . .

well carry on *Macduff*
JIM

/ · /

Merrill Moore: (1903–1957), American poet (one of the Fugitives) and psychiatrist. Moore's work appeared in the first *ND* annual, and his *Sonnets from New Directions* (with a preface by W. C. Williams), published in 1938, was one of ND's first books.

SPEARHEAD: *Spearhead 10 Years' Experimental Writing in America* was published in 1947 by ND. According to JL's Editorial Notes, "This book has both a pleasant and a serious purpose. Its pleasant purpose is to commemorate, and celebrate, the first ten years' activity of New Directions by reprinting some of the best work that was published in the annual volumes *New Directions in Prose & Poetry,* many of which are no longer in print. Its serious purpose is this: to present an impartial historical survey of the significant experimental and advance guard writing in the United States during the past decade." KR's "The Phoenix and the Tortoise" is featured there, along with selections by forty other writers (including Muriel Rukeyser, Tennessee Williams, Kenneth Patchen, Ezra Pound, Djuna Barnes, and W. C. Williams). In his contributors' note, KR writes: "Poetry is best when it is personal, speech from one to another; purposive, written out of some definable subjective need and objective motivation; simple, sensuous and passionate or at least made up of such elements or articulated around them. I find hallucination and rhetoric dull, pernicious and silly. Cataclysms are all alike and it is not a human function to create them. Being human is being totally responsible."

out of his head: According to JL's note in *Spearhead,* written the following year, "The past decade of Pound's life has been tragically clouded by the mental illness which was revealed when a Washington jury brought in a verdict of 'unsound mind' and he was committed to St. Elizabeths Hospital for treatment. During his illness Pound had allowed himself to be used for radio propaganda against the US by the Italian government and he was indicted on a charge of treason. Psychiatrists engaged by the government to examine him testified that he was a seriously ill man, and that, from the evidence of his writings and behavior, this illness had been growing on him for many years. Hence it is to be inferred that his relationship with the Mussolini regime must be judged, as far as moral responsibility is concerned, in the light of his mental condition. This condition was defined as a paranoid state. One of the 'illusions' offered as an example of his paranoid thinking by the psychiatrists was Pound's conviction that the social-political ills of the world can be solved by the teachings of Confucius."

a cheap selected edition: Personae (Ezra Pound's collected shorter poems) had been first published in the United States by Boni & Liveright in 1926. In 1946, JL acquired the rights and plates to the volume and reprinted; in 1949, ND released an enlarged edition, and in 1975 a definitive *Collected Early Poems,* edited by Michael John King. *The Spirit of Romance,* Pound's first published prose book, was issued by J. M. Dent in 1910; a fully revised edition was published by ND in 1952. ND published *The Cantos of Ezra Pound* in 1948; the "best essays" appeared in 1954 as *The Literary Essays of Ezra Pound* (edited, with an introduction by T. S. Eliot; according to JL, in a letter to the editor, "TSE was the only person from whom EP would take any correcting").

24. TLS-2
[May 1945]
[San Francisco]

DEAR JIM,

I would be very flattered if you reprinted the "P[hoenix] and T[ortoise]." You've got a lot of people—Delmore [Schwartz], [Kenneth] Patchen, Henry [Miller], [Paul] Goodman, Laughlin, [W. C.] Williams, [Richard] Eberhart, [John] Wheelwright, [Dylan] Thomas, [Charles] H[enri] Ford, [Lawrence] Durrell; all I remember of [19]41 is [Charles] Snider, besides all the furriners. NOT the Vou group, please. BUT Tasilo Ribischka and Hiram Handspring. It is surprising how many of your bets paid off. Far be it from me to read you a lecture, but you have sort of missed out on events abroad. Where are the Celts? The English Anarchists and the Neolaurentians? . . . Of course, most of this stuff is not "experimental" writing—i.e. you can tell pretty easy what it's about, and I suppose the purpose of ND is to give voice to the "experimenters." The only trouble is, most of the new directions have been in the opposite direction. . . .

Me, personally, I dont think Ezra [Pound]'s criticism is very good. There is too much plain eccentricity. You could select it all together and make one good book. I dont think the *Spirit of Romance* is as much a Modern Classic as any of maybe 500 books I might name. I think the Noh Plays are. "Nishikigi" is the greatest poem of "our time," as they say so liberally in book reviews. Albeit as it may—it is a very very good poem. And out of that book came all the later [W. B.] Yeats plays—which I think are the only dramatic advance—but that's a personal notion, shared by few. Of course, you are really sticking your ass in a buzzsaw by reprinting them at this time. DONT put out a "good cheap selected edition." He's been over selected already. Like the Faber volume, which misses half the good stuff. I think the B[oni] & L[iveright] *Personae* is about as drastically cut as you want his oeuvre. I dont care for the avaunt thee varlet period much, though the later Provençal translations (in *Poems 1918–21*) are very good. But all of *Cathay,* all the epigrams, "Hugh Selwyn Mauberley," "Homage to Sextus Propertius," and the poems of sentiment, like the "Villanelle," and "Your mind and you are our Sargasso Sea." I suppose the high point of Ezra's career was from the River Merchant's Wife to Propertius. The climacteric is marked by the "underworld" "Merde" *Canto,* and his farewell to London. Good heavens, did it all come about just because his best friend fucked his wife? I suppose it did. I have been saying that he was out of his mind ever since 1921–22, but you see, the trouble is, nobody dared admit it, it's like the Emperor's New Clothes. It was Modern Art and ergo mahvellous—that it might just be nutty would invalidate the taste of all his admirers. Myself, I am willing to do my bit—write something, sign anything, you know, the Free the Scottsboro Boys stuff. But personally—I think intellectuals should learn to be responsible for their remarks and be ready to pay up when they come home with all their consequences to roost. There has been too much miscellaneous shooting off of the face of late centuries. A morality that stretches from "If I don't Do It" to "Get Out of It Any Way You Can" has got the world in the fix it is in. I would prefer, on esthetic grounds, that Ezra stood by his guns, said "Yes, you bastards, I meant every word of it" and made what Catholics call a "good death." He would at least not leave a bad taste in the mouth of history, which isn't going to be able to distinguish one side from another in 200 years anyway. Courage is still a virtue, and cowardice a sin. A lot of good young GIs and/or Blackshirts have made good deaths, and all due to a lot of loud mouthed intellectuals. By the way—doesnt it all hinge on Archie Macgimper, who insisted on indicting him in the first place? Or is that a legend? . . .

How on earth am I ever going to make a living?

Marie [Rexroth] will no longer give me money for anything but food and rent. I have to find money for laundry, clothes, etc. somewhere. Which I haven't managed so far. What I really want to do is live as a mendicant in the woods like Buddha—but they arrest you. . . .

c̄ love

KENNETH

/ · /

Goodman: Paul Goodman (1911–1972), American novelist, poet, playwright, social critic. ND published his *The Break-Up of Our Camp & Other Stories* in 1949 and featured his work in *Five Young American Poets* in 1941; Goodman was a frequent contributor to the *ND* annuals.

Eberhart: Richard Eberhart (1904–), American poet, awarded the Pulitzer Prize for Poetry in 1966. ND published his *Poems, New and Selected* in 1944. In his review of KR's *The Dragon and the Unicorn* (*New York Times*, 1953), Eberhart would call KR's style "hard as prose and lithe as lyric." In "Homage to James Laughlin" *(Conjunctions)*, Eberhart recalled: JL "took all my work with him across the water by boat to see Ezra Pound, whose *Cantos* he published through the years, and had the editorial skill to choose what he thought were the easiest poems to understand. The book *[Selected Poems, 1930–1965]* came out in 1965, sold reasonably, and then one day the telephone rang and I was told that it had won the Pulitzer Prize."

Wheelwright: John Brooks Wheelwright (1897–1940), American poet. ND published his *Selected Poems,* with an introduction by R. P. Blackmur, in 1941, in the first Poets of the Year series; in 1972, ND issued his *Collected Poems,* edited by Alvin H. Rosenfeld. KR considered Wheelwright a "close friend." In "The Influence of French Poetry on American" *(Assays),* he writes of Wheelwright: "Too hot for the orthodox, he became an impassioned Trotskyite, Anglocatholic and several other kinds of violent and peculiar exceptionalist."

H Ford: Charles Henri Ford (1913–), American Surrealist poet, translator, editor; with Parker Tyler edited *Blues,* which published KR's early work. His poetry and translations have appeared frequently in the *ND* annuals (and he translated a number of poems by Paul Eluard, which appeared in *ND* 3). One of ND's first books was Ford's *The Garden of Disorder & Other Poems* (with an introduction by W. C. Williams), published in 1938; ND followed in 1949 with *Sleep in a Nest of Flames* (with a foreword by Edith Sitwell).

the Vou group: ND 1938 published a selection of contemporary Japanese poets from "the Vou Club," with a preface by JL: "They will show first of all that militaristic imperialism has not wiped out artistic activity and secondly that there is live poetry in Japan." The Vou Club was founded in August 1935, in Tokyo, by the modernist poet Katue Kitasono and others. Between 1936 and 1940, the Club's magazine published numerous translations of Ezra Pound's poetry and essays, and in his essay "Vou Club" (*Townsman,* 1938) Pound argued that the group's poems were "better work than any save those of E. E. Cummings."

Tasilo Ribischka: JL published work in *ND* annuals as Tasilo Ribischka (including "The Messianic Blues" [*ND* 3] and "Psychomachia in Juke Time" [*ND* 9]); as Hiram Handspring he published a drawing in *ND* 7. According to JL, "Ribischka was the name of a famous ski teacher in Hanns Schneider's Austrian school. Handspring I made up. In my *Selected Poems* there is a selection of humorous verses by Handspring, who became my mischievous döppelganger" (JL letter to the editor).

Modern Classic: ND's New Classics series of "dollar reprints of significant modern books which have gone out of print" led off with W. C. Williams's *In the American Grain* (1941). Later volumes included Gertrude Stein's *Three Lives* (1941), E. M. Forster's *The Longest Journey* (1943), Evelyn Waugh's *A Handful of Dust* (1945), and F. Scott Fitzgerald's *The Great Gatsby* (1945).

the Noh plays: Knopf had published *The Classic Nōh Theatre of Japan* by Ezra Pound and Ernest Fenollosa, with an introduction by W. B. Yeats, in 1917. Pound "cribbed" the fourteenth-century Japanese "Nishikigi" from the sinologist Ernest Fenollosa's notebooks. The story of two dead lovers whose ghosts roam a mountainside, "Nishikigi" first appeared in the May 1914 issue of *Poetry* without reference to Pound, as "translated from the Japanese of [Zeami] Motokiyo by Ernest Fenellosa." Pound and the Irish poet William Butler Yeats (1865–1939) were living together at Stone Cottage in Sussex during this period, and it was Pound's work on "Nishikigi" which inspired Yeats to write the first of his great "plays for dancers," "At the Hawk's Well."

the Scottsboro Boys: In 1931 nine black men were accused of raping two young white women in Scottsboro, Alabama. During the trial, which drew international attention, the defense was split between the NAACP and the Communist organization the International Labor Defense.

Archie Macgimper: Archibald MacLeish (see note, letter 4). MacLeish, who served as Assistant Secretary of State for Public and Cultural Relations in 1944–45, had in April joined with Robert Frost, W. H. Auden, T. S. Eliot, Ernest Hemingway, and others in a deposition asking the U.S. District Court to dismiss the 1943 indictment for treason against Ezra Pound.

25. TLS-2   [August 1945]
                                             [San Francisco]

DEAR JIM,

. . . I read [Delmore Schwartz's] *Genesis* through.
That wilted watch metrical system of his is awful
soporific. I still think Delmore is kinda vulgar, as
well as being a bit of a scissorbill. This ah ah ah ah
ah ah ah ah American stuff après Paul Robeson . . .
cum pink pop. Comrade Schwartz would be better
occupied analysing why America has turned into the
Inferno of organized irresponsibility where bright
young Stalinist college professors named [J. Robert]
Oppenheimer and such, can turn the spigot of the
Apocalypse and no one can stop them. I for one am
hardly proud of being geographically, at least, an
American. Though fortunately, I have never considered myself that ultimate cipher—a "citizen." I
suppose *Genesis* is a good picture of a Jew in the
making—but not a pleasant one. I guess Delmore is
right in disliking me. Try as I will, I must admit we
belong to extremely antagonistic worlds.
. . . I have never seen people so terrified. But just
like it says in the Book. The Last Judgement will
flash thru all the skies of the world like lightning and
the sheep shall be separated from the ghosts. A person's response to this, the opening of the final catas-
trophe, is the strict measure of his sensibility. The
undamnable hordes that will never get into hell or
heaven are jubilant because the boys will be coming
home soon. But it is amazing how many simple
ignorant people are more frightened than they ever
were at Pearl Harbor. For one who has trained himself to live constantly in the apocalypse, for whom
every hour is the end of the world, the judgement,
and the fire, it isnt frightening. It is of course aston-

ishing that it should all come true in one's own life-time. And one is filled with a heartrending pity for the triviality of the world. Just think—before we will have had time to grow old and die naturally—the earth, with the Parthenon equally vanished with the *Partisan Review,* will be rolling through space, first a tiny, briefly bright star, and then a dead ball of rock like the moon.

This is the world so brave and new of your friend [Melvin J.] Laski and the *New Republic.* It was them that did it. I bet everybody connected with this project in an executive capacity subscribes to the *New Republic.*

If I were you, I would go back to Alta and stay there.

c̄ love

KENNETH

/ · /

Genesis: ND had published Delmore Schwartz's *Genesis* in 1943. According to JL *(AP),* Schwartz "had a very uncertain adolescence and out of this perhaps came his fascination with Freud and psychoanalysis. He was deeply into Freud and many of his poems show this influence. So he decided that his second book would be about his personal Genesis, a long poem in a rather loose form with poetic prose interludes. In it he would analyze himself in terms of Freud and, for the society in which he lived, in terms of Marx. An ambitious undertaking, and I think the further he got into it the more he realized the risk of what he was attempting. He began to see, too, that the relaxed verse of *Genesis,* which did not have the great tension of the *In Dreams* poems, might not stand up well. These worries led him to the extraordinary maneuvering in which he involved me. If you go through his folders in the New Directions Archive you'll find two or three letters a week written while the printer was setting up *Genesis.* 'Dear J,' he'd say, 'please write to Blackmur to see if he will review *Genesis.* Let him know that if he does I will write an essay proving that he is the greatest critic since Aristotle.' (Delmore had a great sense of humor.) He was quite open about all this. Maybe he enjoyed literary politics more than writing. I dumped some of his requests off on other friends because Delmore was trying to manipulate about 20 critics. Of course, it just didn't work out. I don't know whether the critics panned *Genesis* because they didn't like being set up or because *Genesis,* and this is just my opinion, is a somewhat dull book. Where *In Dreams* had been a good seller, I think we sold only about 800 copies of *Genesis*. Delmore's *Genesis* operation was like a Rube Goldberg machine."

Paul Robeson: (1898–1976), internationally known Black American singer, actor, and social activist. Robeson, who also was the first Black All-American athlete and a lawyer, had his passport revoked in the 1950s because of his support of the Communist Party.

Oppenheimer: J. Robert Oppenheimer (1904–1967), American nuclear physicist. Central to the Manhattan Project, which culminated in the dropping of the first atomic bombs on Hiroshima (August 6) and Nagasaki (August 9) in 1945.

Laski: Melvin J. Laski (1920–), American writer, editor. During this period Laski served as literary editor of the *New Leader,* and later would edit and publish the English journal *Encounter.* According to JL, "I think Mel Laski was best known for editing the Congress of Cultural Freedom magazine *Der Monat* in Berlin. It was CIA backed and Stephen Spender resigned from the board when that came out" (JL letter to the editor).

26. TLS-2

[September 1945]
[Norfolk]

DEAR KENNETH—

If you really think Phil Lamantia is good and want to select eight or ten poems and get them to me by airmail before October 1st they could go into *ND* 9. . . .

Viking Press has agreed to let me bring out a selected poems of DHL[awrence] in my dollar series. Which poems shall I include? Do you want to write an introduction? If so, get it to me within the next four weeks. . . . Let me know whether to hold for you. Otherwise I'll give the job to some New York name. But I don't want you to reproach me about not having given you a fair chance to try it. You can if you will. But will you? You promptly forgot about the Blake when I got mildly encouraging about it. I don't really think you want to write criticism, though there is no doubt you know enough, and write well enough, and have better ideas than most of the people who do it. Now does that make you mad enough to get some action. . . .

Heard from Ezra [Pound]'s wife and mother. They are OK and they saved his books and papers. Nothing definite from him yet.

What do you think of Pasternak? His prose is something but wonderful I find.

Keep it cleanly

JAS

Miriam Patchen tells me there was a Stalinist American Indian who used to go over to sleep with Anaïs Nin and always left a copy of *The New Masses* on the bed table for the next comer. Ah politics . . .

/ · /

Phil Lamantia: Philip Lamantia (1927–), American Surrealist poet; served as an assistant editor of *View* magazine. *ND* 9 (1946) included five poems by Lamantia, along with other San Francisco writers (William Everson, Kenneth Patchen, George Leite, and KR). In his "San Francisco Letter" *(WOTW)*, KR wrote: "Philip Lamantia is generally considered by his colleagues in San Francisco to be another of the three or four leading poets of the community. . . . Lamantia's poetry is illuminated, ecstatic, with the mystic's intense autonomy." KR contributed an introduction to Lamantia's first book, *Erotic Poems,* published in 1946.

a selected poems of DHL: KR accepted the D. H. Lawrence project. His "Poetry, Regeneration, and D. H. Lawrence" was published as an introduction to *D. H. Lawrence: Selected Poems* (ND, 1947), and appeared as "The Poems of D. H. Lawrence" in *Now* magazine the same year. "My dollar series" is a reference to ND's New Classics series.

Pasternak: Boris Pasternak (1890–1960), Russian poet, prose writer. Pasternak's work in translation had appeared in *ND* 6, and in 1949 JL would publish his *Selected Writings.*

Miriam Patchen: An anti-war organizer in the early thirties, Miriam Oikemus married Kenneth Patchen in 1934. In 1938–39 the Patchens lived in Norfolk, Connecticut, and were employed by ND (see letter 12).

The New Masses: In May 1926, Mike Gold, Joseph Freeman, and others founded the radical magazine *The New Masses,* which would eventually evolve into the primary American Communist literary magazine. KR published regularly there in the late thirties.

---

27. TLS-2

[September 1945]
[San Francisco]

DEAR JIM,

The only trouble with Arthur [Winters] on [E. A.] Robinson is that Robinson is an atrocious poet who never wrote a good line in his life. You can't get wise to the fact that Winters' pseudoclassicism is merely the last word in affectation, he is simply in the business of producing furrier fur-lined teacups than *View* Inc.

HURRAH for [Kenneth] Patchen. Be sure and give him my best. In my opinion he is the only US poet who came thru the war. I consider my contemporaries a bunch of cannibals and whores, the OWI generation that went to hell on a gravy train of human blood.

It is called the Poetry Medal of the Commonwealth Club of Cal. It is all very nice—it means [they] . . . think I am better than Arthur [Winters], Muriel [Rukeyser], or R[obinson] Jeffers, which is a somewhat startling evaluation. Unfortunately, I will once again have to borrow somebody's suit to go to dinner and get it, my own is much too ragged. I wish they would be a little more practical. . . .

I think Blake is a great deal easier to do than Lawrence. But both shd come out in the MML series this winter. You watch and see, a craze for both will sweep the country as soon as the boys get home. English literature has been undergoing a religious, anarchist, personalist revolt against the scissorbill epoch of [W. H.] Auden and [Lytton] Strachey for some years now. Even Auden knows that. I think you should drop the titles you are planning and bring out Blake, Kierkegaard, Berdyaev, Yeats, Lawrence, and maybe one book on several Catholic writers. . . . The books on Blake, Yeats, and Lawrence shd be written by people who both understand them, and believe, basically, what they say. All three were better social prophets than Marx or Lenin, and better philosophers than John Dewey or Bertie Russell. And that is plain fact, not hyperbole. How not to do it is like [Jacob] Bronowski's book on Blake, which reads like it was written by Beatrice & Sidney Webb or Charles & Mary Beard, when it doesn't read like it was written by Mike Gold & Dorothy Parker. But it is a swallow of the spring, it shows that the British commie critics are scared of all this apocalypticism and are trying to give it the old class angle. . . . On the whole I think English writers are more to be trusted, they know more, are better scholars, more humane, and have recovered from the interbellum Marxist pandemic completely. I picked up a copy of the *P[artisan] R[eview]* in Elder's and glanced at it. I hadnt seen one in many months. At last they admit the thing is written of college professors, for college professors, by college professors. No one under 35 in the world takes them seriously anymore. They are as dated as Joe Kling's *Pagan*. More so. After all, cheesecake is a permanent literary theme, John Dewey is not. . . .

I went to church when the war ended. Later we went down town. In comparison c̄ the last war's end, this lacked all spontaneity and creative expression. Last time there was dancing and singing and all sorts of spontaneous group expression in the streets and of course a "class conscious" reaction that touched off a wave of revolt over the world that scared the wits out of the bosses. This time everybody just milled around, drunk. The first night was uproarious, but well tempered, the third, which I didn't see, was apparently a bastard. Most of the windows on Market St. broken, hundreds of naked girls. (The emergency hospitals ran a douche service all night for the rapes. Honest.) It took 2000 city regular and special bulls, 3000 SPs and MPs to keep them from tearing the city to bits. . . .

I guess I had better drop the idea of the Blake. It is pretty obvious that you still are convinced I am not respectable. I wd only do it to get a little money, and I wd have to stop working on my plays, which I dont want to do if I can possibly help it. . . .

c̄ love
KENNETH

/ · /

on Robinson: ND had published Yvor Winters's *The Anatomy of Nonsense,* which includes passages on the American poet E. A. Robinson (1869–1935), in 1943. Winters's *Edwin Arlington Robinson* would be published by ND in the Makers of Modern Literature series in 1946.

View: A literary magazine begun in 1939 by Charles Henri Ford in New York; one of its primary supporters was W. C. Williams. Issue 7/8 (1941) had been a "Surrealist number." In "The Influence of French Poetry on American" *(Assays),* KR would write: "[André] Breton did not carry any of the older American modernists with him. A whole new crop of American poets sprang up—specifically disciples of Breton's brand of Surrealism. The most important of these poets are Charles Henri Ford, Parker Tyler, and Philip Lamantia, all still writing today. Together they edited one of the most dynamic magazines of 'Surrealisme Outremer'—called *View*—which was livelier if less learned than *transition.* All three are certainly among the finest non-French Surrealists."

Patchen: Probably a reference to ND's 1945 publication of Kenneth Patchen's novel, *Memoirs of a Shy Pornographer.*

OWI: U.S. Office of War Information (1942–45), a federal agency devoted to espionage and counterespionage during World War II.

R. Jeffers: Robinson Jeffers (1887–1962), American poet. ND published Jeffers's *Cawdor/Medea* in 1970, with an introduction by William Everson. Rexroth wrote Everson in 1946 that he disliked Jeffers "intensely" because of his "noisy rhetoric," as well as his philosophy of "inhumanism" and his imputed fascism.

MML series: ND's The Makers of Modern Literature series, "critical Baedekers to the great modern writers," led off with Harry Levin's *James Joyce.* A number of announced volumes (including R. P. Blackmur's *Henry James* and Delmore Schwartz's *T. S. Eliot*) were never completed.

Strachey: Lytton Strachey (1880–1932), British biographer and essayist. A member of the Cambridge Apostles and a friend of Leonard Woolf, as well as a prominent figure in the Bloomsbury Group.

Kierkegaard: Søren Kierkegaard (1813–1855), Danish philosopher and theologian. References to Kierkegaard are scattered throughout KR's essays, including "Why Is American Poetry Culturally Deprived?" *(The Alternative Society):* "The profound revolutions of the sensibility, which began with Baudelaire, Kierkegaard, Newman, Dostoyevsky, and Nietzsche and which represent in fact a systematic destructive criticism of the foundations of humanism and humanitarianism, and which have thrown up in the course of their ever-accelerating liquidation all the anti-humane art movements and philosophies of our time, were, to judge from the evidence, totally incomprehensible to the American imitators of their stylistic innovations—even at the remove of fifty years."

Berdyaev: Nicolas Berdyaev (1875–1948), Russian philosopher, exiled by the Bolsheviks. His mystical anarchism was influenced by Jakob Boehme, a central figure for KR.

Marx or Lenin: Karl Marx (1818–1883), German Socialist and political theorist; with Friedrich Engels (see note, letter 96) he developed economic, political, and aesthetic theories characterized by notions of dialectical materialism, surplus value, and class struggle. Vladimir Ilyich Lenin (1870–1924), Russian revolutionary leader and political theorist, served as Soviet premier in 1918–24. KR's notion that capitalism mitigates against community is an explicit theme of *The Dragon and the Unicorn;* further, there is significant reference to Marx in his 1974 study, *Communalism.* In *Excerpts,* KR recalls: "Before the war all revolutionary hope in Bolshevism had been destroyed in the wake of Stalin's terror, the shameful Moscow Trials, the deliberate murder of the leading cadres of the Russian army. . . . In San Francisco we organized an anarchist group called 'The Libertarian Circle.' . . . Our objective was to refound the radical movement after its destruction by the Bolsheviks and to rethink all the basic principles, i.e., in other words to subject to searching criticism all the ideologists from Marx to Malatesta."

John Dewey: (1859–1952), American philosopher, educator; one of the leaders of the Pragmatist school.

Bertie Russell: Bertrand Russell (1872–1970), British philosopher, logician, economist, social activist; inventor of the Theory of Descriptions, his *Principles of Mathematics* and *Principia Mathematica* (with Alfred North Whitehead) are classics of mathematical logic. Russell, a pacifist, founded the Campaign for Nuclear Disarmament.

book on Blake: Jacob Bronowski's *William Blake* (1944), reprinted as *Williami Blake and the Age of Revolution.*

Webb: Beatrice Potter Webb (1858–1943) and her husband Sidney Webb (1859–1947), British economists, Socialists, writers, founders of the Fabian Society.

Beard: Charles Beard (1874–1948) and his wife Mary Beard (1876–1958), American historians. Charles Beard's *Economic Origins of Jeffersonian Democracy* and *The Rise of American Civilization* were important books for Ezra Pound.

Mike Gold: (1894–1967), American poet, playwright, social activist. Under his editorship, *The New Masses* opened itself up to writing by "the working men, women, and children of America. . . . The raw materials of the worker's art." Gold's poetry appeared alongside that of Kenneth Patchen, Muriel Rukeyser, and many others in Granville Hicks's 1935 anthology, *Proletarian Literature in the United States.*

Dorothy Parker: (1893–1967), American journalist, humorist, satirical poet; frequent contributor to *The New Yorker.*

Pagan: In *APTC,* KR refers to "the lonely Greenwich Village maidens and Middle Western women in rut who wrote for Joe Kling's *Pagan,* the outstanding organ of erotic verse in the Twenties." According to JL, Kling also "ran a hole-in-the-wall bookstore in Greenwich Village."

28. TL-2

12 X [19]45
[San Francisco]

DEAR JIM,

No mail has come from you for weeks. I am stopping work on the Lawrence project. I have about 10,000 words written on DHL as a poet etc. out of which I can't cut a selection to fit your wordage. I can only find one modern classic c̄ introduction—

[Harry] Levin on [Flaubert's] *Trois Contes*. Very short, very nicey nice. Is that what you want? Something toney? As is, my stuff sounds like DHL's own letters. . . .

I should never have gone off half cocked with this Lawrence thing. I should know you well enough by now. Trouble is, I get enthusiastic about things, and I forget that you only think you are being taken advantage of. I think it extremely cruel of you to cook up situations like this over things that mean as much to me as DHL's poetry does. . . .

Please let me know immediately the status of this whole business. I shall proceed no farther without some definite instructions and some sort of commitment. No one in his right senses would ever do anything like this for you without an advance. It is easy to see why you have all this work done by what DHL called Willy-Wet-Legs. I refuse to kiss your ass. And I think if you allow some filthy half-born literary swine to touch DHL you might as well get [John] Middleton Murry to do it, and then climb in bed with him. Lawrence does seem to attract Judases like honey does flies.

Now look dear, be a wooly lamb and stop being so skittish, it is more important to do right by DHL than it is to work off one's own frustrations. You are undertaking the publishing of some of the most important work of the greatest religious thinker since Blake, and one of the world's very great saints. Humility is indicated at this juncture.

with love
[KENNETH]

/ · /

Levin on Trois Contes: Three Tales by Gustave Flaubert (trans. by Arthur McDowell, with an introduction by Harry Levin) was published by

ND in 1944 as New Classics 7. In *Conjunctions,* JL describes the American critic and first Irving Babbitt Professor of Comparative Literature at Harvard, Harry Levin (1912–), as one of the strongest influences on ND after KR and Ezra Pound: "A man of enormous learning and taste, and in many literatures. . . ." Levin's *James Joyce* was published by ND in 1941 as the first volume in its MML series; Levin's *Memories of the Moderns* (ND, 1980) opens with an extended "Letter to James Laughlin."

Middleton Murry: John (Jack) Middleton Murry (1889–1957), British journalist, critic, editor. His books include a biography of D. H. Lawrence, *Son of Woman* (1931), and *Reminiscences of D. H. Lawrence* (1933). Murry and his wife Katherine Mansfield first met Lawrence in 1914. His relationship with the writer was intense and difficult, as reflected in Lawrence's *Women in Love;* at a London party in 1924, for example, which ended with Lawrence drunk and ill, Murry said, "I love you, Lorenzo, but I won't promise not to betray you."

29. TPC-1

2/11/[19]46
[San Francisco]

DEAR JIM—

I guess you are plenty mad about something—and I can't figure out what—unless something some malignant person has told you, deliberately to cause trouble between us, or, very remote possibility, what I wrote you about Ezra [Pound]. Maybe I didnt make myself clear on that issue. I worry about it a great deal—it is very complex, and brings up the whole issue of the Artist vs Society and the artist as humanly responsible.

At least be good enough to let me know if you want me to go on with the British poets thing and if you want the DHL[awrence]. We have been pretty good friends for over ten years now.

I am terribly upset—and very sorry if there is any cause for your silence.

c̄ love
KENNETH

/ · /

about Ezra: see letter 24.

The British poets thing: KR's *The New British Poets: An Anthology* would be published by ND in 1949.

30. TLS-1   August 2nd [1946]
                                              [Norfolk]

DEAR KENNETH—

Thanks for your many letters. Things have been damn busy. I'm off for Yurrup in September. . . .

Can you find there in [Chinatown] a [Chinese] who can draw nice characters? Ezra [Pound] needs him. He can make what he wants recognizable in pencil, but can't draw them nice with a brush to make cuts. . . .

Your preface to DHL[awrence] is brilliant. I don't know what the hell you are talking about most of the time but it sounds wonderful and your style is inflammable to say the least. . . .

                                              JIM

/ · /

nice characters: See letter 38. According to JL, "EP needed to unify the style of the characters in the *Cantos,* which was never done. He got characters over the years from different people, and Dorothy [Pound] did some and he did some" (JL letter to the editor).

31. TLS-1   16 XI [19]46
                                              San Francisco

DEAR JAS,

Glad you're back, and sorry that you dont seem to have had a good time. Too bad. But Yurrup is

hardly the place to go looking for a good time. Even
Wally Windsor didnt enjoy herself. . . .

Thanks a million for the [Dylan] Thomas. I dont
like him, but he is a first rate poet alright. It is surprising how conventional neometaphysical it looks,
gathered up in a Selected Works. Just as [T. S.] Eliot
for a generation before him, and WHA[uden] for the
period between, he sort of created contemporary
British poetry, single handed. (That would look good
on a blurb, huh?)

You have mss. of several local poets sent you by
me, dont forget. I cant get anything out of [Robert]
Duncan, who is, after [William] Everson and [Philip]
Lamantia, the best. He is sure you dont like him. A
bit of a bitch, Duncan. Everson is impossible. I have
been trying to get him to send you a book, but he
stalls and postures and strikes attitudes. Too much
Robinson Jeffers in early youth. Then he wanted me
to make a selection of his poems for you—about
which he struck more attitudes. (NOT antagonistic,
would they were—just Great Strong Inarticulate Poet
Against Sunset, Rock and Fog sort of shit.) Afterall,
I am in the same grift myself. Let him talk that way
to the customers. . . .

c̄ Love
KENNETH

/ · /

the Thomas: The Selected Writings, published by ND in November of
1946. According to JL, "I worked for Gertrude Stein one summer when
I was young and she talked about good books making 'the bell ring.' I
listen for the bell when I start on a manuscript from a new writer. It
rang hardest for me, I think, when I sat down on a bench in Red Lion
Square in London after Edith Sitwell tipped me off to buy Dylan
Thomas' first book—the bell rang louder for me then than Big Ben"
(AP).

Everson: William Everson (1912–), American poet who for eighteen years lived as Brother Antoninus, Dominican monk. ND published his *The Residual Years,* at KR's strong suggestion, in 1948. In *SFP,* Everson remembers first coming into contact with KR in 1944 while he was living in the Waldport, Oregon, Conscientious Objectors' camp: "I got a letter from him. Somebody had sent him one of my CO pamphlets, *The Waldport Poems* or *War Elegies,* I don't remember which. On my next furlough . . . I came down to San Francisco to meet him, and his presence here was the real reason I returned after the war. Not only was he the acknowledged leader of the new literary ferment, but as soon as I read his new poems, *The Phoenix and the Tortoise,* I took him to be the best poet of his generation." Everson, KR wrote in his "San Francisco Letter" *(WOTW),* "is probably the most profoundly moving and durable of the poets of the San Francisco Renaissance. . . . His work has a gnarled, even tortured, honesty, and rugged unliterary diction, a relentless probing and searching, which are not just engaging, but almost overwhelming . . . anything less like the verse of the fashionable quarterlies would be hard to imagine." Everson's work appeared in three numbers of the *ND* annual (9, 12, 28). Lee Bartlett's biography *William Everson: The Life of Brother Antoninus* (ND, 1988) offers extended discussion of the KR/Everson relationship.

32. TLS-2   Nov. 22 [19]46
                                                     [San Francisco]

DEAR JIM,

. . . What is wrong with Ted Weiss? He seems to be under the impression he is Phil Rahv and/or Delmore Schwartz as a small boy. Who cares about all that crap anymore. There has been a war. The days of Jo Donne amongst the purple cut glass tigresses and fur lined soubrettes are over but definitely. Nor the people that H[orace] Gregory was "discovering" circa 1935. We've all had some Kafka. By the way, know who "discovered" Kierkegaard amongst NYC highbrows? James Gibbons Huneker. Before him, Mrs. Humphrey Ward. Before her, Emerson—but that was in Boston. Tell Ted he is too young to turn into a dead pissant like Lionel Trilling. His magazine is just something awful, yet he seems a nice feller.

Furiosa red. Very lively, but a little empty. Best things in it, KR and [Richard] Eberhart. Ain't [Wallace] Stevens turrable nowadays? A one book man. . . .

When are you going to get around to the [Ford Madox] Ford Tietjens novels and the [Wyndham Lewis] Apes? You could put *Tarr* in your Modern Classics if you could get it away from Blanchey [Knopf]. And look, why in the hell dont you snatch that Noh Plays of Ezra [Pound]'s?

How about the DHL[awrence] Selected Poems?

Giving a big party for [Philip] Lamantia's book tonight.

[Henry] Miller and [George] Leite get shittier and shittier. I can smell them from here. I think it's that little retired chambermaid of Hank's that is destroying him. Leite is headed for the gas, sure's hell.

I will try to drive a little quiff into the gatherin pasture for you. I have lost my long time negro mistress I always wanted to introduce you to. She was a professional assigneuse. . . .

Use the phone—it's across the street from the ND office.

faithfully
KENNETH REXROTH

/ · /

Jo Donne: John Donne (1572–1631), British poet, preacher. Though he later revised his opinion of Donne (placing him by 1926 in the Romantic line), early on T. S. Eliot had pointed to the Metaphysical wit of Donne as inhabiting the central tradition of English poetry, arguing that it had been lost since the seventeenth century; given Eliot's influence, Donne thus quickly became a crucial figure for the New Critics. In 1931 Edmund Wilson wrote, "It is as much as one's life is worth nowadays, among young people, to say an approving word for Shelley or a dubious one about Donne." In *NBP,* KR would argue that while Richard Eberhart had studied at Cambridge for a time, he survived

William Empson's influence in large part because he "does not believe that it is possible to discover a recipe for writing like John Donne." ND published Donne's *Some Poems and a Devotion* in its first Poets of the Year series in 1941.

H. Gregory: Horace Gregory (1898–1982), American poet, critic, editor. In 1940, Gregory and his wife Marya Zaturenska dismissed KR's *In What Hour* as "regional verse that reflected the charm of the Pacific Coast, and the meditative if somewhat belated contact of a poet with the political and aesthetic 'conversations' of his day," in their *A History of American Poetry 1900–1940.*

Kafka: Franz Kafka (1883–1924), Czechoslovakian writer. ND published Kafka's *Amerika* (trans. by Edwin Muir) in 1940, and Gustav Janauch's *Conversations with Kafka* in 1954.

James Gibbons Huneker: (1860–1921), American music critic and journalist; also wrote about literature and art for the *New York Sun*, 1900–17. In "The Art of Literature" *(WOTW)*, KR takes the work of Huneker as an example of the "role in social change" popular literary criticism can effect.

Mrs. Humphrey Ward: Mary August Ward (1851–1920), British novelist. Her work (including the very popular and controversial *Robert Elsmere*) tended to deal with questions of faith, tradition, and freedom in Victorian England.

Emerson: Ralph Waldo Emerson (1803–1882), American philosopher, poet. In his essay "The Poet," Emerson called for an indigenous American poetry: "America is a poem in our eyes; its ample geography dazzles the imagination, and it will not wait long for meters." He was an active supporter of Walt Whitman.

Lionel Trilling: (1905–1975), American critic. In books like *The Liberal Imagination* (1950) and *The Opposing Self* (1955) he argues for a kind of Freudian liberal humanism. In 1943, ND had published Trilling's *E. M. Forster* in its MML series; Trilling also wrote introductions for F. Scott Fitzgerald's *The Great Gatsby* (ND, 1945) and Gustave Flaubert's *Bouvard and Pécuchet* (ND, 1954).

Furiosa red: Furioso: A Magazine of Verse (1939–52) was begun at Yale by James Angleton and Reed Whittemore; its first issue carried work by JL, as well as Ezra Pound, W. C. Williams, Richard Eberhart, and Horace Gregory. KR's "The Signature of All Things" appeared in the Fall (1946) issue of *Furioso.*

Wallace Stevens: (1879–1955), American poet. KR: "Philosophizing poets have been a dime a dozen in our epoch but Stevens is the only one who is actually a philosopher. . . . [He] takes it for granted that his readers are well-read, cultivated people who have recovered from the post-war disillusionment, abandoned both optimism and pessimisim, and learned the un-American lesson that life is tragic—even if they are not aristo-

crats who absorb such wisdom with their mother's milk. He is what
Nietzsche used to call a good European" *(APTC)*.

Tietjens novels and the Apes: Ford Madox Ford's Tietjens tetralogy,
Parade's End (see note, letter 71); Wyndham Lewis's *The Apes of God*
and *Tarr*.

Noh Plays: ND would publish an edition of Ezra Pound and Ernest
Fenollosa's *The Classic Nōh Theatre of Japan*, photo-offset from the 1917
Knopf text, in 1959.

a big party: KR had arranged a publication party for Philip Lamantia's
first collection of poems, *Erotic Poems,* which had just been published
by Bern Porter with an introduction by KR.

33. TLS-1

Nov 28 [19]46
[San Francisco]

DEAR JIM,

Thanks a million for the two new books.

Temper praise with discretion. "New Directions
the House of Reliable Blurbs." What does it mean
the most compelling force in American poetry since
[Walt] Whitman? I think it is bad advertising and
prejudices the reader against the book. Sometimes I
think [Kenneth] Patchen is simply Kenneth Fearing's conscience. He is one of that outfit that didnt
sell out—the only genuinely revolutionary poet now
writing in the old definition of "revolutionary poet"—
all the rest have pooped out or died, washed up and
bitter in the economic struggle. Fearing, the Robt.
W. Service of the Big Apple, sort of Damon Runyon in verse, and so on down the line—and besides,
Kenny is incomparably more skilled as a workman
than any of them ever were. Further—he has restored
to poetry the prophetic (in the Hebrew sense) role
without which it becomes socially etiolated. He really
speaks with the voice of the prophets, "Woe, Woe,
to the bloody city!" And he really speaks of love—

that profane love which is more sacred than any other, real hot juicy pussy—fuckin pussy as well as eatin pussy in a world which is very very sick in the balls. In other words, Jeremiah and the Song of Songs. And this is what poetry must do to be part of man— it must go back to public speech of the ragged, blazing eyed fanatic shouting in the streets . . . and back to the amorous dialogues sung across the irrigation ditches by the lines of swaying boys and girls all along the hot cloying midsummer night. I dont give a damn how careless Kenny Patchen is. He can afford to be disheveled. If John Crowe Ransom ever took the suspender button out from between the cheeks of his ass for one second—there would be a frightful mess. Honey swat—

As for [Pablo] Neruda. I belong to the school— the only good Stalinist is a dead Stalinist. However. Again—be careful of your blurbs. What is this about Kafka? Just to catch the *P[artisan] R[eview]*-martini trade? Why not Kierkegaard and Hank James, too? Come off it. Neruda writes like [Jean] Cocteau, and that is why he is better than most of these coffee colored brethren who write like calculating horses or walking dogs or organ grinders' monkeys. The "objective correlative"—Neruda is essentially a late cubist poet (like me for that matter)—always the positively referable—the definite situation—the verifiable image—the "ideogrammic method" as E[zra] P[ound] called it—always building the complex out of new collocations of the simple and precise—out of permanent psychological "radicals" like Chinese characters. Neruda greatly resembles Rexroth as of 1927–35. Which I knew well then. [Angel] Flores is not a very good translator. But then I dont think that strange precision and sharpness can ever come over—it depends so much on the use of very incisive, aggressive syllabic tonal evolution—which, when translated, must evaporate. It is like translating Burns. Note—'Preguntas:? Y donde estan las lilas?' Which has a sharpness and kind of anger about it—like Cocteau reading his own poetry—or like Apollinaire sometimes—and this completely evaporates in the literal translation. 'You want to know what has happened to the lilacs?' is probably better—but that is a strictly USA "tone"—Patchen—Humphrey Bogart, for instance—and it doesn't convey that special Spanish—Valentino in the *Four Horsemen* thing, whip-like irony. I suppose Flores, by providing a usually reliable pony, does the best one can ask. . . .

faithfully, and give my congratulations to Kenny
KENNETH

[appended in holograph:]
The Neruda poems after 1935–36 are a frightening indictment of literary Stalinism. The one on Bolivar is one of the most evil, silly, meretricious things I have ever read. And what happened in 1935—that certainly was the last year a man could remain a Stalinist & not be damned. And look at Neruda! What a squalid, tawdry, seedy thing damnation is.

/ · /

two new books: Kenneth Patchen's *Selected Poems* (NCS 12) and Pablo Neruda's *Residence on Earth and Other Poems* (trans. by Angel Flores), both published by ND in late 1946.

Whitman: Walt Whitman (1819–1892), American poet. His *Leaves of Grass* proved a transformative text for many ND writers, including W. C. Williams, Lawrence, Miller, and Everson. In "The Influence of French Poetry on American" *(Assays)*, KR writes: "Whitman, I am afraid, for all the doctors of comparative literature try to do with him, is an autochthone, a real original, and if his roots are anywhere except in the pre-Civil War North with its swarming cranks, reformers and humanists, they are in Isaiah."

Kenneth Fearing: (1902–1961), American poet, for a time on the editorial board of the *Partisan Review*. Fearing's poetry, KR writes in *APTC,* "is rhetorical, denunciatory, agitational in intent, and his satires are directed not at people, but archetypes, stereotypes out of the *commedia dell'arte* of Middle America. He is the Juvenal of the Swing Vote. . . . The first eschatological American poet." In a 1949 letter to Selden Rodman (who included work by Fearing, KR, and W. C. Williams in his *100 Modern Poems*), Williams wrote: "Kenneth Fearing's composition is for me just another revelation of his greatness. He is one of my greatest admirations."

Service: Robert W. Service (1874–1958), Canadian poet; remembered primarily for his poems and ballads on the gold rush in the Yukon, including "The Shooting of Dan McGrew."

Damon Runyon: (1884–1946), American journalist and short story writer.

John Crowe Ransom: (1888–1974), American poet, critic; as a professor at Vanderbilt University, led the Fugitive group (see note, letter 4). ND published his *The New Criticism* in 1941, and *Beating the Bushes: Selected Essays 1941–1971* in 1971.

Neruda: Pablo Neruda (1904–1973), Chilean poet, diplomat, born as Ricard Eliecer Neftali Reyes. Joined the Communist Party in 1939 and served as Chilean ambassador to France under Socialist president Salvadore Allende; won the Nobel Prize for Literature in 1971. A large selection of Neruda's verse (trans. by Angel Flores) appeared in *ND 8* in 1944; in 1972 ND published Neruda's *The Captain's Verses,* and in 1973 the complete *Residence on Earth* (both trans. by Donald D. Walsh).

about Kafka?: A reference to ND's *The Kafka Problem,* published earlier in the year.

Hank James: Henry James (1843–1916), American novelist, essayist, playwright, who in 1915 took British citizenship. "In the Influence of French Poetry on American" *(Assays)*, KR wrote, "Nothing in criticism . . . is quite so comic as Henry James' book on French novelists, with its utter inability to understand what those novels were about. They might as well have been in Swahili or Etruscan. . . . Where did Norah go when she escaped from the Doll's House? She went to town to get a job. Henry James' characters go to art galleries to resolve their mysterious tragedies." In short, KR argues, James's fiction "is writing which has fed on writing. . . . When the chi-chi has died away, cannibalism is an uncommon curiosity, in art as in anthropology." Between 1943 and 1950, ND published four books by James: *The Spoils of Poynton, Stories of Writers and Artists, The Other House,* and *The Aspern Papers* and *The Europeans.*

Cocteau: Jean Cocteau (1889–1963), French poet, dramatist, critic, and film director. ND published Cocteau's novel *The Holy Terrors* (trans. by Rosamond Lehmann) in 1957, and in 1964 *The Infernal Machine & Other Plays* (trans. by W. H. Auden, Dudley Fitts, and others).

Burns: Robert Burns (1759–1796), Scottish poet. Much of his work was written in his native Scots; for the last decade of his life Burns traveled the Highlands and Borders collecting songs for two anthologies of folk music.

Apollinaire: Guillaume Apollinaire (1880–1918), French poet, essayist, art critic. Roger Shattuck's edition of Apollinaire's *Selected Writings* was published by ND in 1950.

Humphrey Bogart: (1899–1957), American film actor, best known for his "tough-guy" roles in such films as *The Maltese Falcon* and *The Big Sleep.*

Valentino: Rudolph Valentino (1895–1926), Italian-born American silent-film actor, the archetypal almond-eyed Latin lover.

one on Bolivar: Neruda's "Un canto para Bolívar" ("A Song for Bolívar").

the last year: Joseph Stalin (1879–1953), Secretary General of the Communist Party from 1922 until his death, initiated mass trials for treason in Moscow in 1936.

34. TLS-2

1/[19]47

[San Francisco]

DEAR JIM,

. . . I get the impression you had a happy time—and got a double barrelled hard on from them twins. I have had double headers—but never with twins—it had ought to be a kind of metaphysical experience—like looking in retreating shaving mirrors—maybe if you sniffed nitrous oxide or smoked muggles you would slip off into samadhi and never come back, the quaker on the box held by the quaker on the box on quaker oats used to trouble me as a wee one. . . .

I honestly can't bring myself to write Ezra [Pound]. I get a sour stomach every time I think of it. I know that is terribly unchristian.

Who is Bunk Johnson? Did you hear from Knopf about the [D. H. Lawrence] Pansies and Plumed Serpent poems? I think the [Christopher] Isherwood novels the best diagnosis of how Germany went nuts in the nuts, or the buttocks, I ever read. Why does Delmore [Schwartz] dislike me so? . . .

DID I TELL YOU THE SIMPLY TERRIBLE THING THAT HAPPENED? For two years I have been very slowly putting together a play, giving it my allest all. A retake of the *Oresteia*. As Orestes is going in to bump off Unc and the Old Lady—Berenike-Electra his sister—"Do you know where you are going?" He (named in this case Menander): "At the end of the universe/There is another Menander/And another Berenike./We have hunted all our lives./At last, tonight, we will meet them." I CHORUS: "That is what the universe/Is, the thing that hangs between/Those double figures." Now please turn to [Jean-Paul] Sartre's *Flies* at EXACTLY THE SAME POINT! Since, in a sense, the whole play hinges on that line—I am going to have to give up two years of the most intense concentration I have ever expended. I was physically ill for a month. This is the ironic justice of a good God—because I utterly despise Sartre and all he stands for. Maybe I should rewrite the material into a JOB—only trouble—the situation isn't "dramatic."

Without any question the worst English poet is WS Graham . . . of all the specious, outdated studio slang I have ever read—his is it. He makes [Henry] Treece read like [Walter Savage] Landor. . . .

All sorts of hyperactivity out here amongst the poets. It would be possible to put out a new POETS OF THE PACIFIC, a nice body of poems by [Robert] Duncan, [Sanders] Russell, [Philip] Lamantia, [William] Everson, Dick Moore, [Leo] Levy. Six poets—128 pp. or maybe 160 pp. 25 pages to the poet if he wanted them—otherwise we could fill up c̄ Duncan & Everson.

KENNETH

/ · /

Bunk Johnson: New Orleans jazz trumpeter. W. C. Williams's "Ol'
Bunk's Band" recalls a New York City performance of Johnson's black
jazz band in 1945.

Isherwood novels: ND had published Christopher Isherwood's *The Berlin Stories* in 1945.

Sartre's Flies: Jean-Paul Sartre (1905–1980), French philosopher, nov-
elist, playwright, critic, political activist; the principal exponent of
Existentialism in France. In the late forties ND would publish Sartre's
The Wall and Other Stories (trans. by Lloyd Alexander), *Baudelaire* (trans.
by Martin Turnell), and *Nausea* (trans. by Lloyd Alexander) in 1949.
Sartre's play *Les Mouches* had been published in 1943.

W. S. Graham: (1918–), Scottish poet. KR would include work by
Graham in his *NBP* anthology, calling him "one of the youngest and
most independent Scottish poets."

Treece: Henry Treece (1911–1966), British poet; identified with English
"New Apocalypse" writers of the 1940s. KR includes Treece's work in
NBP.

Landor: Walter Savage Landor (1775–1864), British poet, playwright.
In "The Function of Poetry" *(WOTW)*, KR compared Landor to the
French painter Jacques-Louis David: "Landor's neo-Classicism was a
typical expression of the revolutionary ideas of his time."

a new POETS OF THE PACIFIC: Yvor Winters's anthology, *Twelve
Poets of the Pacific,* was published in 1937 by ND. It included work by
Winters, his wife Janet Lewis, his students J. V. Cunningham and Ann
Stanford, and others. This sequel volume, if compiled, was never pub-
lished. Richard Moore and Leo Levy were two young Bay Area poets;
Moore would go on to produce a series of films called *Poetry U.S.A.*
for National Educational Television, including programs on William
Everson, Michael McClure, Robert Creeley, Denise Levertov, and
Charles Olson.

35. TLS-1

[Spring 1947]
[San Francisco]

DEAR JIM,

. . . LOOK—have you ever done anything about
running down the legal-copyright questions on that
Macmillan—Noh or accomplishment? IT IS A NACH-

ERAL FOR YOUR MODERN CLASSICS; except for 2 poems in Cathay—it is the best verse Ezra [Pound] ever wrote. The play "Nishikigi" is the most beautiful verse ever produced by an American. Maybe you could get EP to fuck around with the text—cut out, and rewrite most of the explanatory matter—([Ernest] Fenollosa worked from a bad text, an apocryphal edition of Seami [Motokiyo]—and was sometimes misled by his Japanese informants—also—there shd be a certain amount of going over of meanings by a Shingon Buddhist—tho I could do it to some extent. However, it is remarkable how penetrating Ezra's analyses are—tho he was ignorant of the language, and cared nothing for the religion.) Then you could call the thing a new and revised—I think if you really want to do something for the old fool, this is the thing to do. And I betcha a pretty penny, it will sell like hotcakes. I been after you about this for years and years—why dont you get the lead out of your ass? . . .

[Henry] Miller is the 2nd guy to turn down [Richard] Eberhart. It was obvious from his letter—Lepska [Miller]'s rather—that they hadn't the vaguest notion of who Eberhart was. Me, I think it likely Dick will be read when Henry has been gathered to the musty corners. . . . Frankly—H Miller was defended by me only because he spoke against the War, and I think that was the main reason for his fame. Now—I do not believe, what with Palmistry, Chirography, Phrenology, and the Great Cryptogram, he will survive the retooling period. I honestly think he is the most insufferable snob I have ever met—but all reformed panhandlers are like that. . . .

faithfully
KENNETH

/ · /

"Nishikigi": See note, letter 24.

36. ALS-8

14 VI [19]47
[San Francisco]

DEAR JIM—

I am not very pleased. I think you are extremely insulting—suggesting I write for Hearst & I think you would be ashamed to do it yourself. It is my opinion that you, like most rich people, are insane on the subject of money—and the fear that others "only want to take advantage" of you. . . . Further, I resent being treated as though I was some sort of eccentric and feeble minded freak whose association c̄ you causes you intense embarrassment chez Diana Trilling and/or J[ohn] C[rowe] Ransom. . . .

We are homeless and desperately in need of money—and it does not help us to tell me that I can build a mud house, in a place where no one can make a living, for $500. I cannot continue a relationship which has sunk to such a level of mockery. I must have definite, written commitments on the following points:

1) Are you going to reprint the book *The Phoenix & Tortoise?* If not, I want the copyright.

2) I have a new book of verse. Are you going to take that, and if so, when will it come out?

3) I have what you like to call "a valuable piece of property"—over 100 Japanese poems in what is unquestionably the best translation to date. (I was doing this while you thought I was loafing.) . . . Do you want it?

4) I have never believed for a moment that you were serious about that magazine. Will you make a defi-

nite statement, one way or another?

5) Do you want a preface to [D. H. Lawrence's] *The Man Who Died,* or dont you? It is written—but I will not send it off into blank space.

6) Will you give me an advance on the Blake book? How much? I am certainly as trustworthy as [Edouard] Roditi—even if I dont drink martinis c̄ the right set.

7) Have you really any intention of printing the collection of plays? Why not at the back of the book of poetry? In this instance again I think you want to get out of it because of the opinion of certain cocktail critics. . . .

I am really very fond of you—but you must understand that you cannot treat me as though I was some poor cousin, who, out of your beneficience, you permitted to live on the leftovers from the main table, in exchange for a little help c̄ the children, the sewing & cleaning. . . .

faithfully
KENNETH

. . . I have no doubt that you are now and will be in exaggerated tones from now on, telling everybody you meet at cocktail parties that I am 1) insane, 2) an alcoholic, 3) dishonest, 4) constantly trying to swindle you and begging money from you. I have the consolation that I will be in noble company. I am leaving, on Marie [Rexroth]'s money, for a month in the mountains—do not bother to write till April 15.

. . . [Donn] Moir says—to me & Henry [Miller]— "In a way, our aims are much the same as James Laughlin's—*when he started* c̄ New Directions—but we do not intend to degenerate solely into the publishing of moderns who flopped 10 years ago, nor do we wish to complete a circle or coterie of writers

& artists, barring those who do not conform to the circle." Take that—what've I been telling you? Stalin forgot an apothegm not unlike "You can do everything c̄ bayonets except sit on them," and that is—"The future is always young, poor, & dishevelled." Fuck Diana Trilling.

/ · /

Diana Trilling: (1905–), American essayist, editor. Married to Lionel Trilling, she wrote a regular column, "Fiction in Review," for the *Nation* from 1941 to 1948. Her *The Selected Letters of D. H. Lawrence* was published in 1961.

over 100 Japanese poems: Published as *One Hundred Poems from the Japanese* by ND in 1955.

that magazine: KR had hoped that JL would finance a literary magazine for him which he wanted William Everson or the Grabhorn Press to print. The project never materialized.

Do you want a preface: ND published D. H. Lawrence's *The Man Who Died, sans* preface by KR, in October 1947.

The collection of plays: KR's four plays would be published by ND as *Beyond the Mountains* in 1951.

37. ALS-3

[Fall 1947]
[San Francisco]

DEAR JIM,

. . . I am sending off the new poems—title—The Signature of all Things. I will write a short preface, like for *P[hoenix] & T[ortoise]*—it does wonders for reviews. . . .

You'd love the night I saw Zorina! First, I spent till 3:30 eating cheese sandwiches in a depressing restaurant and talking to her—she being very much like most highbrow girls—but still—beneath it all—a really great person. Then—my head in a whirl—I went for a walk. This most dismal she tramp stopped me and told me—while having a violent fit of shakes—that she had been hit over the head, raped, and her purse stolen—and she had no place to sleep. This was all probably true—her back was covered with dirt, she had two handsome eggs on the back of her melon, and she had no purse. Since she was in no state to carry the banner and refused to go to the hospital—I set out to find her a room in the Tenderloin. The town has sure changed. It took me about an hour of trudging around and trying to persuade night clerks. At last I roused an old madam I know, who took her in for $1.75. I then noticed, in her hotel, a light thru the door of a girl I know and being very tired by all this paid her a call. She is not very young—is half Chinoise—tho she looks full blooded Chinese—and has only recently kicked a son of a bitch of a habit. We sat on the bed & talked—her in her negligee c̄ her body spotted like a leopard from shooting gen shi (scrapings of opium pipes, which leave a small ulcer, and then a scar like a bluish vaccination mark). If you put it in a book—nobody would believe it—I suppose there do not exist 3 more dissimilar women. I really do lead a strange life—or rather—I certainly know a strange assortment of people. . . .

c̄ love
KENNETH

/ · /

the new poems: KR's fourth book of poems, *The Signature of All Things*, was published by ND in 1950.

38. Airletter. TLS-1

1/22[19]48
[San Francisco]

DEAR JIM—

Why are you such a dreadful provincial? E[zra] P[ound]'s characters MUST be right—and you dont understand that Chinese calligraphy is a subtle business—you cant just copy his pathetic "sketches" made in crayon, in ink. Go to the library of the nearest city and get a book on the art of calligraphy—there are several in German and others in French and Italian as well as English—and see what you are getting into. Several of those you showed me were wrong, ie. drawn wrong in the first place. Here is an example. The strokes must be in a certain order and the brush must move in a certain, varied direction in each stroke and the pressure must change constantly, as well as the speed. I implore you. Do not make yourself and EP ridiculous. . . .

With your letter I got a note from Frieda [Lawrence] thanking me very beautifully for the Lawrence. This is the first I know it is out. . . .

love
KENNETH

/ · /

EP's characters: In SFP, KR recalls that for years he had noticed that two of the ideograms in Ezra Pound's Cantos were "upside down. I used to pester Laughlin about this. I used to make fun of it. Ezra by this time had gotten very dim-witted, so he didn't notice it. This was after the war . . . Laughlin said something to Eliot about it, and Eliot burst out laughing and thought it was a great joke. Not that they were up-side down, but that it would worry me. He said, 'But, you know, no one pays any attention at all to that sort of stuff. You know, the Chinese thing. Nobody reads Chinese anyway.' Eliot's attitude towards Ezra's interest in the Orient was that it was a great deal more ridiculous than his interest in social credit, or his other crackpot ideas." According to JL, "Ezra definitely did notice the characters that were upside down and raised hell about it, as you'll find recorded in my *Gists & Piths*. The story about Eliot is a KR fabrication. TSE thought *Cathay* was one of the best things Ezra ever did" (JL letter to the editor).

the Lawrence: KR's edition of D. H. Lawrence's *Selected Poems*. In his introduction to the volume, KR writes of Lawrence's wife Frieda (1879–1956), "With Frieda the sleeper wakes, the man walks free, the 'child' of the alchemists is born. Reality is totally valued, and passes beyond the possibility of hallucination. . . . Poetry is vision, the pure act of sensual communion and contemplation. That is why the poems of Lawrence and Frieda on their Rhine Journey are such good poetry. That is why they are also the greatest imagist poems ever written. Reality streams through the body of Frieda. . . . The swinging of her breasts as she stoops in the bath, the roses, the deer, the harvesters . . . the light of the Holy Sacrament of Marriage, whose source is the wedded body of the bride."

39. TLS-1   January 28 [1948]
                                              Milan

DEAR KENNETH—

. . . You may have had a request from [Hubert] Creekmore to airmail me a few phrases about [William] Everson's poetry for the jacket of his book. Hope you will. I always come up with the same old chestnuts on jackets, and Bill deserves better. His book underway now. . . .

If you tell people I am ashamed of your Lawrence preface you are a liar. You know better. Diana Trilling never saw it, nor said anything to me about it. You are as neurotic as hell. Just because I am getting tired of working all day and all night and let things drag a bit, you accuse me of dropping things. In the end I shall get around to doing all the things you have asked me to do, but it all takes time. Now for Christ sake come off it and be a little patient.

I enclose your check for *Spearhead* royalty. The office reports that the book has been doing fairly well.

One thousand went to England, and to my amazement, seem to have been let through the customs, in spite of the hot passages in Henry [Miller]'s section.

Your biblical friend sends you indecent noises made with her mouth. She is really thriving here & very restful. Has an admirer—one [Salvatore] Quasimodo who is about the best Italian poet. Campigli's wife says the Q does it 12 times in a single night and G is having a bad time being ladylike and reserved.

J

/ · /

Creekmore: Hubert Creekmore (1907–1966) worked for ND for many years. His *The Long Reprieve and Other Poems from New Caledonia,* with an introduction by Selden Rodman, was published by ND in 1946. He was also a novelist and translator of Tibullus.

his book: William Everson's *The Residual Years.*

in spite of the hot passages: Henry Miller's "The Cosmodemonic Rigolade" passage from *Tropic of Capricorn* appeared in *Spearhead.*

Quasimodo: Salvatore Quasimodo (1901–1968), Italian poet who won the Nobel Prize for Literature in 1959.

40. Airletter. TLS

Feb. 10, 1948
[San Francisco]

[DEAR JIM,]

. . . Some ideas for Oriental Library. Pick up [D. T.] Suzuki as Routledge reissues. This will sell very well. Very very well. I can do a Buddhist anthology, and illustrate it with pictures of the great sculptures of Borobudur which can be got cheap from Holland. Two Korean books, *Cloud Rim of the Nine; Grass Roof.* The 47 Ronin with Japanese woodcuts for illustration—this is cheap and easy to do, and includes some of the very greatest woodcuts. If the *Dream of the Red Chamber* doesnt come back in print soon—grab it. [Robert] Payne says he knows a complete translation. If Knopf doesnt want to reissue [Arthur] Waley, *The Way and the Power* (Lao Tzu, Tao Te Ching) GRAB IT—I think Unwin has it in print still. There is a great demand for it, it is the best and hard to equal in our time.

WHY DONT YOU BOLDLY PUBLISH [D. H. Lawrence's] LADY CHATTERLEY AND SEE WHAT HAPPENS??? I THINK NOTHING WOULD, AND EVEN IF IT DID, SO WHAT? This is one of my very brightest ideas. After all [Bennett] Cerf did [James Joyce's] *Ulysses*.

Did you ever think of doing [Sacco and] Vanzetti's Letters in the Modern Classics. If not, you should have and should.

YOU TELL [Herbert] READ I AM RESPONSIBLE FOR THE GREEN CHILD AND I THINK HE IS A VERY GREAT MAN AND A VERY GREAT WRITER.

KENNETH

/ · /

Waley: Arthur Waley (1889–1966), British orientalist, translator, editor. Like KR, essentially self-taught in Chinese and Japanese, his translation of Murasaki Shikibu's *Tale of Genji* (6 volumes) appeared 1925–33; his translation of Lao Tsu's *The Way and Its Power* had appeared in 1934.

After all: James Joyce's novel *Ulysses,* originally serialized in *The Little Review,* was first published entire by Shakespeare and Company in Paris in 1922. Copies of both the first and second editions were seized and destroyed by U.S. Customs for alleged obscenity. In 1933 the United States District Court found the book not obscene; Random House subsequently published the first American edition in 1937. JL did not take KR's suggestion that ND publish D. H. Lawrence's *Lady Chatterley's Lover* which, also at first regarded as obscene by U.S. Customs, eventually survived a court test and was published in an unexpurgated edition in the United States by Grove Press in 1959.

41. Airletter. TLS   2/17/[19]48
                                        [San Francisco]

DEAR JIM,

. . . You know—you have yet to fulfill *any* of the
commitments you made a year ago out here. I knew,
immediately you got back, that you had again fallen
under the influence of the *Partisan-Kenyon* swine and
of nincompoops like [Hubert] Creekmore and were
very anxious to shake what you considered some very
indiscreetly undertaken responsibilities. I have consistently defended you to all these people and it has
reflected back to me. For some reason they all think
that I have some sort of influence with you. Sort of
Delmore Schwartz the Second. I suspect this ema-
nates originally from poor scorned Delmore himself. If people only knew! You just keep on taking
the advice of NYC cocktail hacks and printing
warmed over nonsense from the Café Dome and they
will put you in the Smithsonian Institution along with
Fulton's paddle wheel. I am getting very annoyed
placating angry telephoners. . . .

You impress on [Herbert] Read I am responsible
for the *Green Child* publication c̄ you. I think he thinks
I dont like him. And always send complimentary
copies of anything I write to him, [Alex] Comfort,
[George] Woodcock, [D. S.] Savage, and [Nicholas]
Moore—also review copies to *Poetry Quarterly* and
Poetry London. I am much more interested in my
English reputation than my USA one. . . .

I am slow about the Cal Poets because I find it
very difficult to get anything out of them. I am running a very successful Poetry Forum at the hdqtrs of
the anarchist group, which itself is going great guns,
and on an incomparably higher level. The Cal poets
should go off this week.

Here is suggested list of Far Eastern Classics—100 Japanese Poems; 100 Chinese Poems; 100 Indian Poems; A Buddhist Book; A Taoist Book; A Confucian Book; a Vedanta Book (let [Christopher] Ish[erwood] edit); San Kuo; Hung Lou Meng *(Dream of the Red Chamber)* [Robert] Payne says he has trans.; 4 Cautionary Tales, change to 4 Erotic Tales; The Tzuredsure Gesu and Hoojooki in one vol.; A Korean novel; An anthology of Indochinese verse; Selections from the History of Su Ma Chien; Selections from DT Suzuki (or import from Routledge); *Le Livre de Jade* in French & English; E[zra] P[ound]'s Chinese and Japanese translations. . . .

Now you stop being bad. And come back & go to the mts.

Love to you-all

KENNETH

/ · /

Comfort: KR included work by younger British poets Alex Comfort, George Woodcock, D. S. Savage, and Nicholas Moore in his *NBP* anthology.

I am running: Following a memorial service for Sacco and Vanzetti, KR and Philip Lamantia had founded a group which would come to be called the "Libertarian Circle." The group met once a week in KR's apartment (then later rented the top floor of a hall) for discussions of anarchist politics. According to *Excerpts,* the group "had by far the largest meetings of any radical or pseudo-radical group in San Francisco. The place was always crowded and when the topic for the evening was Sex and Anarchy you couldn't get in the doors. People were standing on one another's shoulders." Eventually, the Circle introduced a Poetry Forum to the agenda each Wednesday. Two Wednesdays a month discussion would center on the work of a writer in the group—KR, Duncan, Everson, Parkinson, Rukeyser, and others—led by the writer himself. Alternate Wednesdays, KR led classes in poetry and criticism. In time, the Forum developed into the Poetry Guild of San Francisco, whose founding members included KR, Rukeyser, Everson, Edith Henrich, and William Justema, and whose directors were Duncan, Madeline Gleason, and James Broughton. Further, by this time KR had also organized a weekly seminar for ten members, "preferably those who have written verse of some merit," for discussion of his "A Selected Bibliography of Poetics, Modern Period," which included studies by Empson, Eliot, Pound, Spender, Riding, Yeats, and others, charging each member a dollar a week tuition.

42. TLS-3

February 18th [1948]
Zermatt

DEAR KENNETH—

There have been a lot of letters from you this week and I shall try to answer as many points as I can. You bombard me with so many ideas that you vitiate the force of your suggestions. Decide what is most vital and concentrate on that until done. Then take up the next most vital.

I have tried to read the San Kuo but cannot get into it. The many foreign names baffle me and I get mixed up. The thing would have to be retranslated, I think, because the old customs house man uses so many odd old-time expressions. Are you sure you have not confused your passion for the play in the Chinese theatre with the merit of the thing as reading?

Zermatt is very fine in winter. The mountains seem to stand out more than ever, and are particularly wonderful at sundown. Yesterday, with Heinz and my friend Elias Julen, the guide who took me up the Matterhorn, we climbed over the Theodule Pass, skied down to Breuil, then took the Italian cable car (one of Musso's good works) back to the pass, skied diagonally across that flat glacier to just under the Hoernli Hut, and then down back to Zermatt. Cold day, and the snow windblown, but wonderful air and views. I had never seen the mountain before from the Italian side. It hasn't any sex appeal from that angle, but it is an imposing big chunk of rock. . . .

All what you write about my being under the influence of the *P[artisan] R[eview]* is a lot of horse-crap and you know it. You have more influence on what ND publishes than anyone. As for what I say about you to other people I don't take one half the liberties that I have repeatedly heard you take in being "amusing" about other writers. This may be because I am not as comical as you are. . . .

The ideograms you put on your letters are very pretty, but you are wasting your time—I can't read them.

I think the Far Eastern Series is a good idea, but how can I work with you when you consistently refuse to proofread scripts. . . . So it will have to wait until finances are better. . . .

I don't see that you should take credit for THE GREEN CHILD. I met [Herbert] Read at a cocktail party and he himself told me about the book. . . .

You realize, I hope, that we are having to cut down the number of poems [in *The New British Poets*]. It will be a trim little book. Page has to be small because Italian paper comes in smaller standard sizes than ours. The type is beautiful—monotype Bembo—something you could never get in USA in a commercial book. I think I will print an extra thousand for distribution on the continent. In this way copies will filter into England through travellers and you will get your message across. Will print about 4000 for America, but have them hold the type so we can do more if it takes. The jacket is stolen from a very pretty book I picked up in Milan. It gets all the names of the poets right on the cover in a simple and effective way, each inside the square of a rough mesh or net. Very handsome. . . .

[D. H. Lawrence's] *Lady Chatterley*. IMPOSSIBLE.
Don't you realize that I have to depend for funds on
handouts from aged Presbyterian females who would
stop off everything if there were a scandal.

Thanks very much for the blurb on [William]
Everson. It was excellent, just what was needed,
much appreciated and will be used as written. You
are one of the best blurb writers in the biz, really.
Tragic that you cannot be meticulous on scripts. You
would be a wonderful editor and invaluable in a
publishing house if one could RELY on you to correct
scripts.

The preface for *Signature,* and the jacket blurb, are
both very good, and will be used. . . .

No, I like Philip [Lamantia] personally, but don't
think he has a future as a poet. [Robert] Duncan more
likely. There is a gift of gab there, in spite of the lack
of interior bone.

J

/ · /

blurb on Everson: KR's jacket blurb for William Everson's *The Residual
Years.* Leslie Fiedler reviewed the book for *Partisan Review,* attacking
the anonymous blurb: "The jacket blurb on William Everson's book
. . . is a kind of manifesto: poems are to be no longer 'abstract aesthetic
objects,' but intimate speech, sensuous and passionate. The paired
adjectives suggest, of course, Milton, but it is D. H. Lawrence via
Rexroth and Patchen, who is actually invoked, and we should perhaps
read for the more conventional pair—phallic and sentimental."

preface for Signature: In his introduction to *The Signature of All Things,*
KR notes the absence of overtly political and protest poems: "These
are all simple, personal poems, as close as I can make them to integral
experiences. Perhaps the integral person is more revolutionary than
any program, party, or social conflict."

43. TLS-2   1 iii [19]48
                                          [San Francisco]

DEAR JIM,

O you dirty stinker. You said you had not been impressed by [Herbert] Read when you met him and that he had nothing to say and I told you about the *Green Child* and ordered it from CWG for you to read, and have been annoying you ever since. Now, whatever you think—you tell Read I think it is one of the few perfect masterpieces of Our Time and that I have been urging you to print it for years and years and that I will do the blurb. Dont fail to do this because I have great respect and admiration for him and I think he don't like me, or rather—I have been told by people in England that he thinks I dont like him, due to a review of *Art and Society* I wrote years ago—AND since he is editor of Routledge, I want to butter him, because I think this Far Eastern Library could well do with importing some Routledge titles, who have the best Orientalia list of any trade house in the world. Now you be good enough and do that— its good beezniss.

As for my "scripts" you're full of shit. The mss. of the Britshits is practically perfect. A handfull of errors which could have been done in proof without the printer ever noticing. . . .

You're nuts not to publish *Lady Chatterley*. If you cant publish it now, sew Frieda [Lawrence] up, and publish it later. But if you can publish drivel by Henry Djuna Maldoror, you can sure as hell publish the cleanest book ever written. You're very dumb if you dont at least make an effort to *corner* it. . . .

You're wrong about the San Kuo—this is because you like Prose like is wrote by the lady Donn Byrne and D. J. Barnes. Your blurb on Monday Night is so funny—there are probably fifty detective story writers who are better than Miss Boil. You just think narrative is lowbrow. . . .

I think the Brit Poets should be as small sized as possible. NEVER NEVER publish an anthology that can't be carried in the pocket, at least a big pocket. Anthologies are read on hikes with the head nestled in a coppice of pubic hair. . . . BUT LOOK. THIS IS THE FIRST I HEAR YOU ARE CUTTING THE CONTENTS. YOU LET ME KNOW RIGHT AWAY WHAT YOU ARE DOING. . . . It would be better maybe to cut out some poets than cut down on the representation of the best. I will send you a list immediately of what I think the contents, if cut, should be. . . .

> love, and farts in snow
> KENNETH

/ · /

due to a review: KR's "Marxism?" (a review of Herbert Read's *Art and Society*) appeared in *Art Front* III, in 1937.

D. J. Barnes: (1892–1982), American dramatist and fiction writer. ND reprinted her novel, *Nightwood,* with an introduction by T. S. Eliot in 1949.

44. ALS-3

[March 1948]
[San Francisco]

DEAR JIM—

. . . You are completely off about that *British Poets.* I haven't any objection to the size of the book—BUT you agreed to print the material I gave you last year. All you had to do was say how many pages you wanted. Instead you turned it over—as you did the [D. H.] Lawrence—to an empty headed NYC cocktail fairy whose ideas of poetry are derived from some emasculated English Professor and the *Partisan & Kenyon Reviews* and *Horizon*. So what did he do? He cut out all the personal poetry. (Fairies have no persons.) All the unabashed sentiment—all the humor—all the erotic poetry—all the Scots dialect—all the satire—and produced a book the exact opposite of what I had edited. Certainly c̄ this selection—the introduction is absolute nonsense. You know perfectly well that I would have cut the mss. to any length—and you certainly had no business bundling it off to the printer without telling me—if that is what you did. If it is not set up yet—I can still cut it about 20% without any trouble. Otherwise, I guess you will have to add some pages.

It is not true that my manuscripts are not clean. You have said yourself that they are the cleanest you get. Anyway—they are typed by Marie [Rexroth]. This is part of what has become a very curious neurosis c̄ you. As for my suggestions—I shall stop making them. You do not seem to be able to face the fact that you are no longer an "advance guard" publisher. You publish Miller, Williams, Pound, Rexroth, and one or two others—yourself included—none of them young men. Otherwise you publish junk by people like Kay Boyle & Djuna Barnes who are about as modern as bathtub gin—and the academic writers the conventional houses miss—like Jean Garrigue, who is simply atrocious—the worst of the *PR-Kenyon* lot. Do you realize that you are rapidly becoming an antique like HL Mencken? *Spearhead* was one of the most depressing things I have ever seen. If you dont snap out of it—broaden your list to include a few practical specialties and some young writers—you will find yourself in a complete impasse. . . .

With love, your best friend
KENNETH

/ · /

Kay Boyle: (1903–), American fiction writer. JL included work by Boyle (who, according to JL, had been contacted directly by Ezra Pound) in the first *ND* annual; her *Thirty Stories* was published by ND in 1946. Several of her early novels and collections of short stories have recently been reprinted in ND's Revised Modern Classics series.

Jean Garrigue: (1914–1972), American poet. Her work appeared in ND's *Five Young American Poets* in 1944; her collection, *The Ego and the Centaur,* was published by ND in 1947. In *APTC,* KR wrote, "Delmore Schwartz, Elizabeth Bishop, Jean Garrigue, Robert Penn Warren—what characterizes these people is their narrowness, their lack of broad contact, or even interests, in anything but a narrow range. . . ."

H.L. Mencken: (1880–1956), American writer, social critic. His *American Language* first appeared in 1919.

45. TLS-1

March 18th, 1948
Klosters, Switzerland

DEAR KENNETH—

Your stinging letter makes me realize that perhaps I have been a bit high-handed with you. But your total disregard of everything practical connected with publishing makes it difficult for me to consider you an adult in that respect. You act like a child with your thousand confused suggestions—these coupled with scripts full of simple errors—and I realize that I have been trying to treat you like a wayward child.

Well, I admit that it would be unfair to you to put out a Bowdlerized version of your anthology, and I am willing to add another 64 page signature to the book, even though this means that there is no possible chance of selling the book at anything but a loss. . . .

It is all right about the loan. If you are using it for a house that was what it was for and I am satisfied. But what I objected to was that money sitting doing nothing when I was in need of cash to live on. Will you get it through your head that I am broke? I suppose that means that now you will drop me. Well, that will only be part of the general disintegration. . . .

I don't know whether to consider you my best friend any longer, or whether to think of you as another of the many who tried to get a ride on the gravy train. I don't really think the latter. You have been generous of yourself to me in many ways—very—and the happiest times of my life have been those that I have spent with you.

I sent off the script for a little 32 page booklet of my poems to Milan the other day. It was dedicated to you. I am writing them to remove the dedication—I don't want to embarrass you.

JIM

/ · /

little 32 page booklet: JL's *A Small Book of Poems,* published by ND and Giovanni Scheiviller in Milan in 1948.

46. Airletter. TLS

4/13/[19]48
[San Francisco]

DEAR JIM,

GOT GUG. Thank you for the good word. Now maybe I can afford a trip East this Fall. I think I will use it to live in the mountains for two years. I have it all planned. Altho I just planned it—I never expected to get a Guggenheim. It is good it came—because I need money so badly—now I can get necessary dental and medical work done too. . . .

Now look—you be sure and leave in—G[eorge]

Bruce—[Alex] Comfort, notes for my son; [Keith] Douglas; ALL of [David] Gascoyne; [Denise] Lever-tov, some are too much at home; ALL of [Hugh] MacDiarmid except Hedgeback; [Os] Marron; ALL of Sorely Maclean; [Nicholas] Moore, Incidents and Little Girl—DONT you dare cut these out; most of [Norman] Nicholson; ALL of [Kathleen] Raine if possible—BUT ULLSWATER FOR SURE, this is the best poem in the book, most of [Anne] Ridler; most of [D. S.] Savage; cut only Miracle of Soutar; leave in Refusal to mourn and Deaths and Entrances and Force that thru green fuse of [Dylan] Thomas; cut two of [Vernon] Watkins, and two of [John] Waller, ONLY TWO of [George] Woodcock. If you had only con-sulted me in the first place, I would gladly have cut a third out of the book. But you cannot understand that you have become trapped in the taste of a lot of superannuated homosexual bookreviewers and teaching assistants. The world of [William] Empson and/or Kay Boyle is dead, dead, dead. No more Hound, no more Horn. You stick to [Kenneth] Patchen, [Paul] Goodman, Rexroth, even [Henry] Miller and [Herbert] Read, Savage, Comfort and Woodcock. Us, honey, are the future, or rather, the young people we are trying to raise up. Assuming the existence of the future. . . .

KENNETH

/ · /

GOT GUG: KR was awarded a Guggenheim Fellowship in 1948.

you be sure and leave: In *The New British Poets.* All of these suggestions were adopted, save that Hugh MacDiarmid's "In the Hedgeback" was retained.

Empson: Sir William Empson (1906–1984), British poet, critic. His *Seven Types of Ambiguity* (1930), coming out of I. A. Richards's experiments with Practical Criticism, proved an influential work, arguing through close linguistic analysis for the elevation of verbal complexity over simplicity.

no more Hound: Hound & Horn, a literary journal founded in 1927 by Lincoln Kirstein and Varian Fry (like JL, as Harvard undergraduates) in 1927, took its name from Ezra Pound's "The White Stag" ("Bid the world's hounds come to horn!"). Contributors included Pound, Dudley Fitts, and R. P. Blackmur, among many others.

47. TLS-2   April 20th [1948]
                                          Ascona

DEAR KENNETH—

That is wonderful news about the Guggenheim. I am real pleased. If you are a good industrious boy they will give it to you again next year. Lots of people get renewals. We will surely have the new book out this fall and you can show them that and then line up some imposing project and get a renewal. But don't count on it.

Yes, I think you ought to come East, but you have to consider that all the boys like Delmore [Schwartz] and Foggy [Philip] Rahv will be sitting there waiting to pot at you. It might be strategic simply to ignore New York and center on Boston. I am sure that I can arrange for you to have a reading at Harvard if they are in session, also for you to record.at the Library of Congress. Shall I work on these angles? Might be other readings too, though you will have to compete with the Sitwells, who are arriving en masse in New York in the fall. You should by all means arrange to spend some time with Bill Willyums who is a great man. Perhaps we could get Bill and Floss [Williams] to come up to Norfolk for a visit while you are there, since Rutherford is not much of a place to stretch out in.

Yes, I think you should just ignore the *P[artisan] R[eview]* crowd. I do, for the most part, though I see Delmore now and then. . . .

Zermatt is rapidly going to hell. You ought to get out there right soon. It is becoming very social. People are building chic little chalets with blue shutters all over those pretty cow gardens on the east side of the river, and the place is dripping with awful international set females (who go by names like Annie-Pannie-Pee-Pie) who are busy buttering behinds. . . . It is sad. The trouble is that nice guys like the guides only see the money that these turds bring in and so they encourage it. Real sad. . . .

[Thomas] Merton is so obedient. He writes now that the Abbot has told him he must write explanations of his poems because he gets letters from the faithful that they cannot understand. But he does at least think now that God wants him to be a poet and not just a prayer wheel. . . .

Poor old Ez[ra Pound]. He's catching it now from the wimmen. Dorothy [Pound] wants to keep him in. She wouldn't allow Julien [Cornell] to make the appeal to higher court on release. Apparently she has him now where Olga [Rudge] can't get at him and she means to keep him there. Poor old Ez. She being the legal guardian it's a tough nut to crack. Julien has to do what she says. Other explication is that it costs a lot of money in those private buggyhouses (where he would have to go) and she probably wants to save her money . . . Dunno. Parson [T.S.] Eliot much concerned. He's the best one to tackle her about it. She's scared of him.

JIM

/ · /

Lots of people: KR's Guggenheim Fellowship was renewed the following year.

Merton is so obedient: Thomas Merton (1915–1968), American poet, essayist, translator, Trappist monk. With the 1944 publication of Merton's *Thirty Poems,* ND became one of the monk's primary publishers. According to JL, "He was a kind friend and interested in everything. I often went down to visit him at the monastery in Kentucky. . . . He wanted to read contemporary writers, but the books were often confiscated, so we had a secret system. I sent the books he wanted to the monastery psychiatrist in Louisville, who would get them to Merton. I sent him everyone he wanted to read: Sartre and Camus, Rexroth and Pound, Henry Miller and many more. We talked a great deal about the oriental religions. He was very ecumenical. We talked about his situation and why he stuck it out in the monastery. Once I asked, 'Tom, why do you want to stay here? You could get out and be a tremendous success in the world.' He answered that the monastery was where God wanted him to be" *(PR).* Merton entered the Trappist Abbey of Gethsemani in December 1941; during his first years there he was discouraged from publishing his poems.

Dorothy: Dorothy Shakespear Pound (1886–1973), Ezra Pound's wife.

Olga Rudge (1895–), concert violinist, Pound's companion, and mother of his daughter, Mary de Rachewiltz.

She wouldn't allow Julien: Julien Cornell (1910–), attorney. JL had arranged for Cornell, who during the war had served as counsel for the American Civil Liberties Union, to act as Ezra Pound's defense attorney. ND published Cornell's *New World Primer* in 1947.

48. Airletter. TLS

14/V/[19]48
San Francisco

DEAR JIM,

O boy, what a lemon we picked in [William] Everson. He seems to be one of those ugly bastards who can't stand the thought that someone else has done something for him. The publication of his book seems to have thrown him into a sort of frenzy of hatred for me, and incidentally you, though he is afraid to say much about that, you being influential. He has been telling people that I am a very dangerous man, a faker who has a lot of charm and who leads people on and then exploits them, and that my anarchism and pacifism is all a fake designed to trap the unwary. That is what I did to him, lead him on and then exploit him for my own ends! When I think that I spent two years in a bug ward getting beat up, and sending my wages to the NCRO to keep bastards like him in camp so's they could posture against the sunset! Then he writes me a letter about how ugly the book is and how it was cheap and vulgar and whatnot. When I pointed out to him that 1) he was offered a printing business, in which he could have done the book himself, 2) he was offered the opportunity to set it by hand from which ND could make plates, 3) he was offered the opportunity to design it for another printer—all of which he refused in a most aesthetic manner, 4) [Peter] Beilenson is the most expensive printer you use, and the one he requested, 5) he was shown his—Everson's—stuff and told to use it as a model and spare no expense, 6) the book is the most expensive book of verse ND ever published, and if he would prefer, it would be cheaper to burn it up, because every copy you sell will lose more money. Then he took another tack and wrote me that I was exhibiting him in a vulgar show as Honest Abe the Poem Splitter. That he had nothing in common with Lawrence, that he despised Patchen and had no use for me, and that he wanted, not rejected, academic approval, and a lot more nonsense.

I have, needless to say, been very upset by all this. I feel like I have been played for a sucker, and I have that sick queasy feeling that comes over you every time you realize once again, the hard and dirty way, that almost all men are sons of bitches. And I feel so badly about the neurotic destructiveness of it. You would think he would want to enjoy having his first book published. Marie [Rexroth] and I planned to give him a party and I called him up, happy as a lark, and got a very snotty rebuff, which was followed by the letters. I know now what you must go through with these swine. Christ what a thankless job!

I saw his first wife last night, and we talked about it. She, of course, laid it all to that Dago wench he is shacked up with. But the core of the matter seems to be that he is terrified that he wont be approved of . . . and he is outraged by being placed in the company of such disgusting people as me, Patchen, Lawrence. This is the behavior of a rube from Fresno who is too ignorant to know who is who in the Big City. But mostly it is that deep evil of sick pride that hates all overtures of genuine friendship and concern, and which looks on the receipt of any sort of kindness or interest as the incursion of a hideous debt which must be struggled against with maximum violence. Philip [Lamantia]'s theory is that he is no longer perfectly sane. Which is also Marthe [Larsen]'s. He sent some poems over for the Cal. Poems which certainly read like the products of some sort of mental illness. It is certainly an awful thing to have happened. What a bitched up world it is! . . .

I guess Jack is going to do the Jap poets alright. The U of Cal Press wanted it—but they also wanted it "scholarly" with a lot of notes and crap! Fuck that. I am trying to get a visa for the Orient next spring. If not, England, I guess—especially if you are going back over, I would like to take a trip with you—I'd be afraid of all them buggery British by myself, honey. And I do so long to have that little ole bird fart in my left ear.

lots of love
KENNETH

/ · /

NCRO: National Council of Religious Objectors, an umbrella group created in response to the 1940 draft by the three historic "peace churches"—the Quakers, the Church of the Brethren, and the Mennonites.

Beilenson: Peter Beilenson, founder of the Peter Pauper Press.

I saw his first wife: Everson's first wife, Edwa Poulson.

that Dago wench: Mary Fabilli.

Marthe: Marthe Larsen would become KR's third wife in 1949. According to *Excerpts,* KR recalls that at one of the meetings of the Libertarian Circle, a Mills College student "brought three other students with her, one of them a young man who was a member of the Brubeck Octet, all of whom were studying with Milhaud at Mills on the GI Bill. In due course there were about ten Mills girls who came regularly to the meetings and dances and several of them were to marry members of Brubeck's group. And one became my third wife, Marthe." Before their divorce in 1961, the couple would have two daughters, Mary and Katherine.

49. Airletter. ALS

6/11/[19]48
[San Francisco]

DEAR JIM,

Why does my name not appear in the advertising for *Spearhead*? This is absurd when it appears in magazines like *Retort* where I am one of the persons in whom the readers are most interested. I cannot permit you to use anything of mine in the Annual unless you agree to mention me in the advertising. I am certainly as important as nincompoops like John Berryman and Randall Jarrell. The trouble is—you are ashamed of me. Why dont you mention [Paul] Goodman and [Kenneth] Patchen as well? The readers of *Retort* are certainly not interested in has-beens of *Paris America* or in the stormtroopers of the *P[artisan] & K[enyon] Review.* I have mentioned this to you before. I have had about enough. In fact I am perfectly sore. You are completely under the domination of the NYC cocktail academic set. Cant you *realize* that this is *not* significant writing? They are the *Atlantic Monthly* of the present time. Either I am properly advertised or I dont play anymore.

KENNETH

/ · /

John Berryman: (1914–1972), American poet and critic. His work appeared in *Five Young American Poets*, published by ND in 1940. ND published his *Poems* in 1942.

Randall Jarrell: His work appeared with Berryman's in ND's *Five Young American Poets*, 1940.

50. Airletter. ALS

June 25, 1948
[San Francisco]

DEAR JIM—

Where are you going? Today in the mail came 2 books—Henry [Miller]'s clown & [Kenneth] Patchen's 1st Will & Testament. . . . Pretty soon you'll be a middle aged reactionary printing middle aged reactionaries like Jean Garrygoo. You are losing your grip. You are absolutely insane to let Patchen & Miller slip away from you like this. Especially since last year—when Patchen was quarreling c̄ Padell—you could have got *all* his books. good Christ! Cant you see past these snobs and high-toned sheenies and Anglocatholic English Professors. Your writers are E[zra] P[ound], W. C. W[illiams], [Paul] Goodman—Patchen—Miller-myself—and you should be taking on new-similar—young-revolutionaries. Instead you have now lost Patchen altogether, and for all I know, Miller—and you never did publish

Goodman. Are you under the impression that Dudley Fitts, RP Blackmur, JC Ransom, and their little scholars, are New Directions? Why not just retire. . . . All over the country the young are revolting against the dictatorship of parvenu mediocrities who run the hightoned magazines. Can't you understand that the *Partisan Review* is about as "advanced" as the *Atlantic Monthly* was in its day—or the *North American Review*—and not as well edited.

You said you were going to Frankfurt. If you have been—can you honestly go on printing the Fugitives—*Hound & Horn* bunch & their Bronx disciples and abandon Miller and Patchen and Goodman. It is Lincoln Kirstein who made the rubble heaps you saw. He and thousands like him.

Says Fitts of Patchen—"The bobbysoxers can have him. Let us run, not walk, to the exit." That's right. Righter than he thinks. Cannibalist. Swine like Fitts & his friends *are* running to the exit. And bobbysoxers are, after all, the future—the future he and his precious friends are trying to prevent—literally—by blowing up the world. They will probably succeed—but I can't understand what you have to gain by going over to their side—as you certainly have been doing these last few years.

When, if ever, are you coming to the mountains c̄ me?

c̄ love
KENNETH

/ · /

Henry's clown: Probably Henry Miller's *The Smile at the Foot of the Ladder,* published by Duell, Sloan & Pearce in 1948.

Padell: Between 1946 and 1948 Padell (New York) published three books by Kenneth Patchen.

Lincoln Kirstein: (1907–), American writer, founding editor of *Hound & Horn* (1927–34), founding director of the School of American Ballet (1934) and director of the New York City Ballet Company. ND published his *Rhymes of a Pfc* in 1964.

51. TLS-2   August 11, [19]48
                                              S[an] F[rancisco]

DEAR JIM,

    . . . I was very impressed by Delmore [Schwartz]'s book. It is quietly written without the posturing one expects chez *P[artisan] R[eview]*. But it is fundamentally inconsequential. Being a Jew may be a predicament or an obsession, but it is not a tragic experience properly so called. Sometimes, as in the story about the classroom, due to Delmore's humorlessness, it is ridiculous. Further, it is vulgar to be so concerned with the things that concern him. Everybody was a child once, and everybody labors under some nagging disabilities in life, possibly not always as serious as Jewish birth seems to be to Schwartz. There are, after all, people who are very proud of carrying in their veins the blood of Moses and Spinoza. Paul Goodman's story about the little girl is a hundred times better because it reduces the question to the level of the basic ironies and tragedies of life. Schwartz, after all, is still writing very overdressed "proletarian fiction"—unimaginative thesis writing. However, again—it was better than I expected. . . .

    Maude Hutchins' sexy cliffhanger left me unmoved. That is quite a trick-ending, practically every chapter on a note of unresolved homosexuality. One reads on, hoping that the daisychains of mimeographed pornography will show up in the next few pages. I think Mrs. Hutchins should grow up. And quite a notion, too, a photograph of herself on the back and a pen drawing of her Georgiana on the front. Cute advertising, but I know dozens of girls who are simply dying to stick their tongues in my ear. And they haven't been corrupted by any nasty old Neothomists, either. James, I think you are infatuated. This is circulating library stuff.

[Robert] Lowry's new book came. He certainly writes with great lucidity. But he runs the danger of degenerating into formula writing. He should think of something else to warm up his readers besides his fetish for undressing women. He should draw up a schedule: 1948, crotch cannibalism; 1949, golden showers; 1950, winking-off; 1951, bagpiping; 1952, snarfing, etc.—otherwise he will end up like Ernst Haycox, another great and lucid writer who now turns them out like Gillette Blades or Juicy Fruit.

You be good.

And get the B[ritish] P[oets] and S[ignature of] A[ll] T[hings] out in OCTOBER.

c̄ love

KENNETH

[appended in holograph:]
What is the greatest French poem in the 20th century? Answer this—it is important I know what you think.

/ · /

Delmore's book: The World Is a Wedding (two short novels and five short stories) was published by ND in July 1948.

Maude Hutchins' sexy cliffhanger: Georgiana, a novel published by ND in August 1948. Hutchins's other ND books include *A Diary of Love* (1950), *Love Is a Pie* (1952), and *My Hero* (1953). She was married to Robert M. Hutchins, president of the University of Chicago.

Lowry's new book: Robert Lowry's novel, *Casualty,* was published by ND in November 1946.

52. TLS-2
August 18th [1948]
[Norfolk]

DEAR KENNETH—

I owe you a lot of letters. I can't keep up with anything anymore, let alone the flood of your letters, which I'm glad to get—they cheer me up—but hopeless to try to find time to answer all the points. I'm now trying to save my strength by dictating on a machine for a girl to type, but I can't dictate to you, the way I talk. . . .

Wonderful evening over at Bill [Williams]'s in Rutherford the other night. What a man. But he's aging fast. Be sure to see him when you're here. I'm getting his selected up now, and also reprinting *Grain* and *Paterson*.

I admit that Maude [Hutchins]'s writing is sloppy as hell, but I still think she is damn original as cunt writers go, and I like her. She is living near here now so you can see for yourself. . . . We are neck deep in crappy promotion for the [Giuseppe] Berto. First printing is 42,000 with the Book Find Club. You can imagine the lather. I thought up this one: we get a story on the wires that he wants to find this here nurse that was kind to him when he was in prison camp hospital in Texas, and all he can remember is her name was Mary and she was a small blonde. Like that, like that. And me sort of a poet.

I'm glad you like the poems. I do too, but it's probably just as well that all this mess obtrudes. If I just sat around being a poet they would probably stink.

Gotta work now, will write soon again

J I M

/ · /

his selected: William Carlos Williams's *Selected Poems,* introduced by
Randall Jarrell, was published as *NCS* 21 by ND in 1949.

the Berto: Giuseppe Berto's novel *The Sky Is Red,* translated by Angus
Davidson, was published by ND in 1948, followed by a Book Find
Club edition. Later ND Berto volumes included *The Works of God &
Other Stories* (1950) and *The Brigand* (1951).

53. APC

[Sept. 5, 1948]
[San Francisco]

DEAR JIM—

I notice that advertising for *ND* X does not mention my name. Now look—I have had about enough
of this. Either you promote me properly or I will
get a publisher who will. You are always soft soap-
ing me about how I am the only one of my generation that ranks with the Great Dead—E[zra] P[ound],
T. S. E[liot], W[illiam] C[arlos] W[illiams], etc. but
it is patent that you are ashamed of me. Also—there
would seem from the advs. that there is no Japanese
or German poetry in *ND* X—this is unforgivable.

K R

/ · /

advertising for ND X: No work by KR appears in this *ND* number.

54. TLS-1

7 ix [19]48
S[an] F[rancisco]

DEAR JIM,

Your disgusting letter anent [Kenneth] Patchen was
just brought to my attention. It made me slightly

sick at the stomach. And it sickened plenty of people who have no liking for Patchen.

It does not show you as overly blessed with the courage of your convictions or loyalty to your friends or good sense. Why, pray tell, do you imagine it was published by the worst enemies literature has ever had? To make you, my dear, whom they hate fully as much as Patchen, look cheap and ridiculous. They certainly succeeded.

It is amazing how completely intimidated you are by the academic and cocktail reactionaries. I honestly believe that you cower with shame at the thought of every decent writer you have ever published. . . .

You have definitely lost your grip. Knopf and Liveright were the New Directions of the twenties, you know. Horace [Liveright] is dead, and [Alfred] Knopf at least publishes good standard books. You seem to be unable to see anything but the Nobel Dead, the Great Decrepit, College Professors, Salon Keepresses and Cocktail Fairies.

Patchen is one of your justifications for having existed. Every year New Directions has fewer.

faithfully
KENNETH

/ · /

Your disgusting letter: The following letter from JL appeared in the July 1948 issue of the *Partisan Review* (XV,7:845): "On the back cover of your April issue, in an advertisement for the books of Kenneth Patchen, I was startled to see a rather fantastic statement printed over my name, and would ask you to publish this notice that it is neither authentic nor authorized. While I have a very great liking for the best of Patchen's poetry, I would certainly reserve the comparison with Whitman for men of the stature of Pound, Eliot, Crane, Cummings, and Williams. Patchen is still in his thirties; he has time to grow, and I think he will."

55. APC

[Sept. 24, 1948]
[San Francisco]

DEAR J.

At last I got a ND catalogue from a bookseller. I note that my name is the only one of the introducers left off The New Classics Series. Why not just write to the *Partisan Review*—"I am sorry I ever printed Rexroth—he doesn't like Hank James or Kafka, he isn't an existentialist or a fairy, but a nasty rowdy— I promise *never* to do it again—please dont be mean to me because I did."

KR

/ · /

The New Classics Series: KR's edition of D. H. Lawrence's *Selected Poems* (1947) was published by JL as 19 in his ND New Classics series. Other New Classics "introducers" included T. S. Eliot (Djuna Barnes's *Nightwood*), Lionel Trilling (F. Scott Fitzgerald's *The Great Gatsby*), and Francis Fergusson (James Joyce's *Exiles*).

56. ALS-2

9 [1949]
[Norfolk]

KENNETH,

Stop *threatening* me. It's childish. . . .

Re Patchen. He had no right to put my name on something that I had not officially written. He is good, but not a Whitman yet. Though he may be in time.

Stop *badgering* me! My nerves won't stand it. I'll quit the whole business in a day or two at this rate.

J.

57. ALS-2   Sept. 20, [19]48
                         S[an] F[rancisco]

DEAR JIM—

. . . I am working on the Chinese & Japanese poetry book—I think we will have an incomparably better book than anyone else. I plan to translate from [Judith] Gautier (use [Stuart] Merrill for her) and to translate from French versions of IndoChinese poetry. Nobody has done this. Universities use [Robert] Payne's *White Pony*—which is really very bad. You have some sort of block re the orient. You have no idea of how popular such subjects are in universities now.

As for Patchen—you have no business having official and unofficial opinions and official and unofficial friends. He has been using that statement for years and you never challenged it until it was brought up by the *P[artisan] R[eview]*—a crowd of phonies who have you thoroughly intimidated. Cant you understand how delighted they were when your letter came in—and why? . . .

                         See you soon
                         KENNETH

/ · /

the Japanese and Chinese poetry book: KR's *One Hundred Poems from the Japanese* was published by ND in 1955; his *One Hundred Poems from the Chinese* in 1956.

translate from Gautier: Judith Gautier (1850–1917), French poet, novelist, translator. In his select bibliography to *One Hundred Poems from the Chinese,* KR includes her French translation, *Livre de Jade,* calling it "excellent, a French, or world, classic." According to JL: "I discovered the source of [KR's] first Japanese and Chinese translations, rather to his chagrin. I was poking around in his library one day and I came on some French translations of the oriental poets done in the 1890's, which seemed very familiar. I read them against Kenneth's translations and discovered that he had drawn them from the French of Judith Gautier. Nothing wrong with that. Later he taught himself many Chinese and Japanese characters and worked directly" *(AP)*. KR of Stuart Merrill ("The Poet as Translator"): "Merrill was America's greatest poet between the New Englanders and the post–World War I moderns. He is practically unknown in this country because he lived and wrote almost exclusively in French." Merrill's English anthology *Pastels in Prose* includes selections from Gautier's *Livre de Jade*.

Payne's White Pony: Robert Payne's anthology of Chinese poetry, *The White Pony,* was published in 1947.

58. TLS-4

September 28, 1948
[Norfolk]

DEAR KENNETH:

. . . Yes, my letter to THE PARTISAN REVIEW about [Kenneth] Patchen probably was a mistake. I should simply have ignored the whole affair, but I was angry when he made me look so silly with that ridiculous statement over my signature, which I had never authorized him to use. . . .

With best wishes
JIM

As for some big advances so you can go to the Orient that all depends on how the [Giuseppe] Berto sells. Everything hinges on that. If it fails we are out of biz, and for sure. If it takes mildly we can carry on another year. If it goes big I'll find the cash for your trip. So keep your fingers crossed.

One bad break is the new Tenn[essee] Williams is not good. He pulled us through last year with a 14,000 sale on *Streetcar*. So it's Berto or the skids. . . .

You are crazy if you think I am under the PR influence. I keep the peace with them but am far from chummy and they haven't made a suggestion in years, except [Philip] Rahv's book, which I like, and Delmore [Schwartz], who dates from long ago, and I like. You influence ND policy more than any other single person, but I don't have the strength or the funds to keep up with you. I am dead tired. I've burned myself out with the thing and just don't give much of a damn any more. That's the truth. Exhausted. I just want to go way the hell off somewhere with you know which and never be heard of again. . . .

Enough for now

/ · /

the new Tenn Williams: Tennessee Williams (1911–1983), American playwright, poet, fiction writer. According to Donald Hall *(Conjunctions)*, JL "met Tennessee Williams at a cocktail party—his only literary discovery with a social origin." In his "Homage to J" *(Conjunctions)*, Williams writes: "It was J. Laughlin who first took a serious interest in my work as a writer. My first noteable appearance in print was in a New Directions book called *Five Young American Poets* in 1944. . . . Among all the multitude of persons I've encountered in the world of letters and theatre (if that distinction is permissible), J. Laughlin remains the one I regard with the deepest respect and affection." JL regarded Williams as "a wonderful romantic poet. He comes right out of Romanticism, and no one else has done that kind of thing so well recently. . . . His poetry was swamped by his being such a famous playwright. Readers tend to pigeonhole writers. He was a magnificent story-writer. There are few story-writers today who can touch him for pure narrative drive, psychological penetration, and that lovely fantastic, light, self-mocking style" *(PR)*. Tennessee Williams's play *Summer and Smoke* was published by ND (with photographs from the Broadway production) in November 1948. ND had published *A Streetcar Named Desire* in 1947.

Rahv's book: Philip Rahv's *Image and Idea: Fourteen Essays on Literary Themes* was published by ND in June 1949.

59. TLS-4

December 15, 1948
[New York]

DEAR KENNETH:

. . . I agree with you that there is something a little strange about [Robert] Cal Lowell. I lunched with him the other day with [T. S.] Eliot, and he did strike me as funny. Perhaps it was just the blue blood running down from too much inbreeding. But I think he means well. Certainly, his whole attitude toward Ezra [Pound] has been quite wonderful.

I was a little amazed at your putting into the preface of the new book the statement that you felt it was an honor to have a Guggenheim. I can remember a few years ago, when you said that you would never touch that tainted money. Well, I have gotten practical myself, so perhaps you are entitled to do so as well, but I never thought you really would, and it came to me as a kind of shock. Afterall, it's perfectly legitimate to spoil your enemies. . . .

With best Christmas wishes to you and Marie,

JIM

/ · /

Cal Lowell: Robert Lowell (1917–1977), American poet. KR: "His conflicts and dilemmas are those of Herman Melville and Emily Dickinson and his language is rooted in spiritual ancestors like George Chapman and Du Bartas—he is certainly a better poet than the latter. Overlying religious and philosophical issues was a cloud of storms of personal and psychological conflicts which give his poetry its poignant immediacy. He is certainly the most important poet of his group" (APTC). In his SFP interview, KR recalls: "I was at this big poetry powwow that [Mary McCarthy's] The Groves of Academe was written about. They were having this long discussion on the History of American Poetry, and I said, 'You have left out the whole populist period!' And they said, 'Who's that?' And I said, 'William Vaughn Moody, Carl Sandburg, James Oppenheim, Lola Ridge, Vachel Lindsay.' (Most of whom were Socialist.) With an expression of utmost contempt on his face, 'Cal' Lowell said, 'Well, of course, in the West, Rexroth, you haven't learned that these poor people aren't poets at all.' I don't think they were very good, but it's a matter of history."

---

60. TLS-2   20 XII [19]48
                                              S[an] F[rancisco]

DEAR LAUGHLIN,

I dont know what you can do when you are being printed by a publisher who is ashamed of you, who thinks nobody who is anybody will buy your books (because Mrs M McC Broadbottom doesn't) and who is so obviously doing it for sentimental reasons, and even those no longer cogently felt. If you can't sell a first edition of 1500 of my poems after the work I put in promoting them, you should find something else to do with your time. . . . To you I am one of the "crazies," the people who dont like the taste of Mrs Broadbottom's shit, and whom no one who is anyone reads. If you gave me one tenth the promotion Doubleday gave the completely unimportant [Theodore] Roethke, you would have what you like to call a "valuable property." But you dont even promote Dylan Thomas—only Genuine Old County Families like the Sitwells whom you dont even publish! And you let pass two best sellers by [Thomas] Merton, whom NOW you think is good. Up until recently he too was a "crazy," a hippogriff—the Trappist Monk who contributes to *View*. Ha, Ha. . . .

It was your idea to print that play in ND 10. My objection to the anthology is that it is a complete sellout to the squares, the shanty Irish and Bronx inmates who bemoan the fact that US policemen dont read Proust and Papa unt Mama deent talk it like dot

niice man Henry Jems, so rafined. . . . The eager
beavers of OWI War III, the Drop the Bomb Now
Boys, the people who are willing to destroy civilization to save their own hides from the wrath of the
GPU—a little bunch of convalescent Trotskyites, who
have become the greatest enemies literature has ever
had. You are ashamed as a publisher of all the good
stuff you've ever had. You are ashamed as a publisher of all the good stuff you've ever done by anyone under 60, and you're ashamed, personally of all
the good writers you know, as associates. You know
perfectly well that you were embarrassed to be seen
on the streets of NYC with me. I told you years ago
that you were headed towards the Alfred Knopf of
the 50s—and now you embrace him! But he is just a
scissorbill—certainly in no class with Leslie Fiedler
and Mrs Broadbottom.

I am not discourteous. It is routine good manners
to acknowledge the gift of $2500. If I hadnt expected
to thank them, I wouldnt have asked. The moral
crux is asking in the first place. Also, since my publisher has no interest in using my talents to make
money for either me or him, I must live somehow,
and I think it sensible to be gracious to people who
do honor me—some are *so* ashamed of me. I assure
you that Mr. Moe was much happier to have me in
his office than you were in yours—he didnt seem to
think he had disgraced his "list." Further—I am quite
bored being told that "in time" I will be recognized.
If a publisher doesnt think he can get an author recognized, he should get some other merchandise. That
is his job. As a matter of fact—I found out on this
trip that if you bother to get my books into the hands
of people who already recognize me, I shall do very
nicely.

As for the *B[ritish] P[oets]* I gave the books to the
people I met and liked on my recent trip or to old

friends. I just got a most enthusiastic letter from John Gould Fletcher, an author of whom you never heard, as he doesnt print in *P[artisan]*, *K[enyon]*, *S[ewanee]*, or *V[irginia]* *Q[uarterly]* *R[eview]*, but who does enjoy some standing out in the benighted sticks (every place except 57th st.). He is writing around to get it for review—probably *Poetry*. I think my name should be on the jacket. Everyone says that it is a disgrace that you should be so ashamed of me and that I am at least as well known in the USA as anyone in the book except [Stephen] Spender, and [Dylan] Thomas. I have become so used to your snubs that I hadnt noticed it until people began pointing it out to me in wrath. I am thoroughly disgusted with the whole business and wish I had never undertaken it. And finally, by failing to get the books out for the Xmas season you have simply picked my pockets of any money I might have made on it—it is primarily a "gift book." Of course I was a fool to have done it without a very substantial advance. I have no late addresses for the poets. It is OVER TWO YEARS since I worked on the book and people even then were moving around in a sort of post war shake-down. . . .

REXROTH

/ · /

Roethke: Theodore Roethke (1908–1963), American poet. Although in *APTC* KR describes Roethke, along with Robert Lowell, John Berryman, and Richard Wilbur, as a "significant poet," he feels that "Roethke is in every way a slighter thinker than Lowell and a slighter technician. Roethke's virtues are almost purely personal and his best poems are about his childhood and youth, about a girl student killed falling from a horse, and other simple fragments of autobiography."

that play: KR's "Iphigenia: A Dance Play" appeared in the following year's annual, *ND 11*.

Leslie Fiedler: (1917–). An aspiring American literary critic, Fiedler had published three pieces in *ND* 10. A few months earlier he had attacked William Everson's *The Residual Years* in *Partisan Review* (see note, letter 42). The feud between KR and Fiedler for capo de capo was longstanding. In a 1968 review, "Ids and Animuses" *(New York Times Book Review)*, KR would write, "Leslie Fiedler is possessed by a number of obsessions which destroy his convincingness, except among people who don't know better. First, as is well known, is his favorite term of abuse, 'WASP.' He uses it the way Stalinists used to write 'Trotskyite,' for the most incongruous assortment of writers and tendencies. Since he sees White Anglo-Saxon Protestants under every bed and in every woodpile, it is easy for him to so identify the main line of American culture with their works and to prove that this culture has been continuously challenged and is now collapsing from within. Ultimately this is an incurable distortion of vision due to membership in a small circle of extremely ethnocentric people—the self-styled New York Establishment, triangulated by the *Partisan Review, The New York Review of Books,* and *Commentary*. . . . The United States is a big country, and this tiny set is not even an epi-center, but a small disturbance on an epicycle."

Mrs Broadbottom: Mary McCarthy was at one time married to Bowden Broadwater.

John Gould Fletcher: (1886–1950), American poet. In "The Influence of French Poetry on American" *(Assays)*, KR writes that Fletcher's work "can best be characterized as a deliberate attempt to turn Imagism into a kind of Neo-Symbolism. . . . Five long poems of my own are all deeply indebted to John Gould Fletcher. Had he written in French, Fletcher would have been recognized as a landmark in literary history. As it was, he went out of fashion in his middle age, was little read, changed his style, much for the worse, and finally, as have thirty other important American poets in the twentieth century—committed suicide."

Spender: Stephen Spender (1909–), British poet, essayist, editor of *Encounter*. KR includes five Spender poems in *NBP*. In the introduction to the anthology, he writes: "Reading [Spender], one has the sense of a man trying desperately hard to be absolutely honest. I think it is for this reason that he is still a living influence on younger writers in England."

61. ALS-3   11 I [19]49
                                          [San Francisco]

DEAR LAUGHLIN—

  Look—lets drop the whole *S[ignature of] A[ll]
T[hings]* design and make it just like the *P[hoenix] &
T[ortoise]*. I *dont* want *anything* on a jacket except the
title page. Also—no funny papers. Do you think I
am a whore or a French fairy? Let [André] Gide have
it. You bind in buckram—either unbleached or terra
cotta, and NOTHING else, with label on spine. I think
the 50 copies should be in a slipcase—and you can
bind them any way you think they'll look most
expensive and dignified. No aluminum foil and
chicken coop windows, please. ALSO—I think you
might use the quote from the Tao Te Ching in the
50 copies, and I will write the translation under-
neath. I think this is a wonderful idea—if printed
carefully the Chinese writing will look like original
& I will do a good job on each one. . . .

                                          faithfully
                                          KENNETH

                    / · /

Gide: André Gide (1869–1951), French novelist, essayist, critic, play-
wright. Won the Nobel Prize for Literature in 1947. ND published
Gide's *Dostoevsky* (1949), *Theseus* (trans. by John Russell, 1949), and
Marshlands & Prometheus Misbound (trans. by George D. Painter, 1953).
KR's reference is to ND's production of *Theseus,* which was hand-
printed by Giovanni Mardersteig and included lithographs by Massino
Campiglei.

the 50 copies: In addition to its 1950 trade edition, *The Signature of All
Things* was published by ND in a special edition of 50 copies on Fabri-
ano paper, boxed, and signed by KR.

62. ALS-1

DEAR LAUGHLIN—

Hear you a going abroad. Can you take me if I pay my own way? I am anxious to get some good out of remainder of Guggenheim & am *very* unhappy here. Marie [Rexroth] has become insufferable since I got Guggenheim which she resents somehow. I need to get a long ways away for 6 months.

> faithfully
> KENNETH

63. TLS-2

DEAR KENNETH:

I have just received your two letters asking whether it would be possible for you to come along on the European jaunt next week. I want you to know that I am terribly pleased that you have expressed this wish. It is something that I have always hoped to be able to do with you, and also, it reassures me some-what about your irritation with me when you were in New York. However, I'm not sure whether you would really enjoy this present trip. It is only going to last three weeks, and will be devoted entirely to attending ski races and visiting ski resorts that I haven't seen so far, so that I can write some articles which have been commissioned here by American magazines. I am getting a free ride out of Air France in return for doing an article on some of their places that I've never written about.

I don't honestly think that you would enjoy this trip because I will be associating closely all the time with ski racers and that set of the international crowd who follow them around. I really think we ought to hold back our trip to Europe together until I have a little free time and we can plan to settle down for some good long tranquil stays in places like Swiss mountain towns, or Italian fishing villages.

However, if you feel that you would like to make the trip over with me and then stay in Paris, where you could probably join up with old [C. F.] MacIntyre, and then in a short time you would get to know people there, why that would be fine. . . .

There haven't been any very important reviews yet of the NEW BRITISH POETS. . . .

I will be going out to Alta in April to put on the race there, and possibly after that, we might take a crack at one of the virgin chains of mountains. That time when I drove down through South-western Colorado and Northern New Mexico, I got a terrible yen to light off into that big range that lies there between Ouray and Durango. I think that Walter Haensli, that very nice boy from Klosters, who is teaching this winter at Sun Valley, might like to go along. He is a terrific skier. We could pitch a base tent somewhere, and you could contemplate nature while Walter and I explored the ski slopes. . . .

With best wishes
JIM

/ · /

write articles: See letter 1.

MacIntyre: C. F. MacIntyre's translations of three poems by Paul Eluard had appeared in *ND* 9 in 1946; earlier, in 1941, ND had published MacIntyre's translaton of *Faust* into "American."

64. ALS-3

13 X [19]49
Firenze

DEAR JIM—

. . . The only bad thing about Italy is CIT who are a conspiracy to keep you out of cheap restaurants, 3rd class trains and 3rd or 4th class hotels—and the God awful Americans. My God what freaks & swine. Apparently the douanier takes out his cock and says "suck it" and if you dont they dont let you in. They missed me—but every other American in Italy is queer—*and* square—*nice* queers. I have met none except your two boys by chance in Firenze. . . .

I am sitting in front of the Baptistry and the Campanile is ringing; and I bet you wish you were here. Coming back today—I got a strange frantic letter from Marie [Rexroth] about was I mad at her. This is like chopping off your head and then apologizing for coughing in your face. She apparently wants to come to Europe. This might be a good idea. But I cannot understand the emotional context of the letter at all. After throwing me out of my home & expropriating all my things etc. and maligning me to all my friends—and dropping me about five frigid little notes since I have been here—now I get the frantic, loving letter, all as though we had been on the best of terms up until a week ago. I think a trip to Europe would mean a great deal to Marie—more than it has even to me—I think she has wanted it all her life. So—I hope you advise her to come—and help her any way you can. . . .

love
K R

65. ALS-4

[Florence]
[October, 1949]

DEAR JIM,

This is me, back in Florence, making a decent tour of Italy seeing weirdos like the Gardiners or aged fatal women like Caresse [Crosby]. I bought a fine bicycle in Paris and made a Tour de France—the Loire, Poitiers. . . .

That foul, filthy food fixed by the foul filthy French. Good god! What a vain, dirty and ignorant people! Their favorite substance is shit—they shit everywhere. You should try staying in a 200 franc hotel in Figeac—oh boy! What a pity the Huns didn't hold onto them for a generation and make them wash up. Did you ever notice that the French are the only people in the world who do not wash their hands after they piss? This pensione is about the nicest place I have ever stayed. It is on the Arno—by the arches of the old interpalace gallery, just above the Ponte-Vecchio. Ital / pension is 1700—which is now *very* cheap. [D. H.] Lawrence stayed here. . . .

I think England cured me forever of looking up people. You are never welcome—always treated as an intruder—and always suspect—"What is this guy going to get out of me?" I have met one hospitable man since I left Matticks—D. S. Savage—and he was by far the poorest. [Herbert] Read gave me dinner in his club and seemed glad to see me—but that is all. If you had any sensitivity and went about the world "looking up" people you would soon get to hate the human race unendurably—they are bad enough as it is. I am all for the atom bomb—it will reduce the population of the world 90%—extermi-nate the Northern Hemisphere and cause profound biological mutations in the remainder. And take it from me—nobody needs a good all round mutation more than the human race. Except for Mattick and Savage I have never met anyone on this trip who was glad to see me, or who was 1/10 as hospitable as Marie [Rexroth] & I always were to even the worst tramps. So I will keep strictly to myself in Italy as I did in France. I have talked too much to too many people for too many years as it is. . . .

I just can't bear the prospect of that vast, hysterical worn out boudoir that is Paris. What beastly people! One thing—travel has made me a chauvinist. I have never eaten a dish, not as good as a fair small town American restaurant Blue Plate lunch—but as good as a double milkshake and a rare hamburger c̄ barbeque sauce. I have never met an educated man—or seen anybody who did not suffer far more from the faults they accuse Americans of—commercialism, neurosis, inability to relax, execrable taste, general all round stupid vulgarity and acquisitiveness—and without getting anything for it except the privilege of pissing in the streets, shitting in a hole in the floor, wiping your ass on a piece of dirty newspaper if you're lucky—and spending $20 for a bum pair of shoes, $2.00 for a bum meal.

Of course—the South of France is much better—but what a country of self-satisfied mediocrity. *Everything* is second or third rate—their shoddy, ill-fashioned clothes, their absurd opera & theatre, their dance orchestras that can't keep a beat, their malnourished children. (Do you know what the regimen of a French school is like?!!) The man who most impressed his image on France is not Charlemagne or St. Louis or Louis Quatorze or Napoleon—but Louis Napoleon—that popinjay & parvenu, and France is still living ante-1870—she did not recover from War II or War I—she did not recover from Bismarck or the Commune. With the Thiers government she took the wrong turn—and each war has intensified the dictatorship of the petty bourgeois vulgarity and vanity—and, behind the scenes, the completely non-productive "capitalist," the inconspicuous little offices off the place Vendôme where old men in spats whose offices have not changed their equipment since 1860—control the Beirut raisin market one year, whore houses in Casablanca the next, swing a deal in palm oil the next—always finagling—completely nonproductive—always looking for a 500% profit.

Another thing—when you travel through the south you realize what a series of disasters began c̄ the destruction of Provence. France is *naturally* a Mediterranean power—there is nothing in the north except cathedrals, fortresses, and smelly, gray villages full of disagreeable people. The country has destroyed itself trying to be an Atlantic power—without coal, iron, oil, or any major export—even agricultural—and with absolutely no industrial know how or creative enthusiasm. . . . Imagine what France would be like if its capital was Toulouse! What beautiful cities those are—Toulouse, Nîmes, Aix, Arles. By the way—did you ever see the cathedral at Albi? It is the greatest piece of architecture in France. . . .

faithfully
KENNETH

/ · /

Caresse Crosby: (1892–1970; Mary Phelps Jacob), American publisher and poet. With her husband, their Black Sun Press published Joyce, Lawrence, McAlmon, and others. KR: "Nobody had more flair or more money to spend on publishing than Harry and Caresse Crosby. Crosby was the nephew of J. P. Morgan and Caresse the former wife of a Morgan partner. . . . After Harry's suicide, Caresse continued to publish, and after the Second World War, her *Portfolio* introduced a second post-war generation of artists and writers to the world" *(APTC)*. KR's "Iphigenia at Aulis" appeared in Crosby's *Portfolio* III, in 1946.

66. ALS-4

Mar 29 [19]50
S[an] F[rancisco]

DEAR JIM—

. . . The 3rd play is two acts—full length—I think it might take up too much room in *N.D.* The trick is to write a really cogent preface and give the book a title which doesnt mention "plays." You will see that the plays all go together (there is also a short comedy of Petronius' story of The Widow of Ephesus) and constitute a systematic exposition of all my ideas—as well as containing much of my best poetry. This is my *Cantos, Paterson, 4 Quartets.* It is in dramatic form because I wanted to steer myself always towards maximum communication. Incidentally, Zorina is still hoping to do one—and an outfit called The Living Theatre is interested in putting on the long one in NYC. If you would just have some ideas and be a little help about it, we could probably find production for all of them. All the show business people who have read them think they are producible & communicable for medium high-brow audiences. That is—there is nothing undramatic about them, however unBroadway. . . .

What I have ready for the Annual is a translation of the poems of [O. V. de Lubicz-]Milosz. I dont suppose you would want to make a book of them. . . .

You know—I wonder about the USA poets under 50—my god theyre bad most of them—There is [Elizabeth] Bishop, [Richard] Eberhart, [Kenneth] Fearing, Laughlin, [Thomas] Merton, [Laura] Riding (under 50?), [Muriel] Rukeyser, [Kenneth] Patchen, D[elmore] Schwartz, [Yvor] Winters, [John] Wheelwright (under?), [Karl] Shapiro, [Peter] Viereck, [Robert] Lowell, [Randall] Jarrell—to make up the bulk of the book—but there are some dreary time wasters of cooked verse amongst the minors— and Bishop and the last four are not to my taste, although I have represented them judiciously. Honey—you is really one of the best—as a whole US poetry is sure synthetic & clammy stuff. Your sapphire & the guy boiling in oil are about—99/100 times as personal as most of it.

What in the hell are you doing in Switzerland? What you need to do is retire to a remote spot on the N. California coast for about 2 years. You are going to get a heart attack. Honest—you are, behaviorist- ically, indistinguishable from any of your harried classmates chez Harvard Club. Do you want to die an early death? And furthermore, Mr. Laughlin— you are getting sucked into the new and exception- ally rotten International High Bohemia. New Direc- tions in literature and / or the human spirit are not taking off from the suburbs of Tangiers and Firenze. It is scandalous for you to use the pages of the Annual to pay off social obligations. Wm. J. Smith indeed! Why not Human Crapout? There is nothing New Directions about these alcoholic wanderers on the banks of the Mediterranean with their crew cuts & seersucker jackets. I assure you, cocksucking went on under the impassive eyes of the painted bisons in the caves of the Dordogne. Pretty soon folks will say that to get into *N.D.* you must be 1) richameri- can, 2) queer, 3) mailing address—Harry's Bar.

Dylan Thomas is here. What a problem. It is sure hard to try to keep him from continuously drinking & throwing his money around. You dont realize what a steady reliable character you have got in me. Or do you? I like him very much & he seems to like me. He is sure genuine. A vast relief after these nasty English poets. He is Welsh & proletarian to the core. He . . . says I am a sober [Hugh] MacDiarmid. This is what all the Scots & Welsh say and it is quite a compliment. . . .

If English poets approach you and say I told them so—don't believe it. I was constantly bothered to get you to publish every sort of pig & pissant in collected editions. . . .

love
K. R.

/ · /

The third play: "Hermaios" (originally titled "Beyond the Mountains"). In February 1951, ND published KR's collection of four plays ("Phaedra," "Iphigenia at Aulis," "Hermaios," and "Berenike") as *Beyond the Mountains.* In his introduction to *The Signature of All Things,* KR wrote of these plays: "I have found it interesting to subject my philosophical opinions to the test of dramatic speech. . . . Noh plays on classical themes in which I hope some of my ideas have found a more direct expression than philosophical elegy affords." In a review in the *New York Times* (Jan. 28, 1951), William Carlos Williams praised the collection as "verse with a jolt to it."

Living Theatre: Julian Beck and Judith Malina's Living Theatre staged a production of KR's *Beyond the Mountains* at the Cherry Lane Theatre in New York on December 30, 1951. According to Pierre Biner's *The Living Theatre* (New York, 1972), "In staging Kenneth Rexroth's *Beyond the Mountains* next, the Becks turned toward Japanese, Chinese, and Greek drama. The play was a verse adaptation of the *Oresteia,* and it was exceedingly long—one reason for its failure. It simply did not fit into a single evening. The actors wore masks, and Tei Ko choreographed Noh dances to specially composed music. *Doctor Faustus* had been an indifferent success, but *Beyond the Mountains* was an embarrassment. Judith later said that the two most notable failures in the history of the troupe had been *Beyond the Mountains* and, years later, Pound's *Women of Trachis.* Beck directed the play, while Malina played three roles: Iphigenia, Phaedra, and Berenike (Electra). In Malina's *Diaries 1947–1957,* she reprints a letter from KR, who hoped the play would be "an historic success":

"Dear people—I think you are very mistaken in attempting the four plays at once. Such an idea never occurred to me. I think the audience would be worn out halfway through—as well as the actors. . . . The tempo should be leisurely—even slow—to get across the frozen, hypnotized effect of the people in *Beyond the Mountains*. The whole point is that, during the actual moments of the birth of Christ, they are living through the action of the *Oresteia* like sleepwalkers. . . . [The music] *must* be kept extremely simple—diatonic—"white"— like Satie's *Gymnopédie*—and with a minimum of "effects." It is *very* difficult to get a composer to understand just how stark and hieratic it must be. . . . Once again—put out of your minds the scheme of doing the plays all at once, straight through. I really know quite a bit about the theatre and I assure you you will just be throwing them away. Ask anyone with practical experience—radio—bur- lesque—musical comedy, or vaudeville—or the movies—NOT some highbrows—and you will get the same answer. . . .

Faithfully, Kenneth Rexroth" (Oct. 8, 1951).

"[John] Cage, [Merce] Cunningham, and Johnny Myers," Mal- ina continues in her diary entry for October 10, 1951, "are against our doing *Beyond the Mountains*. They abhor the intensity of its emotions. Isn't it a sign of an overdeveloped culture, to search for a more and more bloodless stylization as in the cool Noh, or the unnatural attitudes of late Hellenistic culture?" Beck wrote in response to KR that "Goethe, too, wrote some long plays," and on October 15, he and Malina received a second letter from the poet:

"Dear Judith and Julian—Goethe was wrong. Go ahead *BMT en gros* if you want—but I think you're ill advised. As to commercial vs highbrow theater, there is more theatrical sense in one old car- nival or burlesque man—or in somebody like Jolson or W. C. Fields—than in all the O'Neills and Tollers laid end to end. . . . I doubt if masks are actually desirable. Actors always mismanage them and actresses naturally hate them. They do permit the dancers to stand in—also they are hard to hear through. . . . What I envisage is an extremely slow but dynamic movement—even more normal than a regular *pas de deux* and very hieratic—especially in the *Phaedra* and *Iphigenia*. There are books of Hindu and Buddhist *mudras* and of Tibetan Buddhas and Bodhisattvas in all the regular *mudras* which would give the dancer a hint of what I mean. And of course the two basic positions are those of the Buddhas and their Shaktis in Tibetan sculpture and painting—one of which represents sexual intercourse sitting, the other standing. You can see these things in any book on Tibetan Art. BUT—the end product should *not* look oriental. The Huns' dance at the end of the book is a typical Chinese military dance of the kind given in the plays based on the three kingdoms. If you ask at the local Chinese movie they can tell you when they are going to give such a movie. They're common enough. Faith- fully, Kenneth Rexroth."

poems of Milosz: KR's translation of O. V. de Lubicz-Milosz, *Fourteen Poems,* was published by Peregrine Press in 1952. KR's only translation from Milosz to appear in *ND* was "Vacant Lots," *ND* 15 (1955).

Shapiro: Karl Jay Shapiro (1913–), American poet, critic, novelist. Shapiro's work appeared in *Five Young American Poets,* second series, published by ND in 1941. Shapiro, who served as editor of both *Poetry* (1950–55) and *Prairie Schooner* (1956–63) magazines, won the Pulitzer Prize for Poetry in 1945 for *V-Letter and Other Poems.*

Viereck: Peter Viereck (1916–), American poet, historian. Won the Pulitzer Prize for Poetry in 1949 for *Terror & Decorum.*

Wm. J. Smith indeed: William J. Smith (1918–), American poet, editor, essayist, translator; his "Eight Poems" appeared in *ND* 11 (1949). Smith first met JL at Klosters in Switzerland on a skiing vacation. ND published his translation of Laforgue's *Moral Tales* in 1985.

Human Crapout: Truman Capote (1924–1984), American writer.

67. TLS-3

April 28 [1950]
Norfolk

DEAR KENNETH—

Please forgive me for not writing for such a long time. There is always a horrible jam of work to get through after I get back from a trip. The trip itself was a great success. . . . For Easter I was up with Ezra [Pound]'s daughter and her zombie husband in their castle in Merano. That is something for the books that outfit. He calls himself King Boris of the Alodjians and has "state" and "military" uniforms that look like they had come from Brooks Costume Co. He will make you a knight or margrave in his order—the Knights of Canossa—for a million lire. That's how they live, apparently. But it sure was pretty there on Easter with the bells drifting up from the valley and all the fruit trees in blossom on the hillsides, and the vineyards. . . .

This Englishman [Christopher] Fry whom *Time*

bills as the new Shakespeare also has a play about the widow of Ephesus theme. It opened on Bway last night and is said to be very windy.

Poor old Dylan [Thomas]. He sure liked San Francisco. I have seen him a few times in New York but haven't been able to get much sense out of him as he always seemed to be half cooked. It's just a shame. His reading at the Museum was very fine, especially on the ballads. He cranks up that big voice and lets it moan.

Do you have David Gascoyne's address? I would like to get a big wad of poems out of him for the next Annual and also have a look at the play he has written. I think he's one of the good ones over there. But hopeless to try a book. You can sell about 300 copies of an English poet until he gets some kind of build up. . . .

I am awfully fed [up] with the literary marketplace, as I believe it is politely called. Money, money, money is all you hear now. The conversion of talent into dollars. [Bennett] Cerf, who had refused the [Paul] Bowles novel, has bought him away from me. Offered him $5,000 for his book of short stories. Naturally I wasn't going to fool with that. Now Cerf is after Bill Williams, egged on by [David] Mac-Dowell, whom I had to fire because he outgrew his britches with the Bowles success and wouldn't do his work around the office any more, whom Cerf hired, apparently on the plan that Dave would show Bennett how to be a success in literature by stealing my authors. I don't think they will get far with it, as Dave is essentially a dumbhead, but I hate to see them mess with Bill. He, of course, wants cash in order to give up his medical check, as we do with [Henry] Miller, but of course Cerf starts waving thousand dollar bills in his face and what can you expect? It would be for his future work, since I have the other stuff sewed up, but even so it makes me feel rather shat upon considering I have nursed him along all these years, stuck by him and got that book written about him, which apparently, he doesn't like, but it has certainly helped him, no doubt of that.

It has suddenly dawned on a lot of those bastards that the day of literature is arriving and being too stupid to find their own they set about to swipe mine. We had the biggest March in our history, at a time when everybody else in the trade was getting nothing. I think the tide may really be beginning to turn. Thornton Wilder has always said that if I just sat tight and waited long enough the public would catch up. But he hardly figured on this despoilment by the barbarians. Fortunately there are still a good many dead authors about whom they can't get at. . . .

Yes, you are dead right, I should retire from it all and go in for rumination if not contemplation. . . .

Be good

J

/ · /

Ezra's daughter: Mary de Rachewiltz (1925–), daughter of Ezra Pound and Olga Rudge. Formerly married to Boris de Rachewiltz, she lives in Brunnenburg Castle in the mountains of northern Italy. Her memoirs about her father, *Discretions,* was later published by ND.

Englishman Fry: Christopher Fry (1907–), British playwright. His "new play"—*Venus Observed,* a romantic chateau comedy.

David Gascoyne: (1916–), British poet; his translations from Pierre-Jean Jouve had appeared in *ND* 7. KR included two of his longer poems in *The New British Poets,* calling him "one of the first English poets to be influenced by Surrealism."

the Bowles novel: Paul Bowles (1911–), American writer, composer. ND published Bowles's first novel, *The Sheltering Sky,* in 1949, and between 1948 and 1950 his fiction was featured in *ND* 10, 11, and 12. Bowles's "book of short stories" was *The Delicate Prey,* published in 1950. According to KR, "The nicest thing about Paul Bowles is that he was a very radical young guy and I remember this midwest magazine, perhaps it was a New Left, sent out a questionnaire asking various writers what they will do if war breaks out, and asking political questions mostly, and Bowles sent them a cablegram saying, 'I will have no further communication with you until I spit upon you from the cockpit of a Fokker.' They printed it, and he had to disappear as a writer for a while! That's when he started composing a lot. They thought it was another Paul Bowles probably. It was years before he could reemerge as a writer" *(Conjunctions)*. Bowles wrote the music for several of Tennessee Williams's plays.

that book written about him: Vivienne Koch's book on Williams in The Makers of Modern Literature series.

Thornton Wilder: (1897–1975), American novelist, playwright.

68. ALS-6   1 V [1950]
                                                  S[an] F[rancisco]

DEAR JIM—

The Greek plays will come to you right away—as soon as they are thoroughly checked. I think I shall omit the comedy—especially if the theme is used by [Christopher] Fry—an extraordinarily empty and pretentious writer. . . . I have a very strong invitation to teach at Black Mt. Should I go? It sounds like a terrible bunch of screwballs & misfits to me. Also, I can teach next year at the University of Washington, Seattle, if I wish. I dunno as I want to teach. It seems to have destroyed most of my contemporaries.

I dont think you miss much but profit in losing [Paul] Bowles. But [W. C.] W[illia]ms is another matter. The trouble c̄ you is that you are simply unable to provide a writer c̄ sufficient publication for him to live on it. As me—if you had the equipment—you would have a steadily working "man of letters" doing miscellaneous jobs every year and producing "Art" every 3 or five years. But you

haven't that much busy work and you dont pay anything for it when it is done, and you can't get the
"Art" out in large enough editions to make any
money at all. . . .

You know Jim—talking about the Neo-Bo-
hemians (read the article in *Fleur Flair*—it makes you
want to reach for a machine gun)—you simply are
not getting the Pounds & Eliots and Djuna Barneses
of today. They arent very good—but they publish
in the *Golden Goose, Glass Hill, Motive, Gryphon,* etc.
etc. . . . I think this represents a rather shocking falling off from the days of *Others, Little Review* and
Egoist—but sociologically & historically this is the
same class or caste. The Harry's Bar, Café Flore,
Time-P[artisan] R[eview] crowd are just a new crop
of squares & reactionaries—only now they make a
lot of money. The others are still poor and bohemian in the good old way. . . .

I also can give you a book of Collected Essays—
people say I write better prose than poetry. I hope
you got [Richard] Eberhart signed up. If you can
keep Muriel [Rukeyser], take all of [Kenneth] Patchen
from now on (I don't think he will be so prolific
now that he is so ill), [Thomas] Merton, [Yvor]
Winters, D[elmore] Schwartz, John Wheelwright
(when are you going to publish a decent collection
of him?)—you have only a few to go—E[lizabeth]
Bishop, K[enneth] Fearing, Laura Riding, maybe
R[ichard] Wilbur—and c̄ yourself and me—you have
corralled the cream of our generation in poets. But
someway they've got to eat. Now that I am through
Guggenheim and separated from Marie [Rexroth]—
I gotta make *some* sort of living writing. . . . I do
hope I can get me a book shop started this year.

faithfully
KENNETH

/ · /

Black Mt.: Black Mountain College. According to Martin Duberman, KR "apparently, at [Charles] Olson's suggestion, did take the first step by applying for a position as lecturer in English or Creative Writing. . . . Rexroth then retreated into a haze of European walking tours and lecture engagements" *(Black Mountain: An Experiment in Community).* In 1954, Rexroth's name appeared in the first issue of *The Black Mountain Review* as a contributing editor (along with Paul Blackburn, Irving Layton, and Charles Olson). Because of an attack by Martin Seymour-Smith in the issue on Theodore Roethke and Dylan Thomas, he withdrew from the editorial board. In *APTC,* KR writes: "Black Mountain never had enough money to realize the hopes of its founders to pay the going rate for its faculty. Therefore it became a refuge for dedicated pedagogues with most advanced ideas, and in its heyday Black Mountain also was a political battleground of intellectuals who considered themselves Stalinists, Lovestonites, Trotskyites, or Norman Thomas Socialists, but who in the struggles on the tiny campus changed sides with the greatest facility. . . . The number of people who went to tiny Black Mountain and who became leading artists, writers, musicians, dancers, and craftsmen after the Second World War was all out of proportion to the school's poverty, primitive plant, faction-ridden faculty, and minuscule student body."

Bishop: Elizabeth Bishop (1911–1979), American poet. Lived most of her adult life in Brazil. JL had included three poems by Bishop in the first *ND* annual.

Wilbur: Richard Wilbur (1921–), American poet, translator. In *APTC,* KR writes of Wilbur as an example of "the rear-garde's avant-garde" and a "significant" poet: "As he presents it in his poetry, life does not offer insoluble problems, nor are good verses hard to write. . . . Wilbur's danger is facility. It is interesting that he has found it congenial to translate French verse of the seventeenth and eighteenth centuries which has the same virtues and the same faults as his own." Wilbur contributed six poems to *ND* 10, 1948.

69. ALS-3

5 V [19]50
S[an] F[rancisco]

DEAR JIM—

. . . Been reading a lot of Provençal & some Italian—Gaspara Stampa. You know—this lady has never been translated—but people know about her via Rilke.

There is only one edition current in Italy. . . . Here's
a poem about her—Gaspara Stampa—bought Libreria
Serenissima, Venezia, giugno 14, 49

I sit here in the evening
With the light of Canaletto
And Guardi changing to the light
Of Turner, looking towards the
Saluta, drinking chocolate
And Vecchia Romagna
On the terrace of the Café
Internationale, and read
These twisting, blazing pages.
Love was agony for you too
Signora, and came to no good end.
All about me is the evening
Sussura of this quiet city
Where the loudest noise is a footfall.
I sit alone with my vino
Under the swallows. Last night
I took a gondola out past
San Giorgio, past the Giudecca,
Straight into the full moonlight.
I wonder if it is possible
To be more alone than in
A gondola under the full moon of June?
All I have for company
Are the two halves of my heart.

/ · /

Gaspara Stampa: (1523–1554), Italian musician and poet of unrequited
love. Rainer Maria Rilke (1875–1926), German poet, refers to her in
his first *Duino* elegy, as well as in *The Notebooks of Malte Laurids Brigge*.
Her work remains untranslated into English, though a selection from
her two hundred sonnets appeared in German in 1930.

Here's a poem: previously unpublished.

70. TLS-4

May 10, 1950
[New York]

DEAR KENNETH,

. . . From everything that I hear, Black Mountain College is a pretty screwball place. I've met Josef Albers, who has, I think, something to do with it, and he seemed to me like a pretty smooth operator in the zany line. I must say, however, that I like those things he draws with horizontal lines. I should think the University of Washington would be a much better place to teach. Bill Williams was out there and he reports that they are a lively bunch. . . .

Your suggestion that I am not getting the right people of the younger new directions may or may not be right. What do you think about the following ideas? Let me give you 50 or 75 pages in the next Annual in which you can have your own little anthology, with comments on why they are good and what about them. . . . I honest to goodness can't see much merit in most of the people whom you mention. But you may be right. . . .

[Kenneth] Patchen calls me up on the telephone every now and then and I believe he is feeling a little bit better. We made a big effort to get him a regular stipend from the Bollingen Foundation, but in the end Paul Mellon turned thumbs down on it. The reason given was that the Foundation was supposed to be a memorial to his first wife, and that there was little connection between Patchen's ideas and work and hers. I suppose that is reasonable enough. He still isn't able to do much work, though he is making an attempt on something now.

The Abbot down at Gethsemani has just ruled that Tom Merton may not publish his Journal until he is dead. They are beginning to get worried about all the talk that is going around about why Trappists talk so much. This is a blow to Tom, as he has put in nearly a year on the Journal, and those revelations of intimate life in the monastery would have made it a big seller, but I think they are probably right. He is now working on a little book for me about the psalter as prayer. I wish he would write more poems, but he seems to think that this is self-indulgence. . . .

As ever

J

/ · /

Josef Albers: (1888–1976), German artist and designer, served as director of the arts program at Black Mountain College.

a lively bunch: In July 1948, W. C. Williams had participated in a week-long Seattle Literary Conference at the University of Washington, organized by Theodore Roethke (who was on the faculty there) and others; during the conference he presented daily lectures and readings to an audience of about 150, followed by an evening seminar for a smaller group of students. His lecture "The Poem as a Field of Action" was written for this event. According to a letter to his wife (July 23, 1948), he was particularly impressed by finding that these West Coast students were "radical in the old American way."

Paul Mellon: (1907–), American philanthropist. In 1942, Mellon and his wife Mary founded the Bollingen Foundation for the purpose of publishing C. G. Jung's *Collected Works* and, according to its charter, more broadly "to stimulate, encourage and develop scholarship and research in the liberal arts and sciences and other fields of cultural endeavor generally." In 1967, KR would write: "Looking back now almost one hundred titles and twenty-five years, it is obvious that the Bollingen Series constitutes an important pivot in the swing of Western culture to a new taste quite contrary to the one dominant between the wars. . . . Whether Suzuki, Eliade, Zimmer, Campbell or Blake or Coleridge, there is a kind of relentlessness about the consistency of the Bollingen program. What is this program? A steady drive toward reclaiming interiority, reinstating values . . . a part of the struggle for revaluation and refounding of a collapsed Western civilization. . . . In no trivial way the Bollingen Series and the Foundation have modified the Zeitgeist" (*With Eye & Ear*).

a little book: ND published Thomas Merton's *Bread in the Wilderness,* a discussion of the Psalms, in 1953.

71. ALS-2   3 VII [19]50
                                             S[an] F[rancisco]

DEAR JIM—

Shocked to see that Knopf got [Ford Madox Ford's] Tietjens away from you. He is going to have a permanent best seller. Why dont you wake up to the fact that you are not what you think you are. You started out publishing the bohemians of the 20s & their warmed over echoes, and as you have got more & more *social* success you have become publisher to the post Djuna Barnes and NeoCapote schools— along c̄ a few bad Dago movie scenarios. I bet you'll have a special spread in *Flair* within the year. What is happening to you is what happens to good bohemian restaurants, and bars—you are being taken over by the fairies. Ask Henri Lenois—they drive away all the other customers and then get tired of you and then nobody comes around. This is the most serious loss of your career—and I have been at you to do Tietjens & *The Good Soldier* since you started and you *have* the sheets available in England.

> The shades of night were falling fast
> When thru an Alpine Village past
> A youth who on a banner bore
> "O Paul and Truman give us more!"
> As on the evening breeze the banner waved
> The girls all cried, "Honey, he's so depraved!"

faithfully
KENNETH

/ · /

Tietjens: Tietjens is the protagonist in British novelist Ford Madox Ford's tetralogy, *Parade's End,* first published 1924–28. In his brief discussion of the novel in *The Elastic Retort,* KR compares Ford (1873–1939) to Dante, writing: "Ford's best novels are all concerned with the struggle to achieve, and ultimately the tragic failure of what before them has been called the sacrament of marriage. Before *Parade's End* Ford's *The Good Soldier* was probably the best of all the novels on this subject which so tortured the Edwardians, in literature and in life. Besides being a much larger-minded work, *Parade's End* is certainly the best 'anti-war' novel provoked by the First World War in any language." *ND* 7 (1942) had included Granville Hicks's essay on the writer, "Homage to Ford Madox Ford" (with contributions by Pound, W. C. Williams, and others), and Edward Naumburg's checklist of Ford's writing.

"O Paul and Truman": Paul Bowles and Truman Capote. The following month (in a letter not collected here) KR sent JL another ditty, "New Directions Author": "An elderly curate of Buckingham / Wrote a book called 'Cunts and Fucking Them.' / It did well for a while / But it went out of style / So he wrote one called 'Cocks, and Sucking Them.' "

72. ALS-6

DEAR JIM—

. . . I have finished an anthology of US poets born since 1900. It features [Elizabeth] Bishop, [Richard] Eberhart, [Thomas] Merton, [Josephine] Miles, [Kenneth] Patchen (if you are so disloyal to your own side as to issue a collection edited by Miles & excluding Patchen—you are a really exceptional bastard— maybe you just forgot to mention Patchen in your letter), [Laura] Riding, Rexroth, [Muriel] Rukeyser, [Karl] Shapiro, [John] Wheelwright, D[elmore] Schwartz, [Yvor] Winters, and you, you bastard you. There are ten pages to each, as in the *B[ritish] P[oet]s,* as a maximum for the better poets. Then the rest are represented by one or two poems each which makes it possible to include everybody of any historical importance from [James] Agee to [Louis] Zukofsky, and not use up to more than another 50 pages. This makes a 200 page book of poems—and then there is the introduction, very simple, lucid & judicious, pitched at the students of English classes. I have already buttered up all sorts of poetry teachers around the country. Not specifically about this, of course, but there is no question but what it is in great demand. . . .

I think you will notice that my list of US poets since 1900 is a good deal more judicious than the one you sent me. Fearing, Bishop, Patchen, Riding, Wheelwright, Winters, and li'l ole you, are important poets, however much they may be out of date at the moment—or disliked in certain circles. Your list was of the academic bon ton—the people most professors approve of. Actually, Patchen is worth most of them put together. I have not sent you this book because I know if I do it will tie up my publishing schedule for years, just as the *BPs* did. You can have it as soon as I see the proofs of *The Dragon & the Unicorn* from the Annual and of the plays.

I must admit that the poets since 1900 dont make the impression that the Sandburg-Frost-Lindsay-Robinson, or the Imagists, or the "Others" generations did. 2 world wars have taken the starch out of them—not as bad as France, but it is really noticeable. Outside of the 10 or twelve leaders—the rest are pretty trivial, but of course I feel that way because I spent a year reading everything they've written. . . . When you only have one or two poems of the lesser ones—they usually come through c̄ something quite impressive. Maybe they actually make a better showing than pages of Miles & Bishop. Certainly the history of US poetry *since The Dial, Broom, Little Review, Pagan,* and *Others* makes interesting reading. There is no question but what is wrong is that so many have cut themselves off from all real experience in the universities. Actually, the best are Eberhart, Fearing, Merton, Laughlin, Patchen, Rukeyser, Riding, & maybe Winters. Only one of these is a professor. None work for Henry Luce. Only one—Rukeyser—may have been a member of the Communist Party—none ever worked for Hollywood. It is these activities which have made contemporary poetry in bulk what it is, scared, bled out, punch drunk and synthetic.

You are so damn sure that I am disgraceful and that some professor is so much more au fait. Look—in the last year I have been offered teaching jobs *on my own terms* at Bennington, Black Mt., the University of Washington, a couple other places that skip my mind—these are the ones that wrote several letters or had me lecture & looked me over. For a guy that went to Harvard you sure have an undue respect for the bunny rabbits who teach in State Universities. The only reason they're there is they're afraid to go out in the rain. You see—you never had to make your living and you simply don't understand what the word compromise means—nobody ever asked you to. I am 45 and nobody now asks me—I can teach anything I want—in fact—it shocks them that I dont plan to give seminars in Nat[hanael] West compared to Kafka. But imagine living amongst the bastards—with their Scottys, their tweeds, their Blue Boar, their New Directions books, sets of Henry James, Kafka, Kierkegaard, and the [C. S. Lewis] *Screwtape Letters*. But these are the best. The rest have been mumbling through every other morning at nine for the last 30 years. I would rather be locked up c̄ Ez[ra Pound] and his cronies in the harmless senile ward at St. Bet's. But, dont forget—they all like me, the older generation because I am learned, the younger because I am a ND author—Like Kafka. Did I ever tell you about Eleanor Clark asking me why I had all the Loeb Greek & Latin poets? I said, "Why, I read them, what do you think?" Says she, "Ah, uh, not for *pleasure?*"

What in the hell will I do with the O. V. Lubicz-Milosz poems? You could put them in the Annual translated anonymously if you want. You see—he is specially good for the Annual because he shot into popularity after the war and after his own death, because he speaks exactly the tone of broken hearted post-war Paris. I suppose I am one of the few people in the world in either French or English who took him seriously before. I dont like to waste all that work and he is not important enough for a book like the [Paul] Eluard or [Jules] Supervielle. By the way, want me to do some Supervielle? I'll send you a couple poems. . . .

c̄ love
KENNETH

/ · /

an anthology: remains unpublished.

Fitzgerald: Robert S. Fitzgerald (1910–1985), American poet, translator, editor. Worked as reporter / staff writer for the *New York Herald Tribune, Time,* and *New Republic.* Fitzgerald's work appeared in three *ND* annuals (2, 4, and 18); his translation of Virgil's *Aeneid* was published in 1983. ND published Fitzgerald's *Wreath for the Sea* (1943) and *In the Rose of Time* (1956).

Miles: Josephine Miles (1911–1985), American poet, critic, linguist. In 1941 JL published eight of Miles's poems in *ND* 6, as well as her *Poems on Several Occasions* in the Poets of the Year series. On the faculty at the University of California at Berkeley for many years. In 1949, Robert Duncan (who had studied for a time under Miles) wrote: "I have been preoccupied with the particular problem of a personal elegiac poem as it was posed for me in the work and immediate criticism and influence of Kenneth Rexroth. And, again, anyone with a shrewd eye will find that I have not been uninfluenced by problems posed for us by Miss Miles: a certain sense of the trick, a strain of sense, and, most important, the problem of the vocabulary of poetry" ("The Poet and Poetry").

Agee: James Agee (1900–1955), American novelist, poet, film critic, screenwriter. A selection from Agee's *Let Us Now Praise Famous Men* (with photographs by Walker Evans) appeared in *ND* 5 in 1940, a year before book publication.

Sandburg: Carl Sandburg (1878–1967), American poet, biographer. Although in "The Influence of French Poetry on American" *(Assays),* KR writes that Sandburg "remained the best American poet until the end of the First World War," in "Why Is American Poetry Culturally Deprived?" *(The Alternative Society)* he argued that the poet's attitude toward " 'the people' was a compound of Chicago police-court reporter sentimentality, Midwest smalltown Populist oratory, and Hull House maidenly magnanimity. The picture of the young Sandburg breathlessly following the debates in the international Socialist movement over Bernstein's Revisionism, the Millerand crisis, Luxemburg and Kautsky disputing the questions of imperialism and the falling rate of profit is so ridiculous it is not even laughable."

Frost: Robert Frost (1874–1963), American poet. In "The Influence of French Poetry on American" *(Assays),* KR writes that while the popular conception of Frost was that he was an "intensely American writer," in fact, he "discovered himself as a British Georgian poet," and "belongs squarely in the tradition" of Edward Thomas.

Lindsay: Vachel Lindsay (1879–1931), American poet. Although in "Why Is American Poetry Culturally Deprived?" *(The Alternative Society)* KR describes Lindsay's work as "immensely popular doggerel" born of "Midwest Populism," in poems like "The Congo," "General William Booth," and "The Daniel Jazz," Lindsay anticipated the fusion of jazz and poetry that would remain a major interest of KR's through the 1950s.

Robinson: Edwin Arlington Robinson (1869–1935), American poet. In "The Influence of French Poetry on American" *(Assays),* KR dismisses Robinson as "a rather vulgar imitator of the early nineteenth-century British narrative poet Crabbe, when he does not imitate those incredibly soft and sentimental productions, the narrative poems of Tennyson."

the "Others" generation: In "The Influence of French Poetry on American" *(Assays),* KR wrote of *Others,* "edited by Alfred Kreymborg, it is with this magazine and the group that grew up around it that modernism in American poetry really begins. William Carlos Williams, Wallace Stevens, Marianne Moore, Mina Loy, T. S. Eliot . . . dozens of others—Kreymborg produced them all suddenly on the literary stage in America, like a conjurer pulling rabbits from a hat. The effect on the press and the conventional poetry circles was terrific. It surpassed by far the noise made by the Beat Generation or the alcoholics of the Hemingway-Fitzgerald Lost Generation."

Henry Luce: (1898–1967), American publisher. KR's "Thou Shalt Not Kill" (an elegy for Dylan Thomas): "He was found dead at a *Time* policy conference. / Henry Luce killed him with a telegram to the Pope."

Nat West: Nathanael West (1903–1940), American novelist. ND reprinted his *Miss Lonelyhearts* as 15 in the New Classics Series in 1946, *The Day of the Locust* as NCS 29 in 1950.

St. Bet's: Ezra Pound, found incompetent to stand trial on charges of treason for allegedly making pro-Axis broadcasts on Radio Rome, was incarcerated in St. Elizabeths Hospital in Washington, D.C., from 1946 to 1958.

Eleanor Clark: (1913–), American novelist, travel writer. Her "Hurry, Hurry" had appeared in *ND* 3 (1938).

the Eluard: In 1950 Trianon Press (Paris) published a bilingual edition of Paul Eluard's *Le dur désir de durer (The Dour Desire to Endure)*, translated by Francis Cornford and Stephen Spender, distributed in the United States by ND. ND published Jules Supervielle's *Selected Writings* in 1967.

73. TLS-3   July 28, 1950
[New York]

DEAR KENNETH,

. . . The question of anthologies is a very confused and complicated matter, and I am not at all clear in my mind about it. I am quite certain, however, that I never gave you a green light on your American project. . . .

I don't see how we can convert your original project over into what I have in mind for a textbook. First of all, as you yourself have realized, your name connected with the book would frighten away a lot of little old maid professors in small colleges. And secondly, I want to limit it to good chunks of about fifteen poets. [Kenneth] Patchen, of course, is to be included. That was a slip if I left his name out. I don't want little odds and ends of lots of other poets cluttering up the main drive of the book.

Please believe me that this is not politics on my part, but simply an attempt to do a certain job as I think it ought to be done. . . .

Best wishes to all out there and keep me posted

J

---

74. ALS-7   31 VII [19]50
                                              S[an] F[rancisco]

DEAR JIM—

The baby came. Too bad we couldn't call it James—it isn't that kind of baby. Looks good—real big—9 lbs.

Honey Bear. There's only one trouble c̄ you—you dont know shit from shinola. J[osephine] Miles has far more standing amongst the bohemian fairies and far less standing amongst academic people than I have. If you really want prestige, I suppose [James L.?] Sweeney is the person. But I know you—you're too tight to pay him what he would ask. The guys that put you in their *Little Magazine* treatise were right— you still have precisely that sort of viewpoint. Anybody'd think you went to CCNY & were born in Bronxville from the way you allow yourself to be intimidated by what you imagine is academic respectability. There are two anthologies of the kind we're talking about, already out in the last year or so—by [John] Ciardi & [Lloyd] Frankenberg—both academic people, and the objection to them is precisely that they *are* academic & reactionary—they haven't sold hardly at all either in schools or bookshops. People teaching contemporary verse are mostly using Oscar [Williams], Selden Rodman or [Conrad] Aiken—the latter two usually taken together. It was funny at the Univ of Washington to see how anxious they were to get me and how anxious they were to get rid of poor old Malcolm Cowley.

What people who are "modernistic" enough to give courses in poets since 1900 want is something from a practitioner who knows what he is talking about and is not a crank or another college professor. "Academic prestige" doesn't mean anything in academic circles in this particular field. But Miles has no academic prestige either, and the cranks and bigots & people c̄ eccentric taste are in the academic world—not outside. Compare [Richard] Eberhart & Yvor Winters.

As for giving me the "green light"—you have been trying to get out of this anthology of mine ever since I told you it was ready. You did plan it, as a companion to the *B[ritish] P[oet]s*—that was the idea. Actually, you would be better advised to do it yourself rather than turn it over to an incompetent like Miles or a person c̄ perverse & eccentric taste like Winters or [R. P.] Blackmur. Cowley would have been good once—but it is a fact—poor old Malcolm has slipped into an early dotage. I guess the Party beat him to death in his Stalinist days (assuming they are over). The great problem is to get someone above schools, tendencies, & cliques. All the poetry is not published in the Neo *Hound & Horn* organs—*Partisan, Kenyon, Hudson, Chimera*, etc. Nor is it all published in *The New Masses* or the New Directions Annuals and / or *Circle*. But there was something—someone—in each. [Horace] Gregory (who is too old) may not be as good as [Allen] Tate or Winters—but he is better for instance than the minor poets of the "Reactionary Generation" (he wouldn't be included, of course, he is way over 50). [Kenneth] Fearing, however, is the right age. I dont like his poetry very much—but an anthology which slighted him & yet pretended to represent his generation would be the work of a bigot. On the other side—most poets are not very tolerant or urbane—I think you will have to seek far and wide to find anyone except you & me who would class Winters c̄ the 15 leading poets under 50. . . . Tate, Blackmur, etc. and the others think if it rhymes it aint art.

You just keep your drawers on and don't commission anybody else to do an anthology until you see mine. In the past 3 years I have read or lectured in some 30 colleges & universities, always to large crowds—got along well at the faculty pushes afterwards and been well paid. You have a mistaken idea of how I rate academically. This is due to the fact that you still look at your own career as though you were a rich George Leite. . . .

I dont know anything about the [James] Decker murder—except his sister, who was living c̄ this fellow Tax, took him out in their car into the woods—shot him & shot herself. What happened to Decker himself I dont know.

The matter of the anthology does raise a serious problem. Normally a publisher who has a clever & ingenious author who can actually write—manages to find enough for him to do to keep said author fairly comfortably alive. You can't even keep up c̄ my "art" let alone any possible hack work I might do. Yet you had a shit hemorrhage when I suggested that I do some editorial work ∴ At the moment I have been translating some of [Leopold] Senghor's *Anthologie Nègre et Malagache* (that means inhabitants of Madagascar—who they say ain't coons, but gooks—Melanesians). It has a preface by Sartre, about which the less said the better—but the poetry—though rabidly, frenetically propagandistic would go through the special market for jig Literature in the USA like a preacher's prick through a calf's asshole. It is really pretty good—and sure hot & fierce. . . .

This is why you can't hold authors. With the incredible decay of education—it is almost impossible nowadays to find anybody who can just plain write. And characters like myself who are an unending fountain of bright ideas and who have the education of the radio quiz masters—are invaluable to "bourgeois" publishers. If you cant figure out how to make your leading authors self-supporting—you are going to lose them, year after year. . . .

Whether [Kenneth] Patchen is dying or not—my doctor tells me I must get out of the city for good or I wont live many more years—I have to buy a house in the country—for which I need about $1000 more—and then I need literary work to keep me after I get there. How are you going to contribute to this? You're my publisher. Dont you see how it is? . . . I'm not beefing. I'm just telling you how it is. . . .

Take it easy
KENNETH

/ · /

The baby came: Mary Rexroth.

Sweeney: Probably James L. Sweeney (1900–), American writer, art critic.

Ciardi: John Ciardi (1916–1986), American poet, translator, editor, critic. Best known for his three-volume translation of Dante's *Divine Comedy*.

Frankenberg: Lloyd Frankenberg (1907–), American critic, whose *Pleasure Dome: On Reading Modern Poetry* appeared in 1949.

Oscar: Oscar Williams's *A Little Treasury of Modern Poetry* (1946) and *A Little Treasury of American Poetry* (1948); Selden Rodman's *100 American Poems* (1948); Conrad Aiken's *American Poetry, 1671–1928* (1929).

the Decker murder: James A. Decker's Decker Press published KR's *The Art of Worldly Wisdom* in 1949. According to KR's note in the 1953 edition, "The man who was running the business was murdered. When I got back to this country, I received from the executor a few copies of the book, all defectively bound, and most of the sheets. As far as I can make out, between one and two hundred copies had been bound; some went to reviewers, a few to bookshops and the rest were defective."

Senghor's anthology: Léopold Senghor's *Antologie de la Nouvelle Poésie Nègre et Malagache de Langue Française.*

75. TLS-1

Aug 2 [1950]
[Norfolk]

DEAR KENNETH—

. . . That is SOME POEM. I am much relieved to see that you have not just been vegetating all this time. The philosophy is so clearly put that even I can almost understand it, and the nature passages are superb, as always. The travelogue very informative and the doings with whores good for the scissorbills, I guess. You will sure not get a job at Sarah Lawrence after that appears.

Yes, it really strikes me as quite a poem, though I can't guarantee that Randy Jarrell and Ta-Ta Tate, as Ezra [Pound] calls him, will concur. . . .

We got to start taking a longer view of you. You are really forging ahead. I don't mean in the opinions of the cocktail crowd but in actual performance. I was worried for a while there and thought you were going to stop writing, but I can see now you are in full cry. Very impressive.

Well it looks like the boys in Korea are going to have to swim for it in a few days, unless the KC Kid is fool enough to get out his little atomizer. . . .

Be a good Papa!
J

/ · /

SOME POEM: *The Dragon and the Unicorn,* written between 1944 and 1950, published by ND in 1952.

the boys in Korea: On June 25, 1950, North Korean forces had surged across the thirty-eighth parallel and captured Seoul, South Korea's capital; the ensuing "conflict" between the North Koreans (aided by the Chinese) and the South Koreans (aided by a United Nations armed force) continued until July 1953.

the KC kid: Harry S. Truman (U.S. President 1945–53), whose Truman Doctrine argued for U.S. funds to "support free peoples who are resisting subjugation by armed minorities or by outside pressures." For KR's assessment of the effects of the Korean War on American politics and culture, see "The Second Post-War, the Second Interbellum, the Permanent War Generation" *(The Alternative Society).*

76. ALS-4

August 14, 1950
[San Francisco]

DEAR JIM—

Will you please go to the Strout agent in Norfolk and ask if she knows any property I can buy for about $1000 down—preferably an old large house (or two houses) pasture in usable shape & family fruit and garden & small cultivatable acrege—stream-watered pasture and usable barn & poultry house. . . . Not *too* near you or I'll go nuts. . . .

DONT cut the 3 parts of the *[Dragon and the] Unicorn* s̄ me seeing them first!!! I dont care if you cut it down—tho I'm not enthusiastic about it—but I want to know what's what because it is all fitted together c̄ the most elaborate care & artiface, "like a Bach fugue" as the boys & girls used to say chez [John] Donne in the days of the Revolving Word. . . .

Love
KENNETH

/ · /

the Revolving Word: Reference to Eugene Jolas's "Manifesto: The Revolution of the Word" (ending with the declaration: "THE PLAIN READER
BE DAMNED") appeared in his journal *transition* in 1929, signed by Kay
Boyle, Hart Crane, Caresse Crosby, Elliot Paul, and others. JL dedicated the first *ND* Annual "To the Editors and Contributors & Readers
of *transition* who have begun successfully the revolution of the word."

77. ALS-3

30 VIII [19]50
S[an] F[rancisco]

DEAR JIM—

. . . I want to thank you for the offer of your house,
which is extremely generous of you. However—I
have to transport Marthe [Rexroth], the baby and all
my stuff c̄ myself, because I cannot afford the extra
transportation. The best way for me to get it all across
the country would be to buy a good second hand
truck and drive. . . .

I feel that by next spring the war will be general—
with a frightened exodus from the cities raising the
price of farm land and a general inflation. Already of
course $100 is worth only $85 as of June. I think it
unwise of you to move to NYC for the winter. There
is no question but the Russians will try to bomb it
as soon as they are ready to move. I think the Chinese
Army will roll in a few weeks, then the German and
Balkan Armies as soon as Russia is safe behind her
snows. At that moment NYC—and Frisco and
Washington—will, if they can manage it, dissolve in
vapor. I dont think they will manage at the first try,
but they will keep trying—and as soon as Truman
makes a gesture towards his atom bomb they are
going to try damn hard. . . .

c̄ love
KENNETH

78. ALS-2   10 X [19]50
                              S[an] F[rancisco]

DEAR JIM—

    . . . I was rereading the [Wyndham Lewis] *Apes of God* the other night. That is certainly a Modern Classic. It is a pity it is so damn long. Not only does it make it impossible as a reprint, but it injures the cogency of the book. It is a pity indeed! because poor old Wyndham is still the most alive human of his generation over there (except maybe [Herbert] Read). His art show, the first in years, was up while I was there and it sure made you feel there were giants in those days. He called me up—but I was leaving London & disgusted c̄ all human contacts there (except for my Nini) so I didnt see him. Another Modern Classic is Sach[everell] Sitwell, who is really a better writer and stronger saner person than the other two, as the real cognoscenti all admit—eg. Edith [Sitwell] herself, [T. S.] Eliot, Lewis, E[zra] P[ound], Read. Again, I dont see how you could ever get Americans to read his long dreamy poems, though the fairies gobble his critical chichi. . . .
    As for the T[ennessee] W[illia]ms. Honest; it is a dreadful book. And such a waste of the material. The Riche Americaine in Italy is almost as horrifying as the Queer American writer, and it is a pity to lose even one opportunity of giving her what she deserves, but the book is just the unraveling of a very small thread of formula. More and more I feel that the USA does not really exist, that I am taking part in a monstrous super-production called "After Hours." T Wms doesn't portray decadence—let alone satirize it—he *is* decadence. Nothing shows this better than his complete lack of humor—compare him & [William] Wycherley or [Sir John] Vanbrugh.

Similar subject—M[ary] McCarthy's story of Peggy G[uggenheim] (and / or Caresse [Crosby]). Mary is just sore that she isnt a Guggenheim heiress instead of a Guggenheim Fellow. She and her kind spend much more time in the Harry's Bars than ever Peggy—who lives in her truncated palazzo & really tries to do something for Aht, besides being an incomparably nicer person. What is the name of that nasty bar near the Am Ex in Florence, full of mid-dleaged gloved & millinered American women, and fading cocksuckers? I need it for my poem. . . .

faithfully
KENNETH

/ · /

Wyndham: Wyndham Lewis (1882–1957), Canadian-British artist, novelist, critic. Lewis's *The Apes of God* was first published in 1930. In "The Influence of French Poetry on American" *(Assays),* KR writes: "Lewis' narrative style is Laforgue reduced to a formula: 'Describe human beings as though they were machines, landscapes as though they were chemical formulas, inanimate objects as though they were alive.' " In the *Conjunctions* interview, KR says of Lewis: "Well, I suppose he was the greatest uncivilized man in England since they gave up Wotan. Lewis was a personal friend of mine. I was very fond of Wyndham Lewis. Fascism and all. Don't forget these people were almost all fascists. And just crazy as hell. You got talking politics to Tom Eliot and you thought you were just talking to a madman. And, of course, Wyndham Lewis just killed himself by writing *Hitler.*"

except for my Nini: "As I cross Romily Street/A girl comes towards me, tall, heavy/Black hair like a Mexican girl,/Exophthalmic, dark blue-grey eyes,/Full hips and the heavy breasts of/Provence . . ./She is a Nizarde, 'Nini' for/Andrée, (I thought Nini was Jeanne),/Certainly the most impressive/Woman to enter a room with/I have ever known and one of/The very best lays. She tells me/She is a sadist 'seulement/Pour le commerce' . . . 'Ah, le monde est méchant, mon/Petit, le monde est très méchant' " *(The Dragon and the Unicorn).*

Sach. Sitwell: Sacheverell Sitwell (1897–), Edith Sitwell (1887–1964), British poets. ND published *A Celebration for Edith Sitwell,* edited by José Garcia Villa, in 1948. According to JL: "when I sat down on a bench in Red Lion Square in London after Edith Sitwell tipped me off to buy Dylan Thomas' first book—the bell rang louder for me then than Big Ben" *(AP)*.

a dreadful book: Tennessee Williams's novel *The Roman Spring of Mrs. Stone* was published by ND in 1950.

Wycherley or Vanbrugh: William Wycherley (1641–1715) and Sir John Vanbrugh (1664–1726), witty, bawdy, cynical, and amoral Restoration playwrights.

M. McCarthy: Mary McCarthy (1912–1989), American novelist and essayist. She satirized KR in the character of Vincent Kreogh, "poet of the masses," in her *The Groves of Academe* (1952).

Peggy G.: In the *Conjunctions* interview, KR wrote: "I have found that the patrons of the arts as people are greatly superior to the people they patronize. I would much rather spend an evening in conversation with Laughlin and Peggy Guggenheim, now dead, and Caresse Crosby, now dead, all of whom are and were very intimate friends of mine, than with almost any author I can think of. They know more for one thing."

79. ALS-6

26 X [19]50
[S]an F[rancisco]

DEAR JIM,

If you are really telling the truth about the T[ennessee] W[illia]ms novel you should shut up the shop and go down to Chestnut lodge for a nice rest. T Wms doesnt need you—he is the queen of Leland's Harry's Bar set—the wet dream of the *Flair* staff come true & represents everything that is wrong c̄ contemporary culture. He is much worse than Truman Capote because Truman is just plain bitch and there is an end of it. Irrespective of his sociological role— books like *Roman Spring* are in just about the most horrible taste imaginable—you wouldn't understand—it is the horrible false sickening homosexual mawkishness with which the whole tale is saturated, as *Time* says—the gimmick is all there in the best written part—to barbershop which ends c̄ the coy nasty covert crap about getting her to suck his cock—

it sounds like a female impersonator telling drag jokes to a bunch of [Helen] Hokinson club women. Finally—the whole book is a cheap fairy spite trick to disgrace & belittle a beautiful woman who was too much for him socially. The peculiar thing about all this scathing satire from the Tangiers boys is that it is always directed, not against the proconsuls of the Marshall Plan, or the Colonels in occupied Germany or Henry Luce—but against people who are infinitely more devoted to the arts & the spirit of man and all that than they are—Peggy Guggenheim, Caresse [Crosby], you, etc. . . . Peggy could easily have started a half dozen *Fortunes* & *Flairs*—instead she has devoted her money & life to the most revolutionary art she could find. I am well aware she got satisfactions, but since they were all satisfactions of ordinary appetites, I am sure better could have been found in other circles—I really am not impressed c̄ Djuna [Barnes] & Max Ernst as fucks.

This world of [Paul] Bowles, Capote, W[illia]m [J.] Smith, T Wms, etc. that you have got into is going to ruin you. Financially because they are a bunch of *very* expensive queens and want everything done up like the circus. Your "artistic integrity" because they are the phoniest writers to show up so far in this phoney civilization. Personally because their social world is one of endless hysteria & tinsel crises. Sexually because if you aren't involved c̄ one of them you will fall for one of their female mascots ("bitch's blinds") who are worse than they are. Socially because nobody will have anything to do c̄ you except their own world & in a few years, after they've played you for all you're worth—they'll drop you completely—and in the meantime they will circulate all sorts of malicious gossip about you. I should think at your age you'd have sense enough to stay away from gorgeous bitches. If you *must* know homos—

associate c̄ frank dirt, like Edouard [Roditi]—who turns his tricks in alleys and parks and lets it go at that. He has more loyalty to his friends in his little finger nail—and more integrity than the whole population of Leland's Bar since [Norman] Douglas & [Ronald] Firbank laid end to end in a daisy chain. . . . Dont you realize that you *are* becoming what the commies call a counter-revolutionary publisher? You are getting mixed up c̄ people who are against everything decent in the world & who for sheer irresponsible reaction cannot be paralleled in the days of Marie Antoinette. If they were to be portrayed exactly as in a Russian movie everybody would say, "See, those bolsheviks have the most childish ideas. What clumsy caricature!"

Maybe you have $500 to lose on Mrs. Stone. But you have no right—with your convictions—to throw away all that work of the publishing house on such crap s̄ even the excuse of money, when you have discontinued things like The Poets of the Month & *The Five Young Poets*. Both of these were invaluable—and whatever time & money they lost were worth it. . . . You are killing yourself for a lot of fairies who will be gone like the morning dew in 10 years and a lot of prick teasing pseudo nymphomaniacs who you wouldnt have guts enough to fuck if you ever got, as you wont, the chance—and the joys of cutting a figure around the Harvard Club as just another rich punk of your year—behavioristically indistinguishable from all the other well curried & thoroughly harried young businessmen. . . .

18 of the ranking US poets of the 20th century committed suicide. Poor [Vladimir] Mayakovsky.

c̄ love
KENNETH

/ · /

Leland's Bar: KR wrote in *The Dragon and the Unicorn,* "After Chase and Sanborn's coffee/At Leland's Bar, the American/Fairies cruise the Lungarno,/Hunting Tall, broadshouldered, hungry/Florentines. . ./I am convinced the Dogana/Allows no heterosexual/American under forty/Past the Italian border."

Max Ernst: (1891–1941), German painter, emigrated to the United States in 1941. In "Disengagement: The Art of the Beat Generation" *(The Alternative Society),* KR writes, "Surrealists like Hans Arp and Max Ernst might talk of creation by hazard—of composing pictures by walking on them with painted soles, or by tossing bits of paper up in the air. But it is obvious they were self-deluded. Nothing looks anything like an Ernst or an Arp but another Ernst or Arp."

Douglas & Firbank: Norman Douglas (1868–1952), British novelist, essayist, travel writer, who spent much of his adult life in Italy. Ronald Firbank (1886–1926), British novelist; a dandy, aesthete, homosexual habitué of the Café Royal (the restaurant in London). ND published several books by Firbank.

The Poets of the Month: Five Young American Poets and The Poet of the Month (later called Poets of the Year) series, published by ND. Designed to promote work by younger writers, *Five* lasted through three volumes: First Series, 1940 (Mary Barnard, John Berryman, Randall Jarrell, W. R. Moses, George Marion O'Donnell); Second Series, 1941 (Paul Goodman, Jeanne McGahey, Clark Mills, David Schubert, Karl Shapiro); and Third Series, 1944 (Alejandro Carrion [trans. by Dudley Fitts and Francis St. John], Jean Garrigue, Eve Merriman, John Frederick Nims, Tennessee Williams). These volumes included poetry, as well as photographs, facsimiles, and an introduction by each poet. PM/ PY were essentially chapbooks, featuring volumes by W. C. Williams, Delmore Schwartz, John Berryman, Vladimir Nabokov, and others. The series was called the Poet of the Month until the Book of the Month Club threatened a lawsuit and the series was renamed Poets of the Year. An annual subscription to the series cost $4 for twelve issues, 35 cents for single copies; it ran from 1941 to 1944, issuing forty-two pamphlets, each printed by a different fine printer.

Mayakovsky: Vladimir Mayakovsky (1893–1930), Russian poet. In "Why Is American Poetry Culturally Deprived?" KR wrote: "To products of environments as troubled as those which produced Rilke, Mayakovsky, Paul Eluard, or Dylan Thomas, even the most tormented American poet must seem singularly content, but so it is."

80. ALS-4   30 XI [19]50
                               S[an] F[rancisco]

DEAR JIM—

Thanks very much for the [W. C.] W[illia]ms
C[ollected] P[oems] & the Stendhal. You know I think
Wms the equal of [T. S.] Eliot and [Ezra] Pound &
superior to anyone else in contemporary US poetry.
[Carl] Sandburg & [Robert] Frost who might compete for 3rd place have too much fake in them—and
it gets worse every year. [Wallace] Stevens is fun-
damentally a trivial writer, and has not written a first-
rate poem in 20 years. The thing of his Comedian as
the Letter C is a versification of [George] Santayana—statistical probability will insure that an arith-
metical mean of humans will have a preponderantly
happy life in this naughty and draughty world if they
confine themselves to the more civilized sensual
gratifications. This is true, but fatuous, and is the
perfect expression of the mind of a well-bred insur-
ance executive. Wms is certainly the realest poet since
[D. H.] Lawrence and in spite of, or because of, his
suburban innocence and chronic hot nuts, by far the
most adult poet in the USA. The Pink Church should
be illustrated by Boucher's *La Petite Morphi* or
Renoir's naked house maid—it is certainly the finest
celebration of the sacrament of female flesh in modern poetry. He is sure pussy simple, ole Doc Williams.

All the above is for quotes if you want it.

I think it very touching of him to dedicate the book
to you. especially after the way you have kicked him
around in favor of his namesake and the Harry's Bar
fairies. . . .

                               faithfully
                               KENNETH

/ · /

Wms. CP: William Carlos Williams's *The Collected Later Poems* was published in 1950 by ND.

the Stendhal: An English translation by Louise Varèse of Stendhal's *Lucien Leuwe* was published by ND in 1950.

a versification: George Santayana (1863–1952), American philosopher and writer. In "Why Is American Poetry Culturally Deprived?" *(The Alternative Society),* KR would write, "The one specifically philosophic American poet of the twentieth century has been Wallace Stevens and his work has been a kind of versification of the philosophy of George Santayana, of what Santayana called skepticism and animal faith."

The Pink Church: W. C. Williams's *The Pink Church,* published by Golden Goose Press in 1949, was dedicated to JL. François Boucher (1703–1770) and Pierre-Auguste Renoir (1841–1919), French painters.

80. ALS-4

30 XII [19]50

s[an] F[rancisco]

DEAR JIM—

Finally read over everything in *N.D.* 12 and I am afraid the final impression is the same—of idle, decadent perverted people—fairies and nymphomaniacs running around to international hotels. . . . These are the rotten dying bourgeoisie—and these are their authors. American imperialism is about to dynamite the world and 20% of the male children of Naples sleep in the streets & live on garbage & prickly pears. The only things that really stand out are [Richard] Eberhart's & mine—and your preface—altho the "goody two shoes" style this time really *is* overdone—it sounds like a personal letter of Bill W[illia]ms—the sentiment's exemplar.

No money. Aren't you *ever* going to pay me *anything?* . . . I am *not* a fairy from Leland's Bar. You have got to realize that I am too old to be impressed by my own name in print. I *must* make at least an appreciable portion of my income as a writer, or stop writing. . . . If I am going to go on writing I must get out of the city. I can no longer work here at all. Also, the flat is not suitable for the baby—and of course within a year San Francisco will be obliterated. So how about it?

faithfully
KENNETH

/ · /

Eberhart's & mine: Richard Eberhart's poems "Letter I" and "A Legend of Viable Women" and KR's "The Dragon and the Unicorn" appeared in *ND* 12 (1950).

goody two shoes: Randall Jarrell had reviewed the ND Annual in the *New York Times,* calling JL "goody two shoes."

82. TLS-1   January 2, 1951
                                                    [Norfolk]

DEAR KENNETH—

. . . I am sick of arguing money with you. I am bankrupting myself for writers like you—spending money I have no right to spend since it should be handed on to my children, as mine was to me—and all I get for it is slander and abuse.

Your constant letters of criticism don't help much either. Why don't you just stop writing me about what you don't like in ND? It just wears me down and discourages me. If I quit business you are likely to be without a publisher. Can you name anybody else who would have brought out these plays in these times without a good fat subsidy?

God knows why I don't tell you and all the rest of your kind to go straight to hell and publish your stuff yourselves. I must be nuts. And when I do try to make a dollar by publishing a few things that are not too bad that the public will buy you scream your head off at me. Really it is unendurable.

J

83. ALS-4

6 III[19]52
[San Francisco]

DEAR JIM—

. . . I think you are returning the 300 lines of the D[ragon] & U[nicorn] for purely personal reasons. OK—but where are you going to find 2 pages to replace the Paris incident which are *not* "dangerous"? I am not going to excerpt the "philosophy" because *that* is all a continuous exposition and the conclusions, or even implications, are far more "dangerous" than any episodic material. I will try to round up something else for you & shoot the typescript back right away.

You are, out of naivety, I think, kidding yourself in what you are trying to do. The Voice of America, and other State Department broadcasts, present a large amount of American cultural material abroad. Poetry of mine is constantly translated abroad, especially in German, and the source of these handouts is the official information service. While I was in Paris RDF gave an hour to my work—the speaker & reader were representatives of the Embassy staff. Next week or so, by the way, the hour was devoted to [Kenneth] Patchen. They apparently never ask permission or pay for this stuff, which is why you dont know it. It was unaware of it all—and was lying in bed with Leontine when my name came over the radio—following a hillbilly song. . . .

NOW the material they use is consistently "radical" and "dangerous"—they apparently want to give the impression of absolute freedom of criticism in the USA. Just recently the poem beginning "Coming back over the col between" appeared in translation in Hamburg—from an official handout. Bear in mind—all this is to build up support for American capitalism in its oncoming war c̄ Russia & China.

You, presumably, are trying to build up the impression abroad that there still exists in the USA a "3rd Force" not committed to bombing Moscow next week. Yet you already admit to constant superveillance—"clearances" and "security checks." So—"working for peace" and before you have even started—you turn out to be more reactionary than the war mongers themselves. I do not worry about my own role—I think I can bring out an issue of the magazine which will be inoffensive to the Jesuits and Silver Shirts who dominate your board and which *will* accomplish the ends you seek. But this will be because I am much more astute in these matters than you—and considerably better informed. You like to kid yourself that you are very "practical" and level-headed and worldly wise in comparison, especially with a crazy poet like me. (You have a fixed idea that I am Ezra Pound Jr.) I am afraid you are a babe in the woods in these matters.

Nothing could show this better than your innocent query about poor old Henry. My God, Jim! What rock do you live under? Let me brief you briefly—Henry Cowell was until quite recently an admitted Stalinist. Furthermore, he is what is known in the trade as a pee hole bandit—he did a year in San Quentin (about 1935–36) for pederasty *with minor boys*. All this has been forgotten & forgiven—and last I knew he was teaching at both Julliard & The New School. I am quite familiar with his work on

[Charles] Ives. In fact around 1932 Henry & I were the only people in the USA who knew about Ives. . . .

You have got to realize that almost every intellectual in the USA who is not a Fascist like [Lionel] Trilling and the *Kenyon Review* crowd or an exTrotskyite Bomb Moscow Now advocate like the *Partisan Review* is going to be suspect of your "board" of retired businessmen and Jesuits. How about Jack Farrell? Do you know that there is not a book by him in the SF Library—due to the Church? Do you realize that I am one of the very few intellectuals in the USA who has never been an actual member of the Communist Party—and this because I started out in life considerably to the left of the Bolsheviks—If you keep on you will end up with Willa Cather . . . who [has] graced—quite innocently—Commie Front organization letterheads. . . .

faithfully
KENNETH

/ · /

you are trying to do: A reference to JL's editing of *Perspectives USA* for the Ford Foundation, publishing sixteen issues between 1952 and 1956. In *PR,* JL explains, "The original project was to do *Perspectives* in four languages: English, French, German, and Italian. There'd been a big gap during the war when nothing cultural from America came to Europe, and the magazine was planned to fill that gap. We had articles on architecture, art, philosophy, etc., and, of course, stories and poems. The idea was to give a catch-up course in recent American culture." KR's "At sixteen I came West, riding" ("A Living Pearl") appeared in the first issue of the journal, Fall 1952.

Coming back over: KR's "Strength Through Joy."

Henry Cowell: (1897–1965) and Charles Ives (1874–1954), American composers.

Jack Farrell: James T. Farrell (1904–1979), American novelist. Farrell, a realist and a Marxist, had in 1936 published "A Note on Literary

Criticism," an attack on Michael Gold's "revolutionary sentimental-
ism" and Granville Hicks's "mechanical Marxism."

Willa Cather: (1876–1947), American novelist.

84. Airletter. TLS

3 V [19]52
[San Francisco]

DEAR JIM,

Any further moves on my part await your decision on the use of the poem in *Perspectives*. If you
decide not to use it, I am breaking with you absolutely and permanently. One by one you have broken every promise you have made to me this year.
. . . The acceptance or rejection of the 300 odd lines
of the D[ragon] & U[nicorn] will be determinative.
I cannot permit you to sacrifice me to the priests
who run you now. (This is of course the real reason
you are rejecting the poem.) For if you get away
with this, you will dictate the contents of the issue
you want me to do. . . .

Before we go any further—here is the contents of
the issue of *Perspectives* as I see it now: Narrative—
[Kenneth] Patchen, Letter to God; [B.] Traven,
Selection from *The Death Ship* (or from his new
book); Ed[mund] Wilson, a story about an halluci-
natory woman sort of Turn of the Screwy, once in
P[artisan] R[eview], a science fiction shocker; ART—
[Morris] Graves et al. . . . MUSIC—[Charles] Ives,
Henry Cowell; Criticism: [Henry] Miller on [Blaise]
Cendrars; MOVIES Parker Tyler on *M. Verdoux;* DRAMA
Paul Goodman or e e cummings; POETRY a selection
from [Richard] Eberhart, [Muriel] Rukeyser, [Hor-
ace] Gregory, Laughlin; and now for the historical
piece—George Woodcock has done a book on
Proudhon from which a chapter on Proudhonism in

the USA could be developed—that is—the Mutual
Banking, Social Credit, Single Tax, and extreme
libertarianism of the 19th century in the USA. But
it would have to be commissioned and Woodcock is
not an American but a Canadian. He was living in
SF for a year, but is now back in Canada. I wish
somebody decent would write on [Antonin] Artaud.
But almost alone [Henry] Miller, altho he is a bag of
wind, writes what Europeans would consider criticism. The sort of academic doodling which appears
in the *Ku Klux Kenyon* would send them off into
peals of laughter.

Before I go any further with this you must OK it.
I notice that my name has never been mentioned in
any of your publicity, altho you have mentioned some
eight other editors, all academicians . . . I will not
stand for any cutting which I feel to be ideological
or political. You must realize that I consider your
board a bunch of clerical neofascists—but nowheres
near as timid as you are scared of them.

faithfully

KENNETH

/ · /

Traven: B. Traven (?1882–1969), German novelist. His *The Death Ship*
(1925) recounts the wanderings of an American sailor after World War
II.

Ed Wilson: Edmund Wilson (1895–1972), American writer and critic.
Wrote regularly for the *New Republic, Vanity Fair,* and *The New Yorker.*
His *Axel's Castle* (1931) is a study of Symbolist literature, while *To the
Finland Station* (1940) traces Socialist theory from Michelet through
Marx and Lenin. His third wife was the novelist Mary McCarthy. In
"The Influence of French Poetry on American" *(Assays),* KR writes:
"The best poet of the *Divan* style in America is the critic Edmund
Wilson, who has a genius for conveying the very taste and smell of
old, unhappy, far-off seductions—a regular heterosexual Cavafi. His
rigorously unsentimental contemporaries refuse to take him seriously
as a poet."

Cendrars: Blaise Cendrars (1887–1961), French writer. Henry Miller includes a chapter on Cendrars in *The Books in My Life* (ND, 1969), and cites "virtually the complete works" of the writer on his "The Hundred Books That Influenced Me Most" list. He also gives a charming description of Cendrars in a 1934 letter to Anaïs Nin: "I had a date at the Café de la Paix . . . Cendrars looks rough, like a sailor—he is one at bottom—and he speaks rather loudly, but very well. He has only ône arm, the empty one, or half-arm slung affectionately around my neck while he tells the whole restaurant what a great guy I am, what the book is about, why it must be published in French, where I belong in the great Catholic tradition, etc. Perhaps the finest moment in my life. . . . Finally we go out, four of us now, and we must have some more alcohol in the bars along the Boulevard in Montmartre. Whores hanging on to us, and Cendrars hugging them like a sailor, and urging me to take one, take two, take as many as you want. After two or three of these bars and more whores hanging on our necks I ducked. . . ."

e e cummings: e(dward) e(stlin) cummings (1894–1962), American poet. JL included a number of cummings's poems in the first two *ND* annuals. In "The Influence of French Poetry on American," KR writes: "He is a conventional and sentimental poet whose typographical and syntactic oddities are the pranks of an incurable Harvard Boy. . . . Everybody pretends not to notice that among his comical cut-ups are some of the most scurrilous bits of anti-Semitic doggerel in any language, including German. Anti-Semitism is unknown in America except among lunatics. So in the sense that he is a sane and educated man and an anti-dreyfusard, he may be said to show French influence" *(Assays)*.

George Woodcock: (1912–), Canadian poet, critic. Between 1940 and 1947, edited *Now,* which published KR's D. H. Lawrence essay and his poem "Lyell's Hypothesis Again." Woodcock remembers KR in "Rage and Serenity: The Poetic Politics of Kenneth Rexroth" *(Sage-trieb)*.

Proudhon: Pierre-Joseph Proudhon (1809–1865), French Socialist and writer. In *Communalism,* KR writes that while Proudhon is "generally considered founder of individual anarchy, mutual credit, and cooperative labor exchange . . . Marx was right about Proudhon. He was a confused thinker and a confusing writer and far from being a practical man."

your board: "It might be amusing to note that one of the members of the board of Intercultural Publications, the name of the 'independent' organization set up by Ford to insulate the Foundation from my wickedness, was William J. Casey. He was put there by the Foundation to keep an eye on me" (JL letter to the editor). Casey later served as Director of the CIA under President Ronald Reagan.

85. Airletter. TLS

18 V [19]52
[San Francisco]

DEAR JIM,

It would seem you have me over a barrel. But do not expect that I will ever have the slightest respect for you again. You are both a trimmer and a victim of the latest person to gain your ear, especially if that person be a fairy. I do not want to write poems to fill space in bourgeois magazines. If I wished to do that, dont you think I would send stuff to the *New Yorker,* the *P[artisan] R[eview]* and *Harpers?* Dont you realize that these people ask me for poems and never get them? The reasons you give for rejecting the selection from the *D[ragon] & U[nicorn]* in your last letter are in complete contradiction to the reasons you gave in your first and second letters as you began to get cold feet but were ashamed to admit it. It is also obvious that you have *never read* the selections I sent you last. I can't imagine anything more suitable of mine than the section on Paestum. Nothing shows better the kind of person you have become and the kind of people you associate with than your remark, "The French are all pretty preposterous with their inflation." What French? All my friends are just barely able to keep alive. A pair of shoes costs a week's work. If you expect me to sell to the French the system of the American Bankers who are responsible for their starvation, you are very mistaken. Since Marthe [Rexroth] works full time and is tired when she gets through, it is necessary for me to have all stuff typed commercially. All your monkeyshines with the selection from the *D&U* have cost me quite a bit. As soon as the *nice* lyrics come back from the typist they will go on to you by air. I guess you are too obtuse to realize that ALL my poetry is tendentious. Why do you think the *Klu Klux Kenyon* hates me so? . . .

Every list of proposed contents I have sent you, you have objected to. As soon as you clear a list I will write to the people. My God! what a rigama-role. I am damn sure you dont act up like this with the Fascists [John Crowe] Ransom and [Lionel] Trilling. I am not at all sure [B.] Traven's *Death Ship* can be excerpted. The narrative runs along like the elephants on parade with their tails in each other's trunks. But rereading it after all these years I am dumbfounded at how good it is. How about putting it in the New Classics? It is Huck Finn in the Century of Horror.

Isn't it disgusting that I should JUST be worried about the money due me for a mss you had accepted? So unprincipled, these mercenary poets!

Do munch a truffle for me in Laperouse, where everyone in France eats these days.

faithfully
KENNETH

[appended in holograph:]
How strange a sense of values you have that you would throw away one of the oldest and best (and fewest) real friendships you have to pacify the spite of a fairy. What on earth is it worth to you?

/ · /

Paestum: An ancient coastal city in southern Italy; the extant ruins include three Greek temples and a Roman amphitheater.

86. Airletter. ALS

[May 29, 1952]
S[an] F[rancisco]

DEAR JIM—

It is *you* who should resign from this job. But I think you are already destroyed. I have never read more mealy mouthed hypocrisy than your letter dictated May 23. 1) You know [B.] Traven is an anonymity. This is the first time I have heard of passport requirements for magazine publication. I happen to actually have known him once. He is an ex Wobbly from Chicago, born in Wisconsin of German parents. He is NOT the person *Life* thinks he is. That man, whose middle name is Traven, is his agent. You know that you object to him because of his politics—or lack of them. 2) "You want so much to have me represented in this issue." What swinish effrontery! 3) I would of course under no circumstances permit my stuff to appear in a magazine run by Polish Fascists. You are insane to tie the Ford Foundation up with such a thing. 4) *I devoutly hope that I have never written a line which was not offensive to good taste* . . . I seriously advise you to consider where you are headed. NeoThomists, Fascists, Jesuits, now—leftover Flagellants & Jew killers of [Jozef] Pilsudski.

Have you asked Horace Gregory to edit an issue? In his day he was certainly the most wide-awake high brow editor around. . . .

faithfully
KENNETH

/ · /

Traven: According to W. Wyatt's *The Man Who Was B. Traven* (1980), Traven was actually Albert Otto Max Freige (later known as Ret Marut), born in Swiebodzin, a Polish town in Germany.

Pilsudski: Jozef Pilsudski (1867–1935), president of Poland, 1918–22; premier, 1926–28, 1930.

87. Airletter. ALS

23 X [19]52
S[an] F[rancisco]

DEAR JIM—

I just got a depressing letter today from an exfriend of yours, beginning: "There is a new cobra in India," and going on c̄ a long histoire of duplicity & snobbery. I really think you should quit the F[ord] F[oundation] *right now*. I believe it is destroying you. You have, socially, become the instrument of a Right Wing Plan Marshall—intellectually, you are the captive of the gestapo of New York cocktail fascism. The peculiar thing is—you think you're just becoming "respectable." Are you stupid, or neurotic, or both or what? Honest to god, how can you stand five minutes in the company of a popinjay like Lionel Trilling? And poor you, you think you've "arrived"! One could stomach your adventures— knowing that eventually you are due for a rude cold miserable awakening. But it is sickening to see you ditch your former friends c̄ such expedient embarrassment. Listen kiddo, you didn't get where you are via the literary quarterlies & the Drop the Bomb Now poetasters. Neither Elizabeth Hardwick nor John Crowe Ransom "made" *New Directions,* but people named Miller, Patchen, Williams, Pound, Goodman, Roditi, Rexroth, etc.—*shameful people.*

Another thing—the swizzle on your time machine is backwards. *"New Directions"*? You are not headed toward the future, but deep into the past. *NO* young people read these squares except as "assignments" in their own classrooms. Even magazines like the *New Republic* are getting scared of being stuck c̄ them. But you—perched on the dizzy heights of Mary McCarthy's cocktail toothpick and hobnobbing c̄ the *Atlantic Monthly* Set in their private ossorium. . . . You be careful, when you are playing ProConsul amongst the small busted nations and coffee colored brethren, a riot dont break loose & you get busted down, corona and all, like a rabbit. You know—I dont enjoy writing letters like this. I think—poor old Jim—lost and astray—I'll just forget all this mess and write him a good old friendly letter, like in the old days, before he became respectable—and then some new folly breaks loose.

By the way—if you go back thru Japan—one of the very greatest modern novels is *Kokoro* (it means "heart") by Soseki Natsumi. I think he still lives. . . .

c̄ love
KENNETH

/ · /

Elizabeth Hardwick: (1916–), American essayist, novelist.

Soseki Natsumi: (1867–1916), Japanese novelist. His novel *Kokoro* was published posthumously in 1941.

88. 2 airletters. ALS

4 XI [19]52
S[an] F[rancisco]

DEAR JIM—

As for your complaints about Selden [Rodman]— I of course side c̄ him. *Perspectives* is just a great advertising stunt of USA imperialism, designed to represent the country as exactly the opposite of what it really is—the most inhospitable environment for an artist or just a sensitive & decent man since Carthage—if that. I have never read a story in any European commie or Russian magazine which even remotely approached the reality—you have to live in it to know how frightful it is—you can't sit in Moscow or Paris and imagine it. I hope you see in my issue plenty which would "give the trustees apoplexy"—but which they will be too stupid to understand. As for Mort[imer] Adler—I consider him a crackpot and fascist as well as a very silly & vulgar man. I write you this because fascist lickspittles like [Lionel] Trilling & [John Crowe] Ransom approve of what you have set him to do. I should imagine that if you start shoving Selden around several of us will quit then and there. . . .

I do hope you all behave responsibly in India, meet the right people, and get some good stuff out of the trip. I suppose you have found that the richer Indian intellectuals are the more likely they are to be Stalinists, and if they are not, with NO exceptions, their attitude to USA culture is exactly mine. If you havent found this out you're meeting the wrong people. As for your fellow Connecticutian—old time imperialist gunmen used gatling guns—now we envelop the niggers in marshmallow spray. You can have him. . . .

[second airletter:]

My radio review is going good—people like it. Wish it paid me some money. Did Henry [Miller]'s book very favorably—though I actually think it is pretty foolish. I would never give the swine the satisfaction of saying so. I'll do [Choderlos de] Laclos next. . . .

As for my publication schedule—if I am so hard to sell, why are other publishers so anxious to get me? Dont worry—I am not going to sign any leases on myself. At most I may peddle a few translations of French novels which you dont want anyway. . . .

Things go pretty good here. I am busy—reviews & other hack work—just took on SF correspondence for *Art Digest*. I am trying to organize a lecture-reading tour. . . .

Mary [Rexroth] had an Indian costume and a small rubber—very real—witches mask—just hideous! and trudged along in the Halloween neighborhood parade creating a tremendous sensation. She can draw fish & pumpkins and daddy, count to five and sporadically to ten, read over names, identify the animals of the zoo, the common birds, some flowers and Venus, the Great Bear and The Dog (Sirius). And she is only 25 months!

The 1st issue of *Perspectives* just came & looks very nice. It is certainly a lot less square than the pilot issue. I think you have every right to be proud of a fine job! I have no objections to it—except—the mention of *Witness,* a silly evil book—[Reinhold] Niebuhr—a fascist. Glad to see *The Invisible Man,* a fine book—I recommend it to you. . . .

lots of love
KENNETH

/ · /

Selden: Selden Rodman (1909–), American critic, poet, translator, editor. Rodman's review of KR's *The Signature of All Things,* "Gnomic, Fastidious Verses," appeared in the *New York Herald Tribune.* The popularizer of Haitian primitive art in the United States.

Mort Adler: Mortimer Adler (1902–), American philosopher. Adler served as editor-in-chief for *Encyclopaedia Britannica*'s "Great Ideas" program.

fellow Connecticutian: Chester Bowles, then U.S. Ambassador to India.

my radio review: KR regularly reviewed books on his KPFA Radio program.

Henry's book: Henry Miller's *The Books in My Life* was published by ND in 1952, as was Choderlos de Laclos's *Dangerous Acquaintances.*

Witness: Whittaker Chambers's *Witness,* an account of his years in the American Communist Party, and Ralph Ellison's novel *Invisible Man* were published in 1952.

Niebuhr: Reinhold Niebuhr (1892–1971), American theologian and philosopher.

89. ALS-2   22 IV [19]53
                                               [San Francisco]

DEAR JIM—

I just suggested to Lawrence Lipton, who is the principal author of the Craig Rice books, that he take a try at an article 2000 words on the alienees—[Horace] McCoy, [Chester] Himes ([Ralph] Ellison & [Richard] Wright as disalienating themselves), [Nelson] Algren, [B.] Traven, [Kenneth] Patchen, [Henry] Miller. Nobody seems to know what I want. Alex Comfort could do it—but he says he has never read *any* of the authors except Miller & Patchen. Lipton does, for sure. I have NOT commissioned the article. . . .

Here are 4 [Morris] Graves—I plan to use 4 more from San Francisco. I dont know a good color photographer of paintings (different from just a color photographer) in Seattle . . . *Owl of Inner Eye, Bird with Possessions, Waning Moon, Ever Cycling.* . . .

Just to make you feel good—here's a quote from the letter I wrote just before this to you—"I should say Laughlin was more uninvolved than most. He had a very modest fortune. He gave it all away and

worked hard doing it to make the giving most effective. Now he lives on his salary, doing work he thinks
is of great social benefit. He lives a good deal poorer
than I do far as food, clothing & shelter is concerned. He's a kind of saint in his way."

Just the same, you bastard, you get my royalty
account straight this year.

Mary [Rexroth] sure loves that elephant.

We all loves you, honey

KENNETH

/ · /

Lawrence Lipton: In 1957, Lipton would publish his "Notes Toward an
Understanding of Kenneth Rexroth, with Special Attention to the
Homestead Called Damascus" in *Quarterly Review of Literature* (9,2).

McCoy: Horace McCoy (1897–1955), American journalist, novelist,
screenwriter. During the 1920s much of his fiction appeared in the *Black
Mask,* which featured the "hard-boiled" school.

Himes: Chester Himes (1909–1984), American novelist. His 1945 *If He
Hollers Let Him Go* centers on a black shipyard worker whose dream
of upward mobility is crushed when he is accused of raping a white
woman.

Ellison: Ralph Ellison (1914–), American novelist. Ellison's novel
Invisible Man focuses on the life of a young Black American boy and
his experiences in the Deep South and Harlem.

Wright: Richard Wright (1908–1960), American novelist. Joined the
Communist Party in the 1930s, but left in the 1940s, as recorded in *The
God That Failed* (1950). His *Native Son* (1940) and *The Outsider* (1953)
deal with the social, political, and economic plight of Black Americans.

Algren: Nelson Algren (1909–1981), American novelist. His *The Man
with the Golden Arm,* the story of Frankie Machine (a card dealer with
a heroin habit), won the first National Book Award in 1950. In "Disengagement: The Art of the Beat Generation" *(The Alternative Society),*
KR writes: "At its best, popular literature, coming up, meets highbrow literature coming down. It has been apparent novel by novel that
Nelson Algren is rising qualitatively in this way. In *A Walk on the Wild
Side,* thoroughly popular in its materials, he meets and absorbs influences coming down from the top, from the small handful of bona fide

high-brow writers working today—Céline, Jean Genet, Samuel Beckett, Henry Miller."

4 Graves: Morris Graves (1910–), American painter. In "The Visionary Painting of Morris Graves," which appeared in *Perspectives USA* (Winter 1955; *BB*), KR wrote: "It is none too easy to sum up such an accomplishment as that of Graves. Certainly he is one of the greatest calligraphers of all time. . . . [He] has also been one of the many around the world who in this generation have freed painting from the exhausted plasticism, the concentration on architecture alone, which formed the residue of subsiding Cubism."

90. ALS-4

28 V [19]53
[San Francisco]

DEAR JIM—

Where are my royalties? My God what a cast iron coat wealth is! Dont you understand that I must have the money? . . .

[Selden] Rodman's essay on [Richard] Eberhart at hand, or did I tell you? Unbelievably square. The name Ford certainly postdates these people. Shows what sycophants they really are.

Eberhart's essay on Rexroth for Rodman also at hand. This is a farrago of snobbery, ridicule & patronizing contempt eked out c̄ cheap patrioteering & invocation of Jesus—*and* 50% avid and assiduous disclaimers of any sympathy or identification c̄ such a dangerous & comic character. The real motive is simply that Dick is moving heaven & earth to get [Theodore] Roethke's job another year and is terrified Heiman might offer it to me and so has written, *and already circulated* the article at Washington (mimeo'd) to make sure I am on record as a person no university could tolerate for a minute. The pathetic thing is—the job was offered to me a year ago and I recommended Dick. When I was up there this Spring—it was offered to me again—and I did not want it under any circumstances & saw no reason why Dick should not stay there till Ted came back. I think the portrait of Eberhart the article gives is best not exhibited. He is, usually, a better person by far. As for me—I dont care. There are some minor errors of fact which should be straightened out.

Re / Education. "Never matriculated" does not mean "never attended." I have attended the University of Chicago, The Chicago Art Institute, The Art Students League, a ballet school, The New School for Social Research. Eberhart has some sort of complex about his own lack of a Ph.D. I dont think all this is germane. Neither do I think remarks about my worn furniture or my "iron stove" are germane—what is the Eberhart stove usually made of? Joy beans? Or that "The Village" was 20 years in advance of San Francisco. I was in the Village in 1920—Eberhart was not. Nor is Morris Graves an abstract artist.

Apparently Eberhart is trying to clean his skirts re the Harvard reading. This is all invented and should be cut out. . . .

"America" has not "maintained" me and I have *often* not had enough to eat. All my life I have worked at "jobs"—hard, working class work. When Eberhart met me I was an attendant in the San Francisco psychopathic hospital—I still have the broken back to show for it. What he means is not "job" but "position." I held those too in my young days. I have been a newspaper man, trade journal editor, adv. copy writer & publicity man. I quit this particular kind of whoring young because I saw that no one can live by *writing* and keep his integrity as a writer—not in "our democracy." My ancestors, incidentally, came here in *1680*.

The "segment" of the faculty who disliked my ideas

was a New Critic. . . . What did the *students* think
of me? Fuck the professors.

What has the Charles Eliot Norton Professor's
Funeral in Christ Church Cambridge to do c̄ me?
And of what interest is it an hour's walk away from
the Charles River? Hardly in Europe.

I would like it mentioned that I was one of the
first abstract painters in the USA. That I am now a
Romantic painter. That I have exhibited in Chicago,
New York, Los Angeles, Santa Monica, and several
times in San Francisco, always one man shows. I do
not believe in art juries & never submit paintings to
group shows. I have paintings in many collections
around the country and abroad.

lots of love
KENNETH

/ · /

Eberhart's essay on Rexroth: Richard Eberhart's review of *The Dragon
and the Unicorn* appeared in the *New York Times,* February 15, 1953, in
which Eberhart called KR's style "hard as prose and lithe as lyric."

91. ALS-2   25 IX [19]53
                                         [San Francisco]

DEAR JIM—

You should really begin to think seriously of
resigning from the Ford Foundation job. Soon. While
you can do it c̄ dignity & before you have compro-
mised c̄ everything & everybody you have fought
for all your life. It is absurd to have given your youth
& several hundred thousand dollars away in the

struggle against this evil society in which we live
and then, as you approach 40—to capitulate to it for
a measly $25,000 a year—most of which you have
to spend in "keeping up c̄ the Joneses." . . . Realize
that the Luce publications are probably the most
vicious form the written word has ever taken since
its invention. . . .

Know you are "busy" but every minute snatched
away from what you are now doing to correspond
c̄ your friends shall be credited to you in Heaven
where, on the whole, your time keeper has been using
the other side of the ledger.

faithfully
KENNETH

92. ALS-5

14 IX [19]53
[San Francisco]

DEAR JIM—

. . . As for the Annual. The real thing to get is
modern French poetry. In the USA [Henri] Michaux,
a man in his 60s, passes for the latest thing. I suggest
the Seghers book of selections from all those post-
war booklets of young French poets he has done &
translate a substantial selection. You can print it
anonymously. I dont want my name all over *ND*.
Or—of course—you could get somebody else to do
it & save me work. . . .

Golf!
Golf, indeed . . .
Elderly, that's what you're getting.

Love & kisses
KENNETH

/ · /

Michaux: ND published Henri Michaux's travel book, *A Barbarian in Asia,* in 1949, and *The Selected Writings, The Space Within* (trans. by Richard Ellmann) in 1951. A selection of his work had appeared in Seghers *Poètes d'aujourd'hui* series in 1949.

93. TLS-1   May 10, 1954

[Tokyo]

DEAR KENNETH,

Well, here I am in Japan, and it is very fascinating, a bit harder to grasp, I think, than any of the other countries where I have been.

I'm sorry that you are not here to see it with me, but, as you will doubtless have grasped, I no longer have much to say about a lot of things. The collection of material from Japan is being done by a group of earnest young men who are out here on Ford grants through the Board of Overseas Training. . . .

Yesterday morning I went out to see [Katue] Kitasono. He is a nice guy, a rather tired looking little fellow, but most friendly. He is the librarian for a dental college but has his poetry group and magazine on the side. We sat in his tiny parlor, on the floor, which I am gradually getting used to, sipping tea, and mostly just smiling, as he speaks no English. The little wife knows quite a few words, however, and with her dictionary we were able at least to exchange a few amenities. Unlike most Japanese houses which are starkly empty, he had his books piled around him, and the general feeling was not too different from your place or the one Ez[ra Pound] used to have in Rapallo. Outside it was raining to beat the band, pouring down into his little garden, just a few yards of space between his house and the board fence. It is sad that it is so difficult to communicate. The language barrier is a big one. Apart from Nisei, most of the Japanese I have met just can't speak English at all, though some of them have French or German. This seems to me an only natural resistance to the occupation. All these soldiers around make me feel very uncomfortable. It is quite clear, through the politeness, that the Japs all just want us to go home and leave them alone. As one man put it to me, a rich textile factory owner who certainly has much to lose if the Reds take over here, they would rather just be Asians and suffer their fate, no matter how bad it may be, than be under the heel of the Whites.

I shall be here about a month—hope to make some trips to the old cities and the country and mountains—and then coming through San Francisco about June 7th. Will you be there? I wish there were time to make a trip in the mountains but I have to rush back to New York to be liquidated. These past months have been a respite from all that horror in New York, except that the letters come through to plague me. . . .

As ever

J I M

/ · /

young men: The editor of the *Perspectives* of Japan was Faubion Bowers, formerly a wartime aide and interpreter for MacArthur. According to JL, "Intercultural's 'outflow' project was *Perspectives*, in English, French, German, and Italian; the 'inflow' were the 'country perspectives' which we planted in the *Atlantic*, quicker than trying to build up independent circulation. There were about 10 of these: India, Brazil, Italy, Indonesia, Japan, Holland, and etc. Along about 1957, when Bob Hutchins had been booted out of the Foundation, I was also very politely 'discontinued' with a nice golden handshake of half a million to let Intercultural's projects taper off. Actually I was glad to be done with it. When Hutchins was running the Foundation I could do anything I wanted to do, but when he was out, there was endless groupthink:

reports, meetings, etc. And no real interest in cultural affairs" (letter to the editor).

Kitasono: Katue Kitasono (1902–1987; given name, Kenkichi Hashimoto), Japanese avant-garde poet. His extended correspondence with EP is collected in *Ezra Pound and Japan: Letters & Essays,* edited by Sanehide Kodama.

94. ALS-2   May 20, 1954
                                                      [Tokyo]

DEAR KENNETH—

   Well, you really do seem to be in one of your foul and ugly moods again! You ought to be ashamed of yourself. What is the use of all your philosophical learning if you can't accept your fate and be even-tempered? Poets before you have had to wait for fame, and some don't get it ever. You complain that you only got $14 in royalties, but [William] Everson, who some years doesn't even get a dollar, doesn't make scenes, nor does Vernon Watkins, who for 2 years had more returns than sales and got nothing. There is no good your saying it is my fault or Bob [MacGregor]'s. We fill every order we get from the stores or libraries. But we can't *make* them take books their customers don't ask for. Really, you make me tired. It never seems to bother you whether I get back what it costs to print your books, let alone the cost of distributing them. Well—get along with you— go find yourself another publisher if you want to. I will always be around if you really need me, but I'm tired of taking your endless bad manners. Bob MacGregor is a finer, better, honester person than you are, who has gone out of his way to try to help you, and you ought to be ashamed of yourself to keep running him down. You are just off your head. . . .

Now you get yourself a little enlightenment up in those mountains and stop acting like a crazy. I admit that I have been annoying with the delays over the Jap poems, but if you would just be honest for once you would realize that there have been compensating factors. But I'm not going to go on turning the other cheek much longer. Or rather, I am just going to disappear on you till you stop being so disagreeable.

Love to all
J I M

/ · /

Vernon Watkins: (1906–), Welsh poet. ND published Watkins's *Selected Poems* in 1948 and Dylan Thomas's *Letters to Vernon Watkins* in 1957.

Bob MacGregor: "A wonderful publisher. He founded Theater Arts Books. I got him in to run ND while I was working for Ford and then he stayed on and became a valuable right hand" (JL letter to the editor).

95. ALS-6

21 VIII [19]54
[San Francisco]

DEAR J IM—

. . . I do not want to stress [Morris] Graves' "symbolism" in the first place, it is *not* Oriental, but personal and *very* odd. "Whatdoes it now pillar apart" is not a question from anything—just Graves' jabberwocky. There is a rather silly quotation from Graves accompanying it in the catalog of the Bronze painting, which Mrs. Willard showed some years back & which did Morris incalculable harm. *Time* had a hilarious time c̄ it! PLEASE forget all this crap. You must realize that painters are just like poets— their verbalizations of their performances are about as reliable as Dylan [Thoma]s' or [Richard] Eberhart's. Also—modern people just think all their Vedanta etc. is crazy. Use the pictures I talk about which are discussed for their virtues as paintings and not as illustrations of Morris' goofy, homemade interpretations of the Mystic East, about which, incidentally, he knows practically nothing. For God's sake keep Mrs. Willard at arm's length. This is just not capriciousness—I cannot go into Morris' "philosophy" s̄ making him ridiculous, for the simple reason that it is intrinsically ridiculous as well as being not just ill informed but positively ignorant. I implore you not to go off on this tangent—I tried to make Morris respectable as a *plastic artist*—which he certainly is. All this Alone to the Alone crap is what has kept him from being appreciated on his real merits instead of as the spokesman of "West Coast Occultism." That damn Woman at Delphic, who used to be my dealer, did the same thing to [José] Orozco &: it took years for her swami propaganda to wither away. . . .

A "vajra" incidentally is a ritual bronze instrument; "The Diamond Club" a symbolic thunderbolt, derived from Hinduism, where it is an appurtenance of the sky deities, primarily Indra but also Garuda and even Shiva. It is much more common in Buddhism where it is an aspect of several Tantric or Lamaist Buddhas and Bodhisattvas, for instance Vajrapavi, and is often carried by others in their "fierce" aspects. It exists as an actual thing, a small bronze made with usually four bent prongs, sometimes five, nine, or even one, held by monks, especially those of the Tantrist sects, like Japanese Shingon, during meditation. In some monasteries it is a symbol of office. In whole or half it is often used as an ornament or finial, especially on the bells which are rung during the chanting of sutras. In this form it is a fairly common piece of Oriental bric à brac in the West.

The painting which you ask about is called "Ceremonial Bronze Taking the Form of a Bird." There is a note by Morris in the catalog—you must realize that these "explanations" are intentionally misleading. I know what he means—but I dont think it advisable to publish—it would just lead to mockery. Briefly—the minnow is the beginning spark of spiritual illumination—The "Inner Light" "scintilla animae" the Scholastics called it—both "illumination" & the primary impulse of the ethical will. The bronze is pseudo person—a "kammi" as the Japanese call it & a great work of art which is so powerful that it becomes a "deity" (a lesser being than a man, because unable to escape from the karmaic flux) (the background of my crane—or of the dragon painters). The bird is the fully achieved form of the kami or deva as manifest to us. Birds, says Morris, are devas, men are bodhisattvas. All beings eventually become Buddhas—but only by turning away from karma. The beginning of & this whole process is represented in this picture. Just as it is represented in the Noh play *Ka Kitsubata*, where the spirit of the iris is "saved."

KENNETH

/ · /

I do not want: This discussion centers on KR's Graves essay for *Perspectives USA*. See letter 89.

Orozco: José Clemente Orozco (1883–1949), Mexican artist.

96. ALS-14

10 III [19]55
[San Francisco]

DEAR JIM—

Ruth Witt Diamant, professor at SF State College, is going to put in an application to [Clarence] Faust for some dough for the Poetry Center. This semester McLeod (Norman) is teaching at the school—he has a notice of termination & will *not* be there in the Fall. Meanwhile he is busy representing himself as a very important piece of cheese. He is not. The Center was my idea and the work including putting up the poets at her house (including Dylan & Caitlin [Thomas]!!!) has been entirely Witt Diamant's. So if anybody asks you, dont put the quietus on it because of Norman because he ain't it. As a matter of fact Dick Moore is on the local educational TV station which is moving to the college & enlarging itself and the probability is he will help Ruth next Fall. But in any case it would be the white haired terror of the gutters of Bohemia. I *do* hope you will help any way you can to get a little dough for Ruth. She is a perfectly reliable middle aged woman & absolutely devoted to the Center. She has already made it a much superior thing to the YMHA. We've had & are having this Spring [W. H.] Auden, [Stephen] Spender, [Dylan] Thomas, [Theodore] Roethke, Rexroth, [Allen] Tate, [Karl] Shapiro, W. C. W[illia]ms. Next Fall starts off c̄ Lou[ise] Bogan. This is all on the other side of the country. In addition Ruth acts as a booking agent & gets them all a circuit tour in the Coast & Intermountain colleges. Tate is due here the 17th on an Easter vacation tour that will make him a nice piece of dough if it dont kill him. I really dont know how we got it all packed in. We made Auden a couple of thousand dollars. This is so to speak a separate letter from the following pages. There is nothing in this for me—I dont want academic work. . . .

I wrote Henry [Miller] & suggested he delete that business about the 11 year old girl going down on them & then submit it to you. What in the hell did he put it in for—just to be difficult? You know I am the only person who talks turkey to him. By an oversight he sent me his latest begging letter & I bawled the shit out of him. I've always wanted to—I think he & [Kenneth] Patchen foul the nest of letters. Patchen has some excuse—he is *much* sicker, by the way—but Henry has none. . . . His poverty has always been imaginary—in Paris he worked steady on the H-T—which didnt keep him from gobbling the contents of Anaïs [Nin]'s purse as well as the rat gnawed muff & cadging everbody met. [Hilaire] Hiler once threw him downstairs. Still Plexus is a good book. Age has slowed him down but it is still better than almost anything else in the way of prose fiction likely to be published in the decade it appears. I think if you promote it as a hotty-part of the Rosy Crucifixion along c̄ the banned-in-Paris Sexus & just like the Tropics you may sell some & reinstate poor old Hank c̄ the young. You sure did his reputation & yourself as a publisher a disservice c̄ all that dismal crap you did print. Aint you never heard of Gresham's law? . . .

I think you are seeing trees instead of woods in the nonEuropean literature question. You must realize that you are witnessing the development of a world culture—but a very uneven altho highly accelerated development. Colonial & subcolonial countries have got to develop a really critical assimilation—a digestion c̄ organic acceptance & rejection of the vast material of Western Culture. So—the nearer they are to the bushes, like Africa, or to an alien older culture—the more they have to rely on what teacher says—even tho they go to Oxford to hear teacher. Muslims of course are awful square anyway—19th & 20th century literature is dominated by Baudelaire, Dostoyevsky, Whitman, Melville, etc. etc.—it is a literature of rejection of the official culture. In the Muslim world there is simply no social mechanism of rejection & nothing in the society to make one out of. Again, of course, never forget that in any acculturation process assimilation & revolt go hand in hand & begin c̄ the deracinated. A highly civilized mandarin or a successful witch doctor does not "revolt" against western civilization—he just ignores it. It is the houseboy who was a foundling educated by missionaries who reads Herbert Spencer, Engels and Sartre and butchers his employers in their sleep or becomes a professor at London University. The process is a long and painful one—the American Negro—the largest body of original settlers left in the USA—is only now beginning to write & paint on a parity c̄ the white population. Between you & me American Negro literature prior to War II is mostly in the performing dog & calculating horse class. One reason is that the most intelligent members of the upcoming race are always too busy laying the foundations of a culture—conquering, their own careers, the essentials. You've got to have a lot of Negro doctors & engineers before you can have good Negro painters & poets. Music of course does not require education or status for its appreciation & so the Negro quickly became the best American musicians, bar none. Dont forget, too, that there was no literary tradition in Africa S. of the Sahara at all—and Muslim culture & Indian too—is so antagonistic to Western European that a crossing

of the two has yet to prove fertile. Just read Hafiz or
Rumi or the *Ramayana*—this is a world unknown to
Aristotle!

The Chinese of course are far closer to us—there
the problem has been due to the sudden collapse of
absolute resistance. . . . Even as sophisticated a man
as Hu Shih was writing bad imitations of Browning
only 20 years ago. Mao Tse's famous poem is a very
impressive combination of tradition, modern real-
ism & imagism, & Marxist revocation—it really is
one of China's great poems—in addition—the great
cities—especially Shanghai—had bred a whole crop
of young decadents—mostly homosexuals—who
were evolving a modern, rather weary poetry which
is still in the main line of development of Chinese
verse & was rather better than anything to appear in
a long time—since the Ming Dynasty probably. Of
course Mao is not the only Communist poet—just
the most famous—others were very good. None of
them owed much to Russian examples, by the way.

Too much is made of the resemblance of Japanese
literature to modern French. The Japanese were doing
it first. Proust can't come near the *Tale of Genji*—on
his own ground. Similarly—the Cubist poets—Reverdy—Cocteau—probably owe as much to Japanese—via Judith Gautier, etc. as Katue [Kitasono]
owes to them. Similarly the more imagistic or
objectivist surrealist poets are full of tricks which were
old in Japan before [Jean] Racine. Again—black bile
was a natural expression of Japan's predicament &
the trap which was closing in on her writers in the
first quarter of this century. The older generation
. . . are saturated c̄ "spleen" because they lived in a
very splenetic world. And if you dont think Post
War II Japan is in the situation existentialist you better look again. But—to speak of somebody you
know—Katue sounds like Reverdy c̄ a dose of Bre-

ton & lots of despair—but he would have to write pretty much like that if France had never existed. You must realize that Japan is *not* a colonial or sub-colonial country—and it proved utterly impossible to make her one in the decade 1945–55.

As for Europe—there doesnt seem to be anybody left in Germany & not much in France. If Surrealism was the art of the 4Fs of War I—what do you think survived War II? You can't crop 2 generations down to the roots & expect a field of Homers. If you want to know what's wrong with French literature, go into the churches on Toussaint & see the crowds weeping for their dead sons & husbands. And this is the 2nd time around. The Italians of course enjoyed a brief flurry living thru the period from 1925 to 1945 that Mussolini had robbed them of—at a vastly accelerated pace. Now that they have caught up c̄ the 20th century it turns out they have nothing to say.

And finally—never forget that nobody under 35 in Europe, England or America expects to be alive in 10 years. They hate our generation as a gang of cold blooded murderers out to destroy them, our-selves, and the solar system. If they tell you different they are deliberately lying to you. This attitude is not conducive to the fine Hellenic line—it is better for the heroin trade—literature after all is a kind of responsibility—and what is there left to be respon-sible for?

That's your briefing ref *[ND]* #15! My good-ness—I wrote that all in an hour! . . .

> Love & kisses.
> Wear your rubbers when it's nasty
> KENNETH

/ · /

Faust: Clarence Faust was the president of an independent grantee organization of the Ford Foundation, the Fund for the Advancement of Education.

Poetry Center: According to KR, "Another remote by-product of [the Libertarian Circle's] activities was the San Francisco Poetry Center. Robert Stock and his small circle of friends migrated to New York so we reabsorbed his poetry readings. Although our audiences were quite large, we felt that the place—The Workman's Circle—and the auspices—or Libertarian Circle—definitely limited the audience. Madeline Gleason, Robert Duncan, and I decided to move the readings to the small auditorium at San Francisco State College which was then downtown. In the course of time, we were able to get poets of national reputation. For these readings we charged admission and paid the poets. A faculty member, Ruth Witt-Diamant, was very interested and facilitated our use of the State College facilities. Eventually she took over most of the planning and administration" *(Excerpts).*

McLeod: Norman McLeod (1906–1985), American poet, novelist. McLeod worked as assistant director of the Poetry Center, 1954–55.

Richard Moore: Produced "Poetry U.S.A." film series for National Educational Television; included interviews with Everson, Snyder, McClure, and Whalen among others.

Lou Bogan: Louise Bogan (1897–1970), American poet and critic.

Herbert Spencer: (1820–1903), British philosopher; Spencer's system of thought was based on evolutionary theory. "In Lafcadio Hearn and Buddhism" *(WOTW),* KR writes: "It is not Spencer's Darwinism, red tooth and claw, but Spencer's metaphysical and spiritual speculations that have influenced Hearn's interpretation of Buddhism. We must not forget that Teilhard de Chardin, who certainly is not out of date, is, in the philosophical sense, only Herbert Spencer sprinkled with holy water."

Engels: Friedrich Engels (1820–1895), German Socialist writer; collaborated with Marx on *The German Ideology,* the *Manifesto of the Communist Party,* and *Das Kapital.*

Hafiz: Shams ud-din Muhammad Hafiz (d. c. 1390), Persian poet, philosopher. His primary work, the *Divan,* is a collection of short lyrics called *ghazals.*

Rumi: Jalal ud-din Rumi (1207–1273), Persian poet and mystic.

the Ramayana: An Indian epic dealing with the life and adventures of Rama and his wife Sita.

Hu Shih: (1891–1962), Chinese scholar, diplomat, poet.

Browning: Robert Browning (1812–1889), British poet. In "The Art of Literature" *(WOTW),* KR writes of "multiple-aspect narrative . . . first perfected in the verse novels of Robert Browning, in fact reached its most extreme development in the English language in poetry: Ezra Pound's *Cantos*, T. S. Eliot's *The Waste Land*, William Carlos Williams' *Paterson*, and the many long poems influenced by them."

Mao Tse: Mao Tse-tung (1893–1976), Chairman of the Chinese Communist Party, 1943–76, of which he was a founding member. Wrote about forty poems (most in the tz'u form) in classical meters.

Reverdy: In 1969, ND published KR's translation of Pierre Reverdy's *Selected Poems*. In his introduction, KR writes: "Of all modern poets in Western European languages Reverdy has certainly been the leading influence on my own work—probably more than anyone in English or American. . . . He seeks, as all Cubists did, to present the spectator with a little organism that will take up all experience brought to it, digest it, reorganize it and return it as the aesthetic experience unadulterated."

Racine: Jean Racine (1639–1699), French playwright.

97. ALS-2

31 III [19]55
[San Francisco]

DEAR JIM—

Here are some sample poems of Denise [Levertov]'s. She has a lot of stuff, including her English book which should be excerpted. If you want me to I will do the selecting & editorial work & blurb the book—as well as review it . . . I have written to her to send you some poems—not a whole book. . . .

I think someday you should have an article on jazz *and* "race records"—now called "R&B"—rhythm & blues—this is the bobby sox music craze now & has even reached *Time* this week. This is something I've been urging on you since the start. Nobody knows much about this except me—jazz people call it "jump music" and despise it.

Love & kisses. Faithfully
KENNETH

/ · /

Denise: Denise Levertov (1923–). Of Levertov, JL writes: "As a technician, Denise has the gift that Williams had for knowing where to break the line. . . . When my own students [at Brown] ask me about 'organic form' I always urge them to read her 'Notes on Organic Form.' It is the clearest statement I know on the poetic structure which now informs so much of the best contemporary poetry" *(AP).* In *Conjunctions,* KR: "Denise is probably the best American poet at the moment. I feel that all these atoms and cosmic rays and all these vibrations of the modern world are doing something to the male of the human species, and most good poetry today is written by women." ND would become Levertov's primary American publisher. "The Springtime" was her first contribution to the *ND* Annual (16, 1957), and soon Levertov became a frequent contributor; her first ND volume was *With Eyes at the Back of Our Heads,* published in 1960.

an article on jazz: KR's own "Jazz Poetry" appeared in the *Nation* (March 29, 1958; *WOTW*). In *SFP,* KR argues: "You discover that jazz audiences don't know shit from wild honey . . . and that includes a lot of the musicians. . . . They didn't know what 12 / 8 was, but they dug the 12 / 8 which was the essence of Jimmy Yancey, of boogie-woogie. Yet they didn't know it was Latin music. Dig? They were jazz habitués. In the Five Spot at least one night a week. That's one of the things that's heartbreaking about jazz."

98. TLS-2

April 6, 1955
[New York]

DEAR KENNETH,

Please forgive my delay in answering several recent letters. I have been very busy rewriting material and reading proofs on our "Perspectives of Greece." . . .

You didn't enclose the snapshot you wrote about of Mary [Rexroth] being confirmed as a Buddhist. I would certainly like to see that. I find it a very touching idea. . . .

Now about the first chapter of the novel that you sent in—I really don't know what to say about this, and wish you could do a little bit more so that I could get more the feel of the thing. It seems to me

that it is rather self-conscious and that the tone wav-
ers. There is a considerable disparity in style between
the descriptions of nature and of the girl. It seems to
me that you are falling between two stools, so to
speak—the way you would write it if you were
pleasing yourself, and the way you would write if
you were simply trying to do something that would
sell in the Gold Medal series. I will ask Bob
[MacGregor] to have a look at it and see what he
thinks, and then let you know further. But the best
would be if you could crank out another chapter so
that I could get more of the drift of the thing and the
feel of how it is to go. The idea for the plot sounds
good. . . .

As ever

J

99. ALS-2   8 IV [19]55
                                            [San Francisco]

DEAR JIM—

. . . I think Denise [Levertov] is at least as good
as Jean Garrigue—whom you did publish. And she
is certainly the best of the jeunesse. Otherwise you're
left c̄ Cid Corman & Chris Bjerknes & that's about
all. As for not having "much effect" on you—I honestly think you have been so conditioned by the good
ole fort under the Stars & Bars run by Marse Allen
[Tate] & Con'l [J. C.] Ransom and been taken in by
imposters like [Robert] Cal Lowell—who would
never have been printed if his name warnt spelled el
oh doubleyou ee el el—that you surely are inaccessible to poetry by young people. I will never forgive
you for paying for a cocktail party in Americanitaly

by publishing Wm J. Smith—who cant write home to mother. . . .

faithfully
KENNETH

Happy Easter to you & your children who seem to be c̄ you.

/ · /

Cid Corman: (1924–), American poet, editor of *Origin.* ND published Corman's *Livingdying* in 1970.

Chris Bjerknes: American poet. Bjerknes's *First Communion* appeared in 1954.

100. Airletter. ALS

1 VII [19]55
S[an] F[rancisco]

DEAR JIM—

Just to give you the terrible news that—as far as anybody knows—since he left no note & his body was not found—Weldon [Kees] threw himself off the Golden Gate Bridge last week.

We all saw it coming—but what can you do? Anne was in a mental hospital most of the winter and is still very psychotic—what has happened to her since this I dont know, they were separated.

Isnt it awful, this world we live in?

c̄ love
KENNETH

/ · /

Weldon: Weldon Kees (1914–1955), American poet, short story writer, editor. Had appeared in *ND* annuals (4,5,6, and 8). Of Kees, KR wrote in *APTC*, "He was a profoundly moving poet, playwright, and painter, and an influence on the early days of the formation of the group in San Francisco."

101. ALS-4

DEAR JIM—

Your pal—fellow statesman John Marshall was out here in his pinstripe suit. Do you *honestly* think an educational institution which breeds an absolutely uniform adolescent type and jinxes that type unchangeably for life is an educational institution? Dont you think you might be well advised to, come New Years, resolve *never* to enter the portals of the Harvard Club again? Anyway—I guess he is going to set up the Poetry Center for 3 years c̄ a small revolving grant. I do not think it is enough and advised refusing it but Ruth Witt-Diamant of course was all for gettin what she could and Dean Bell and President Leonard thought it wasn't worth any more trouble & effort. It wont expand much—but at least it is absolutely sure of continuing on the present level. For the coming years we are having Louise Bogan, Dick Eberhart, Malcolm Cowley and if possible a furriner—first choice Larry Durrell, 2nd René Char, 3rd (or 1st, except that it is most unlikely he could come) [Hugh] MacDiarmid, 4th Edwin Muir. We planned to ask [Herbert] Read but it seems to be pretty well agreed by people who've seen him lately he is getting senile, and *most* uninteresting.

Is [Juan Ramon] Jimenez still alive in NYC? He is probably the best living Spanish poet likely to get in the USA—the others are Stalinoid—e.g. [Raphael] Alberti, [Pablo] Neruda. If he is still alive he must be quite old. Let me know any possible visiting Elks. The trouble c̄ all these activities—The Poetry Center, KPFA, etc.—is that they take an immense amount of work on my part, and I am the one who never gets *any* money out of them whatever.

I think Miriam [Patchen]'s collapse really threw quite a fright into Marshall. He went white at the words "multiple sclerosis"—as well he might. It is a horrifying situation. It is certainly the final argument for the setting up of a USA Civil List or Privy Purse. I should think all these Foundations could create a small pool to which they all could contribute & which could be administered by a small staff—one person & a secretary would be enough and which could be advised by everybody. . . . The Patchens are very surely going to need to be supported the rest of their lives.

I was highly amused the way Marshall seemed to think he was really out in the sticks c̄ the weed monkeys. . . . My treatment consisted of being told first that his—Marshall's—best friend had been Jack Wheelwright and *then* that he thot John Berryman the best "young" poet and Eleanor Clark the best proser! He was utterly unaware of the existence of a living avant garde. The people young people talk about—[Jean] Genet, [Samuel] Beckett, the late Céline, [Antonin] Artaud, [Jack] Kerouac, the bonefide little magazines (e.g. *Origin, Golden Goose, Black Mt Review,* etc) even [Charles] Olson, [Robert] Creeley, Denise [Levertov] and the rest—he actually did not have the slightest inkling suspicion that this world existed.

Some time ago Malcolm [Cowley] said that "most poets under 50 are now teaching in colleges" & I answered "you are the victim of a bow tie conspiracy, the *only* poet of my generation who teaches is Dick Eberhart and that is because he is a pure natural

and doesnt know any better." I told this to Marshall
& he looked very funny and said "Malcolm repeated
this exactly, without mentioning its source, when I
sent him a list of what I considered the most prom-
ising young writers in America." He named some of
them for me & I said I thought they were not writers
at all but petty Fascist politicians. It is easy to see
what is happening—a Rockefeller-Ford-Guggen-
heim-Mellon Potemkin village is being erected.
Hundreds of academic bed pissers c̄ literally billions
to put them across. And absolute utter stark igno-
rance on the part of the expert advisors of what is
actually going on inside American culture—which
of course is 100% rejection and disaffiliation. Just
incidentally this is what went on in 18th century
France and pre 1918 Russia—except that the alienees
at least got printed.

You know all this shit is just a nice way for the
3rd and 4th generation rich to exploit not just the
Bahrein Arabs and the Standard Station attendants
and the workers at River Rouge and Butte and Pittsburgh—but *me*. What guys like Marshall are doing
are living on *me*, not vice versa. I hope you enjoy it.
The night of the Long Knives is bound to come.

Love & kisses

KENNETH

/ · /

John Marshall: In *Excerpts,* KR writes: "After the Poetry Center was
well under way, operating quite without income, John Marshall of the
Rockefeller Foundation paid us his periodic visit, looking for culture
to patronize. We immediately sold him on the Poetry Center. Marthe
was secretary to the administrative Dean of the State College and was
expert at drawing up grant applications. Marshall went to lunch with
Ruth Witt-Diamant. When he came back to our apartment in the after-
noon to go over the grant application with Marthe, he said, 'How
about this Witt-Diamant lady? Do you think she'll make a good
administrator?' I said, 'Why don't you quit the Rockefeller Foundation

and run the San Francisco Poetry Center?' He said, 'I wouldn't dream of it.' I said, 'I wouldn't dream of it either. Ruth wants to do it, she's enthusiastic, knowledgeable, perfectly competent. . . .' So it was set up to flourish to this day although its great days are in the past due to the deterioration of contemporary poetry and decline in funds. For a few years we had everybody from William Carlos Williams to Dylan Thomas."

Larry Durrell: Reviewing Lawrence Durrell in 1957, KR wrote: "I enjoy Durrell's poetry more than that of anybody else anywhere near his age now writing in the British Isles. . . . It is a poetry of tone, the communication of the precise quality of a very precious kind of revery-animalism and skeptic faith." By 1960, he would write of Durrell's fiction: "What had been complex and subtle and ironic turned into something flimsy, schematic and flashy" ("Lawrence Durrell," *Assays*).

René Char: (1907–), French poet. Selections from his work appeared in *ND* annuals 5, 10, and 14.

Read: Sir Herbert Read (1893–1968), British art and literary critic, poet. In addition to *The Green Child,* which KR introduced, ND published his *Phases of English Poetry* and *Collected Poems* (with Faber & Faber) in 1951.

Jimenez: Juan Ramon Jimenez (1881–1958), Spanish poet.

Alberti: Rafael Alberti (1902–), Spanish poet, painter. ND published his *Selected Poems* in 1944. A friend of García Lorca and a Communist spokesman during the Spanish Civil War, Alberti went into exile in 1939 in Argentina. He returned to Spain in 1977 as a member of the Cortes.

KPFA: KPFA Radio station. According to KR *(Excerpts),* "I will never forget the night that Lew Hill, who had been the director of the Committee for Conscientious Objectors in Washington, showed up unannounced at a large meeting [of the Libertarian Circle]. He presented what was really a very simple thesis. There had been a great structural change in society and the days of street meetings and little pamphlets were over. New, far more effective means of communication were available. It was comparatively easy and inexpensive to set up a cooperatively run listener-sponsored FM radio station whose signal would cover at least the entire Bay Area, which could be supported by subscriptions without any commercials. . . . At first a large share of the money came from well-to-do Quakers and other religious pacifists. None came from the rich Communist fellow travelers of which there were dozens in the Bay Area. Eventually my friend John Marshall, the cultural administrator of the Rockefeller Foundation, arranged a grant that would finally total more than two hundred and fifty thousand dollars." In *SFP,* KP continues: "The station was devoted to the reeducation of its audience on what you might call libertarian principles. There was a constant dose of poetry, for instance. . . . The first tapes

Dylan Thomas ever made. I was in England immediately after the war and taped readings and interviews and sent them back to San Francisco. These things were priceless. David Gascoyne, Dylan, Henry Treece, Alex Comfort, Herbert Read, and George Woodcock . . . discussions with the whole English anarchist circle. We kept pumping in stuff from all over, in German, in English, in French. . . . For years and years, Alan Watts and I were back-to-back on Sunday. Alan was handing out the Sunday sermon. . . . KPFA has given hundreds of programs in the past twenty years on the ecological crisis. And I, on my own program, have never let up on it."

Genet: Jean Genet (1910–1986), French novelist, playwright. KR: "Genet we can lay on the side—he has always seemed to me a one-man rubberneck bus of the sins of Paris, an up-to-date and conscienceless Eugène Sue" ("Revolt: True and False," *WOTW*).

Beckett: Samuel Beckett (1906–1989). Irish playwright, poet. He contributed to ND's 1962 Symposium on Joyce, *Our Exagmination Round His Factification for Incamination of Work in Progress*. Nobel Prizewinner.

Céline: Louis-Ferdinand Destouches (1894–1961), French novelist. KR: "We can, if we confine ourselves to the two great novels, forgive Céline for being an anti-Semite" ("The Hasidism of Martin Buber," *BB*). In *PR,* JL remembers: "Céline I met once. I went out to see him when he was living in Meudon, an industrial suburb of Paris near the Renault plant. He had a small house and outside it there was a high barbed-wire fence. He had two very fierce dogs that barked at me when I rang the gate bell. He had to come out and tie up the dogs. He had them because Denoël, his publisher, had been murdered on a street in Paris. Denoël had been a collaborator, too. Céline was rather paranoid, but he was friendly to me. I had had contact with his wife, who was a ballet dancer. While they were in exile in Denmark during the war, she couldn't get ballet shoes for her practice. So she used to write to me and I'd go down to Capezio in New York to buy her ballet shoes and air-mail them over to her." ND published Céline's *Death on the Installment Plan* (trans. by John H. P. Marks, 1947), *Journey to the End of Night* (trans. by John H. P. Marks, 1949), and *Guignol's Band* (trans. by Bernard Frechtman and Jack T. Nile, 1954). According to JL, "The Marks translations of *Death* and *Journey,* first published by Little, Brown, had been Bowdlerized for the rough slang. We had new ones done by Ralph Manheim some time later" (letter to the editor).

Kerouac: Jack Kerouac (1922–1969), American novelist. A central figure of the Beat Generation, with such novels as *On the Road* (1957), *The Dharma Bums* (1948), and *The Subterraneans* (1958). ND published excerpts from Kerouac's *Visions of Cody* in a limited signed edition in 1960. There were contributions to *ND* 16 and 17. KR was an early supporter of Kerouac's, though very soon he would become disillusioned with the novelist. In *Jack's Book* (New York, 1978), Allen Ginsberg describes the first meeting of the two writers: "I once went to Rexroth's salon with Jack. Rexroth had read his work, knew of his reputation, admired him a great deal, had said that he was the greatest unpublished writer in America. Or maybe he told that to Cowley, maybe that's where Cowley got it. Jack was a little drunk and, unless I'm mistaken, was sitting on the floor laughing, and Rexroth got upset that Jack was going to wake his baby—his daughter—and got mad at him, called him a son of a bitch and ordered him out."

In *SF*, KR recalls: "I have always said that the greatest shock Kerouac ever got in his life was when he walked into my house, sat down in a kind of stiff-legged imitation of a lotus posture, and announced he was a Zen Buddhist, and then discovered everyone in the room knew at least one Oriental language." According to Ginsberg *(Jack's Book)*, "Later, '58 or so, or whenever it was *Mexico City Blues* came out [1959], Rexroth wrote a really damning, terrible *[New York Times]* review saying that this form of poetry separated the men from the boys, and Kerouac was obviously a boy and couldn't write, and it was a disgrace that he would present this book in public." Kerouac's Reinhold Cacoethes *(The Dharma Bums)* is modeled on KR.

Olson: Charles Olson (1910–1970), American poet, essayist; rector of Black Mountain College, 1951–56. Olson's work appeared in three *ND* annuals: 12, 13, and 30. Though Olson's essay "Projective Verse" and his epic poem *Maximus* were extremely influential, in *APTC* KR writes: "What his theories sum up to really is the objectivism of Louis Zukofsky and William Carlos Williams and a prosody based on the cadence, the breath strophe, whether natural or induced by unconventional breaks in the line. There is nothing here that was not in H.D. The test is practice, and in practice Olson turns out to have had a heavy and conventional ear."

Creeley: Robert Creeley (1926–), American poet, fiction writer, essayist. A substantial selection of Creeley's work appeared in *ND* 13, introduced by Olson; ND published a number of Creeley's collections in the 1970s and 1980s, including *Memory Gardens* and *Later*. KR: "There are certain American poets, like Robert Lowell or Robert Creeley, whose work is haunted by anxiety, but this is, in each case, an individual psychological problem and very far from a judgement as to the meaning of life" ("Why Is American Poetry Culturally Deprived?" *The Alternative Society*).

102. ALS-2

5 X [19]55

[San Francisco]

DEAR JIM—

  Maybe I was too sharp about that Dharmapada— just dont say that it is the words of the Buddha. It is a sort of omnium gatherum from all sorts of sources—something like the O.T. Book of Proverbs—sentiments & "proverbs" and apothegms which could be assimilated to Buddhism on a popular level. The great trouble c̄ Buddhism—and c̄ Buddha himself—assuming that the most primitive layers of the Pali Texts represent him—is that Buddhism is essentially, almost exclusively, a religion for monks. The Dharmapada was probably the first attempt . . . to give Hinayana a "mass base" of some significance to the masses who were being asked to do the basing—that is—support the monks and nuns. As such it served the same purpose as the Lotus and the Diamond [Sutra] in Mahayana (it is of course itself a Mahayana text too) and as such has incomparably more ethical content than either of those sutras—or selection of sutras—in modern times, especially in Japan, and in NeoBuddhism in the West & back once more in India—it is very popular. Sects like the Japanese Shin . . . once very far from the ethical directness and simplicity of the Dharmapada, now use it for teaching "Sunday school" and even chant it antiphonally in congregational worship. But dont forget that this congregation activity is directly patterned on Xtianity and was unknown only a few years ago. Actually I know of no single document which gives more of the feeling—the sentiment—of what must have been the uniquely *immediate* personality of the historic Sakyamuni & which perfumes even the most remote & "decadent" Mahayana & Amidist Sutras—but which of course in these cases has to be disentangled. Here it all is set out for those to whom the further reaches of Buddhism are incomprehensible.

love
KENNETH

/ · /

that Dharmapada: ND published the twelve page *Selected Verses from the Dhammapada* (trans. by N. K. Bhagwat) in 1955.

103. ALS-2

12 X [19]55
S[an] F[rancisco]

DEAR JIM—

. . . I MC'd a reading at the 6 Gallery last Friday. Allen Ginsberg read a terrific poem—a real jeremiad of unbelievable volume—"This is what you have done to my generation." When he finished the audience of 250 stood and clapped & cheered and wept . . .

Love
K R & family

/ · /

Allen Ginsberg: (1926–), American poet. JL published work by Ginsberg in *ND* 14, 16, and 17. Of the Six Gallery reading, in *Jack's Book,* Ginsberg recalled: "The Six Gallery reading had come about when Wally Hedrick, who was a painter and one of the major people there, asked Rexroth if he knew any poets that would put on a reading. Maybe Rexroth asked [Michael] McClure to organize it and McClure didn't know how or didn't have time. Rexroth asked me, so I met McClure and Rexroth suggested I go visit another poet who was living in Berkeley, which was Gary [Snyder]. So I went right over to Gary's house and immediately had a meeting of minds with him over William Carlos Williams. . . . He told me about his friend Philip Whalen who was due in town that day, and within three or four days we all met. . . . And then Philip Lamantia was in town, whom I'd known from '48 in New York, and then there was Michael McClure. So there was a whole complement of poets. Then Gary and I decided we ought to invite Rexroth to be the sixth—the sixth poet—to introduce at the Six Gallery, be the elder, since he had linked us up."

Jack Kerouac was in the audience, as were Neal Cassady and Lawrence Ferlinghetti. In his advertisements, Ginsberg had promised a "Happy Apocalypse"; writing later he noted, "Like this was the end of the McCarthy scene. . . . The evening ended up with everybody absolutely radiant and happy, with talk and kissing and later on big happy orgies of poets." Ginsberg's "jeremiad" was *Howl*. Although, as with Kerouac, KR would soon attempt to dissociate himself from Ginsberg, in his "San Francisco Letter" of 1957 *(WOTW)* he wrote: "*Howl* is the confession of faith of the generation that is going to be running the world in 1965 and 1975. . . . Purely technically, Ginsberg is one of the most remarkable versifiers in American. He is almost alone in his generation in his ability to make powerful poetry of the inherent rhythms of our speech, to push forward the conquests of a few of the earliest poems of Sandburg and William Carlos Williams. This is more skillful verse than all the cornbelt Donnes laid end to end. It is my modest prophecy, that if he keeps going, Ginsberg will be the first genuinely popular, genuine poet in over a generation."

104. ALS-9

10 XII [19]55
[San Francisco]

DEAR JIM—

. . . Nothing, in my opinion, is more remarkable than the steady growth of Buddhism since about 1935—in the most unlikely places—whether in India, where it has been dead for almost 1000 years, USSR, where, needless to say, its growth has hardly been facilitated—or Greenwich Village & Madison Avenue. I suppose the reason is that it is really the only one of the so-called World Religions in which a civilized man can believe without Tertullian's "sacrificum intellectis." It has no god or gods, no soul or other immortal entity, no afterlife—and preaches loving kindness, unselfishness, and the religious experience, as an empirically valuable end in itself. And finally—it has no sin, guilt or impurity in the barbarous Xtian-Jew sense whatever—not even any taboos—you are perfectly free to eat meat for instance if you wish to assume the responsibility.

I dont believe, since you bring it up, that it is to [Ezra] Pound's best interests to leave St. Elizabeths. I think he is slowly deteriorating from the advanced

paranoid hebephrenia of the time of his commitment—and if released will go down hill rapidly. He
is not, after all, in a prison, but in a hospital—and
altho I do not approve of the operation of most loo-
ney bins—he is in the best, probably the best, public
or private, in the world. Anyway—I dislike him
intensely both as a man & a poet and am opposed to
all this shit about how he is a martyr to his "ideals."
The ideals being the gas ovens of Poland. . . .

That is very sad news about Alvin [Lustig]. Altho
I have felt for several years that ND was relying too
exclusively on his work & that he himself was tend-
ing to repeat himself & to stick in the 1920 Bauhaus
style—nevertheless he was a beautiful designer—he
sort of grew up c̄ ND & his jackets certainly gave
the books an absolutely unique distinction. I only
met him two or three times—he was extremely quiet
and very likeable. His death & the preceding years
of increasing blindness were tragic enough, certainly. At least, unlike so many of the New Directions people he was not pole axed by the evil society
in which we live, but seemed to have managed to
outwit it, more or less.

I dont like to sound ghoulish, but now that he is
gone you've got to make every effort to develop as
distinctive a style c̄ someone else. You could do worse
than try Jonathan Williams on several jobs for which
his style would be suited. I am very fond of J.W.
and think that his [Kenneth] Patchen *Fables* is a real
masterpiece. . . .

> Love & kisses—more B4 Xmas
> KENNETH

/ · /

growth of Buddhism: According to JL, "I remember that Rexroth placed
a great importance on giving himself empty days for meditation. He

and I were skiing once up at Mineral King, a very remote place in the Sierras. You have to walk in about twenty miles. We made camp there and pitched a tent. Next day I climbed up the mountain on my skis. But Rexroth spent the entire day sitting on a stump in the sun meditating. I could see him from up on the mountain. He never moved all day. He just sat on that stump and meditated. He was taking an 'empty day' to think. To contemplate. He was a Buddhist, you know, as well as being an anarchist, though he converted to Catholicism on his deathbed. It was his way of purging himself of surface preoccupations" *(PR)*.

Alvin: Alvin Lustig, one of ND's primary designers, produced the jacket of KR's *Beyond the Mountains*, as well as a number of ND's Patchen titles.

Jonathan Williams: (1929–), American poet and publisher. ND published Williams's *An Ear in Bartram's Tree: Selected Poems 1957–1967* in 1969. Williams quotes KR in his "In Lieu of a Preface": "90% of the worst human beings I know are poets. Most poets these days are so square they have to walk around the block just to turn over in bed."

Patchen Fables: Jonathan Williams's Jargon Press had published Patchen's *Fables and Other Little Tales* in 1953.

105. TLS-3   December 23, 1955
                                                   [Norfolk]

DEAR KENNETH,

Thank you so much for your invitation to come out there for Christmas—I was deeply touched. I certainly wish I could do it—I always had such a good time with you out there—but I am afraid it is just out of the question. . . .

You may be right about Ezra's situation. In fact, though she would never say so, I often think his wife feels that where he is is the best place for him. And it is true that they are kind to him there and let him have a lot of visitors. Nevertheless, I feel it is all just too sad, and that his declining years should be spent in happier surroundings. While I disapprove thoroughly of his intolerant views, I believe they are part and parcel of his disease, and that that factor should be taken into consideration in judging him.

Please get it out of your head that we are "ashamed" of certain authors. That is nonsense. We wouldn't publish anybody we were "ashamed" of. . . .

Thanks very much for sending me the little book of Spanish poems, it is most attractive. When are you going to start work on the Sanskrit stuff? How about the Gita Govinda? The way Sir Edwin Arnold translates it sounds like a May Day celebration in Sussex, but I am told that the original is absolutely breathtaking. Maybe we could get one of [Alain] Danielou's pundits at the Adyar in Madras to do you a literal translation and then you could put it into poetry.

Thanks again for your kind thought about Christmas and I hope that you all have a good one out there.

As ever

JIM

/ · /

little book: KR's *Thirty Spanish Poems of Love and Exile,* published by City Lights Books the following month.

Sir Edwin Arnold: (1832–1904), British poet, translator; principal of the Poona College, Bombay Presidency, 1856–61, before becoming editor of the *Daily Telegraph.* His best known work, *The Light of Asia, or the Great Renunciation* (1879), attempted "by the medium of an imaginary Buddhist votary to depict the life and character and indicate the philosophy of that noble hero and reformer, Prince Gautama of India, founder of Buddhism."

Danielou: Alain Danielou's *Hindu Polytheism* appeared in 1964. ND later published Danielou's *The Way of the Labyrinth: Memories of East and West.* In his *PR* interview, JL recalls that he first met the Frenchman Danielou, the brother of the Jesuit Cardinal Danielou, in India: "He had gone to India as a young man and had become a Hindu. He was living, when I first knew him, in a tiny palace on the banks of the Ganges in Benares. I liked him immediately and we've become great friends. He told me about a wonderful old-time Tamil classic, the *Shi-lappadikaram, The Ankle Bracelet,* a beautiful mystic novel of early Chola days. He had already translated it into French. He's perfect in English, so I persuaded him to retranslate it into English. It is certainly one of the most important Indian books that I have published." In 1989, ND published Danielou's translation of another Tamil classic, *The Mani-mekhalai.*

106. ALS-2

[n.d. 1957]
[San Francisco]

DEAR JIM—

I want a blanket quit claim to any poems of mine I may record *myself,* with band. I have a contract c̄ *Fantasy* records and believe we have a big thing. It has attracted nationwide attention & is very hot. Therefore we must get it out as soon as possible— that means *next week.* I offered the deal to N.D. & met c̄ thunderous distinterest. Dont fuck this up, but answer immediately with a waiver to me & a copy to Max Weiss. . . .

While you have been away I seem to have been hit by a burst of fame. The jazz poetry sessions I have been doing have drawn immense crowds—a *Life* story—and are the talk of jazz circles all over the country. . . .

Love
KENNETH

/ · /

Fantasy Records: Fantasy Records released KR's *Poetry Readings in "The Cellar"* in 1957, *Kenneth Rexroth at Black Hawk* in 1960.

a Life story: "Big Day for Bards At Bay," *Life* (September 9, 1957). The article, prompted by the obscenity trial of Ginsberg's *Howl and Other Poems* in San Francisco, is a photo-essay on San Francisco poets "shouting their poems in nightclubs, at dance recitals, in art galleries, on radio and TV . . . a 'James Dean school of poetry.' " It includes a photograph of KR reading with a jazz group: "Elder statesman among city's poets, Kenneth Rexroth, 52, who has a national reputation, recites to jazz music at poetry jazz session in nightclub." KR's brief essay "Jazz Poetry" appeared in the *Nation* (March 29, 1958): "In the past two years it has spread from The Cellar, a small bar in San Francisco, to college campuses, to nightclubs in Los Angeles, St. Louis, New York, Dallas and, I believe, Chicago; to the Jazz Concert Hall in Los Angeles, where Lawrence Lipton put on a program of Shorty Rogers, Fred Katz, two bands, myself, Stuart Perkoff and Lipton himself, heard by about six thousand people in two weeks. Kenneth Patchen and Allyn Ferguson followed us, and played there for the better part of two months. Dick Mills and his band have performed with me at several colleges and at the San Francisco Art Festival, and we are now planning to take the whole show on the road" *(WOTW)*.

107. TLS-2   November 29, 1957
                                                 [Norfolk]

DEAR KENNETH—

I hope the LA readings were a big success, and that you also had some fun down there. . . .

Had a long complaint about you from [Kenneth] Patchen, something you had said over the radio after his, I thought, rather unmannerly press release about not being a San Franciscan, which was silly on his part, of course, but I'm sorry you didn't just ignore it. Every little thing gets him in a twitch. I think his Cadence record sounds pretty nice, though the jazz, which is lovely, often drowns his voice. Their jazz is not as pleasing as what you wrote for your record, which really relates to the text, as theirs doesn't, but I like the way Kenneth modulates his voice. It comes through with personality. I hope the next record you do will try to vary the voice more. . . .

Actually, you know, we must begin thinking about

some long range planning for a Collected and Selected KR. Not something to be rushed into, but carefully thought out long ahead. . . .

Things should open up before long, and I should be able to concentrate on ND work, and my own, which, as you have often observed, is what I should have been doing all along, yet I wouldn't have missed getting to know Asia, and that wouldn't have come about except for this five-year sidetracking. In that respect, it was certainly not a blind alley.

Best to all
JIM

/ · /

his Cadence record: Kenneth Patchen Reads His Poetry with the Chamber Jazz Sextet.

a Collected: ND would publish KR's *The Collected Shorter Poems* in 1966, *The Collected Longer Poems* in 1968. A *Selected Poems* (edited by Bradford Morrow) appeared posthumously in 1984.

108. ALS-2   11 I [19]58
                                          S[an] F[rancisco]

DEAR JIM—

My god what a lot of trouble! I wont go into a NYC night club for less than $50 a night—that's the minimum I get on the Coast. And I wont go s̄ a good band & rehearsal. This is a dignified, musically skilled thing & has nothing to do c̄ weedheads like [Jack] Kerouac who has really loused things up. 16–NYC—18 St L.—23rd LA. So I have only the 20th, Monday night, at all possible for a jazz poetry thing in NY—or maybe the 21. . . .

I'm not tight—but I have a horror of being alone in a NY hotel. Hotel rooms make me positively suicidal. I wish I could stay c̄ somebody. Cost is important too because I will have to hire a full-time maid for the period I am away—but most important is not being alone in a hotel. Really—it horrifies me. There must be hundreds of people in NYC—especially girls—who would be delighted to put me up. . . .

Thanks many millions
KENNETH

/ · /

weedheads like Kerouac: On January 4, Lynda Simmons of New Directions had written KR that at the request of JL she had attempted to schedule performances at various NYC clubs: "At the Five Spot, the man's name is Joe Termini. . . . He said the Kerouac engagement was a pretty bad fizz. Probably this puts everyone in NY who would like to try jazz-poetry readings in a cautious frame of mind."

109. ALS-9

[Fall 1958]
San Francisco

DEAR JIM—

I think there is much to be said for 2 books of essays, if there was any surety you would publish the 2nd book. Trouble is, when confronted by a book, you have an automatic incorrigible response— how to "save" money, never how to make it. Since in publishing of all places you have to spend money to make money—you always lose money. I want to get a complete representation of myself & opinions into print & I think, like [James Gibbons] Huneker or [Edmund] Wilson, I can make money c̄ frequent books of criticism. You simply cannot understand that 100 people read or hear me for one who knows the name of the *Partisan Review,* of Phil Rahv or Kleagle [J. C.] Ransom. My stuff is the "most popular" on KPFA by far, more people (on check) listen to me than to any other program *including* music. I am extremely popular in the *Nation* and am responsible for a definite change in their audience—along c̄ one or two others—I've got younger people reading it after it had sunk almost as low as the *New Republic.*

Pieces by me in the *Times* or in a slick magazine always result in reader response—the same is true of tv and radio. Besides, I've got all this publicity via the jazz poetry recitals as well as all the dubious bullshit re/"Beatism." The problem is to cash in on all this. You simply do not run a publishing house for popular authors. Also, of course, you don't believe in this kind of exploitation. I dont know what to do about this because I dont want to be published by Doubleday—it's a good deal more trouble as well as more money. It means continuous problems of a kind I find *most* distasteful.

One thing you *must* realize is that I am not, as your Fall list implies, terribly erudite. This is part of the same *Little Review* perspective. The "middle brow" audience that reads me is actually incomparably better informed & better educated than the highbrows who read & write for the pillowcase headdress highbrow quarterlies. What you call "academicians" are a bunch of illiterate exTrotskyite bohemians who have swindled their way into a few college jobs. Christ, I dont see why you cant understand this. You are yourself not a highbrow—you are incomparably better informed & educated than the best of them—say Randall Jarrell. Cant you sense the difference talking to someone like [Edmund] Wilson or Cyril Connolly & to someone like Bill Barrett? Even children, dogs, horses can smell fraud. The good ones get out of that world in their early thirties—look at [Louis] Kronenberger, he knows more & writes better than all of them wrapped in one bedsheet. . . .

As of now we plan to live about six months in Shropshire & then go to France, Italy & Greece. If we could live cheaply in Aix we'd go there straight off.

Love n kisses
KENNETH

/ · /

Wilson: Edmund Wilson enjoyed KR's essays, as he wrote Alfred Kazin in 1962: "I don't quite agree with you about Rexroth, whom I usuallly read with delight—and this does not date from his tribute to my poetry in his last collection of 'Assays'—which I hope to have engraved on my tombstone. He has an absurd judgement or inaccurate statement on every other page, and I get tired of hearing him say that something or other is the greatest something or other 'in any language.' But he amuses me, and I approve of his reading so widely and think it is a good idea to disturb the accepted opinions by throwing the books around" (*Letters on Literature and Politics,* 1977).

The Nation: KR's first contribution to the *Nation,* a review of Fung Yulan's *A History of Chinese Philosophy,* appeared in 1953. Over the next eleven years, he would publish more than fifty reviews and essays in the journal. Through the late fifties and early sixties, KR regularly reviewed for the *New York Times Book Review.*

Cyril Connolly: (1903–1974), British writer and critic, founding editor of *Horizon* magazine (1939–50); ND reprinted his novel, *The Rock Pool,* in 1948. Connolly had included an excerpt from KR's "Another Spring" in his *The Golden Horizon* (London, 1953).

Bill Barrett: William Barrett (1913–), American philosopher; *Partisan Review* editor.

Kronenberger: Louis Kronenberger (1904–1980), American critic and editor.

110. ALS-2

7 III [19]59
[San Francisco]

DEAR JIM—

. . . I will only write the autobiography if paid monthly in advance. You are too tight to risk one month's advance. You are still publishing S4N—go right on. Soon they'll put you in a museum.

Tillie Olsen is an old time SF Staliness née Tillie Lerner. "Olsen" was for many years a Party functionary. During the great agricultural strikes she wrote a chapter of a "proletarian novel" (about 1933). When the publishers looked her up—she was in jail in Sacramento. This created a sensation in NYC. About 10 different publishers offered her advances. She accepted them all—a matter of several thousand dollars—and then never produced. "The hell c̄ the dirty bourgeois!" This led to her eclipse for a generation. Recently she took a course in "Creative Writing" from Wally Stegner who "discovered" her. Actually, back in those days she was a better writer than any other proletarians & today of course shines out in the general gloom of flaccid pointless writing. Nothing is *ever* said about her being the same Tillie Lerner. She's about my age and has some kids now I guess grown up. When young she was a very pretty girl. . . . Jack Olsen was a handsome lad—but a really lifeless marionette like most functionaries. Neither actually were born either Lerner or Olsen—both are Jewish. Tillie's novel was about an unknown part of America—the coal mining district in N.W. Iowa, where she grew up. So now you know.

Love n kisses
KENNETH

/ · /

the autobiography: KR's *An Autobiographical Novel,* which Doubleday
would publish in 1966.

Tillie Olsen: (1913–), American writer. Her works include *Yonnondio,
Silences,* and *Tell Me a Riddle.* Her story, "Tell Me a Riddle," won the
1961 O. Henry Award as best short story of the year.

Wally Stegner: Wallace Stegner (1909–), American novelist, Stanford
professor of English.

111. TLS-1   25 X [19]59
                                                San Francisco

DEAR JIM,

    You are under a serious misunderstanding. I am
NOT Bravig Imbs. I want $1000 now and $500 a
month while the mss. of that autobiography is coming at you. There are now about 30 hours on tape.
Furthermore NO office processing. When I am edited,
I do the editing. Essential is the free colloquial rhythm
and the offhand, simplistic narrative. If this is not
agreeable, send back what you have IMMEDIATELY,
there's plenty others lined up waiting for you to turn
it down. KPFA now has 200,000 listeners and KPFK
about twice that and it is our second most popular
show, the first is "Rexroth—Books." . . .
    I am sick of your "social" tricks. I told you you
could not publish *Bird in [the] Bush* if you censored
that remark about [Robert] Oppenheimer. You were
simply terrified you might encounter a split second
of embarrassment at a cocktail party upon encountering one of your Ivy League pals. I cant sue—but I
dont have to eat anymore such shit. This is very
embarrassing—much more than you would have been
on encountering the man who would be God. . . .
    You promised, and I have it in writing, to take

Weiss's type and publish that book four years ago. I wrote it when I was 16.

faithfully

KENNETH

/ · /

BRAVIG IMBS: (1904–1946), American novelist, poet, biographer. His *Confession of Another Young Man* (1936) describes Parisian literary life of the 1920s.

that book: The Homestead Called Damascus.

112. TLS-2   October 29, 1959
                                                            [Norfolk]

DEAR KENNETH:

I am much dispirited by the tone of your last letter. I had hoped so much that things between us would get back to the happier, calmer plane of past years, so that we could work together effectively for your benefit. These constant attacks, many of them so unfair, and not at all based in the facts of the case, are simply a discouragement to all of us here. . . .

As I wrote you before, we are very much interested in the autobiography, but have only seen one installment so far, and are hardly in a position to make any kind of offer on that basis. In any case, the extremely large advance which you mention in your letter is way out of our scale, and I don't think we could come anywhere near that. I suggest, however, as is the normal procedure in such cases, that you let us see a sizable portion of the autobiography, and we will make the very best offer that we can, and if it isn't good enough, you would be free to look elsewhere. I really don't think it is fair of you to ask us to make a decision where an advance is expected on the basis of such a fragment of the work. . . .

I can't make out from your last paragraph whether or not you want us to plan on the "Damascus" poem for the "World Poets" series, if we are able to get it going. Certainly inclusion in that series would be far more desirable than a separate publication since it would then benefit from series promotion.

I do wish, Kenneth, that you would try to be a little more considerate and cooperative, instead of simply muddying the waters further by accusing me of all sorts of things which are pure fantasy.

> With best wishes to all, as ever
> JIM

/ · /

"Damascus" poem: The Homestead Called Damascus appeared in ND's World Poets series in 1963, with a preface by JL. Other poets in the series included Octavio Paz, Alain Bosquet, and Chairil Anwar.

113. ALS-4

6 XI [19]59
San Francisco

DEAR JIM—

. . . The autobiography is a very valuable property. Right now its publisher should be arranging serial sale somewhere. You have plenty of typescript—if you haven't, you've lost it. I'll send another copy.

As you well know—the main issue is the censoring of my remark on [Robert] Oppenheimer—which was pure cast snobbery. [Haakon] Chevalier stands to make a small fortune on a book which is nothing but one long "actionable" attack on the swine. I am really tired of this attitude on your part. My ancestors came to Pennsylvania in *1680*—I am NOT Ivy League—but something far better, the descendant of Oberlin students since its founding. Did you know, there *are* people (who do not wear pillow cases when they write poetry) who *prefer* Oberlin to Harvard? Just imagine from now on you're back on that park bench. . . .

Yes, yes—you can do *The Homestead Called Damascus*—but you must make it clear I wrote it in 1922–24, and I would like you to publish it c̄ [Lawrence] Lipton's essay c̄ a brief note by me clearing up the date & a few slight errors of Lipton's. I would, as you know when you took it away from me & gave it to an Ivy League, Nelson Rockefeller financed academic crony—I would *still* like to do a *decent* little book of Rafael Alberti. . . .

Love n kisses
KENNETH

/ · /

Chevalier: Haakon Chevalier's *Oppenheimer: The Story of a Friendship*.

Lipton's essay: Lawrence Lipton's "Notes Toward an Understanding of Kenneth Rexroth, with Special Attention to *The Homestead Called Damascus*" appeared with the poem in *The Quarterly Review of Literature* in 1957.

academic crony: Rafael Alberti's "Concerning the Angels," translated by Geoffrey Connell, would appear in *ND* 19.

114. TLS-1   December 14, 1959
                                                [Norfolk]

DEAR KENNETH,

I have been studying and thinking about the chapters of the "Autobiography" which I have received so far (I believe we have had eight tapes from KPFA and have paid them $40 for the typing) and I must confess that I don't know what to suggest about publication.

The material interests me—because I am interested in you—but I don't think that—in its present form at least—it would sustain the interest of the general reader. It doesn't have the bite or the narrative flair of your best conversation. It may be fine for radio, but for reading it seems awfully long-winded and discursive, the remembered scenes not boiled down, or the best incidents pointed up. In other words, it needs a great deal of work and a tremendous amount of cutting—in short, a big job of editing.

I wonder, therefore, if it wouldn't be better for you to do this one with a firm having a larger staff. . . . Please don't misunderstand me. I'm not "rejecting" the project—just worrying about our ability to do right by you on it. . . .

As ever
JIM

115. TLS-3
June 30, 1960
[New York]

DEAR KENNETH,

. . . What we are trying to do with this paperback is to get you into the new market for poetry, which is so astonishing. You will know yourself a little bit about what very low-priced paperbacks are doing from your experience with the book that Larry [Ferlinghetti] did for you. There is a whole new market for these inexpensive paperbacks, and a whole different approach, and way of marketing, which has nothing whatever to do with the old system. What matters now is not what some critic says but what kind of deal we have with some independent magazine jobber in a given area.

There has really been a complete revolution in highbrow publishing. Let me give you a good example. Two books of ours that came out at about the same time. There was Denise [Levertov]'s book, in hardbound, nicely printed by [Peter] Beilenson, done in this way at her insistence though we recommended paperback, and it has sold to date slightly over 300 copies, though getting good reviews. Then there is [Gregory] Corso's little book in paperback, poetry which is perhaps not as fine as Denise's though it certainly has its special merits, and this has already gone past 5,000 copies! Totally without benefit of reviews, as far as I know.

So that is the picture. I know how you feel about handsome books—I feel the same way myself. But we would just be fools, and has-beens, if we didn't take into account what has happened, and act accordingly.

We'll be going out to see Bill Williams in Rutherford tomorrow. As you may have heard, Obolensky and McDowell came to a parting of ways, and Bill has asked us to take over his books again, which is certainly a pleasure.

As ever
JIM

/ · /

this paperback: Bird in the Bush was published by ND in 1959 as KR's first simultaneous hardbound and paper edition.

that Larry did: Thirty Spanish Poems of Love and Exile, published by Lawrence Ferlinghetti's City Lights Books in 1956.

Denise's book: Denise Levertov's *With Eyes at the Back of Our Heads* was published by ND in 1960, Gregory Corso's *Happy Birthday of Death* in the same year.

Beilenson: Peter Beilenson printed a number of early ND books at his Walpole Printing Office.

Obolensky and McDowell: McDowell and Obolensky had published Williams's *The Selected Letters* (edited by John C. Thirlwall) in 1957. David McDowell (1918–1985) worked for ND as sales and promotions manager from 1948 to 1950 before moving to Random House. In 1957, he left Random House to form his own publishing company with Ivan Obolensky. In 1940–41, McDowell had served as secretary of the *Kenyon Review*.

---

116. ALS-2   30 XI [19]60
                                                [San Francisco]

DEAR JIM—

I hope to write a new 800 lines if I can get some time free.

Just offered $1500 a week by Hearst. Honest. TV shows—I get the commercials—$1000. Column 3 times a week & Sunday $500—besides unlimited travel allowances anywhere in the world—ships & hotels—for me *and* my family. I turned it down.

You have got to get off the dime & make me some money. The ND cheque doesn't begin to pay my secretary.

I am under constant pressure from Doubleday etc. to be a celebrity—altho I must say Doubleday are the least bothersome. But all kinds of people want to buy my little oink flesh. *PRINT The Essays.*

Your idiotic Ford Foundation is doing its best to destroy the Actors' Workshop.

Love to all
KENNETH

117. TLS-1   December 7, 1960
                                                [Norfolk]

DEAR KENNETH,

I was so pleased to hear about your TV show! That
sounds just marvellous, and I hope it's a big success.
Wish there were some way we could get it here. But
you say you may turn it down? For heaven sake,
why? You say you want to be a journalist, as well as
a poet, and isn't TV just a kind of Journalism—with
laughs? . . .

I liked your bit on [James McNeill] Whistler and
[Joseph] Turner in the last *ARTnews*.

Very mild here—I never saw such a warm fall—
but I suppose winter will hit us soon.

                                        Best to all, as ever
                                        JIM

                            / · /

Whistler and Turner: KR's "Turner and Whistler: Aristocratic Vulgarian
and Vice-Versa," *ARTnews* (November 1960; *Assays*).

118. ALS-2   1 June [19]62
                                                San Francisco

DEAR JIM—

Guess I'll give the book back to Doubleday. . . .

The Annual has seemed very dreary indeed to me
for years & years—an outstanding demonstration of
the thesis: "L'Espirit Moderne has simply *failed*." Like,
man—it dont work no more.

That Exagmination thing came recently. How
pitiable! And go back & read even the best part of

the [James Joyce] "Wake"—say Anna Livia Plura-
belle. He simply failed at what he tried to do. And
what a loathsome intellectual prig he was! Aren't you
glad you weren't born one of his blighted children?

Love & kisses
KENNETH

/ · /

The book: An Autobiographical Novel.

that Exagmination thing: ND published a new edition of *Our Exagmination Round His Factification for Incamination of Work in Progress* (the symposium on James Joyce by Beckett, Jolas, McAlmon, and others) in
June of 1962.

"Wake": James Joyce's *Finnegans Wake,* first published entire in 1939.

119. TLS-1

May 1, 1963
[New York]

DEAR KENNETH,

Thanks ever so much for sending the color prints
of the pictures recently taken, but I'm sending them
back as all agree that they just aren't good enough
of you, though very sweet of the girls.

Imogen Cunningham wrote me that she wanted
to do pictures of you again, and perhaps you can get
together with her. But do try to take them outdoors
in a woodland setting, which would fit in with the
nature poems, and not in "party" clothes. Couldn't
you sort of rig yourself out, and the girls, the way
you would be on a trip to the mountains, and find
some spot over in the Presidio, or Golden Gate Park,
or along the wild coastline there by the Lincoln Park
golf course, and do some shots that would look like
the wilds?

Could you think up poem titles for the poems from *The Phoenix and the Tortoise* and *The Art of Worldly Wisdom* that now only have numbers? The numbers were all right for the original volumes but they look sort of odd in the selection, when almost everything else has titles. I also think that it is good psychology for anthologists to have titles for poems. I don't think that an anthologist likes to pick for an anthology a poem that has no other title except a number. I feel this is important. . . .

I was going through the poems again the other day on the train, checking for little inconsistencies, and such, and they really are extremely beautiful. Some of them had me almost weeping, especially the one about dear old Bill Williams. . . .

As ever

JIM

/ · /

Imogen Cunningham: (1883–1976), American photographer.

dear old Bill Williams: KR's "A Letter to William Carlos Williams" originally appeared in *The Signature of All Things.*

120. ALS-2   [Summer 1964]
[San Francisco]

TO: JAMES LAUGHLIN

Copy of letter concerning travel book tentatively titled TRAVELS OF AN EPICUREAN PHILOSOPHER, sent to: *McCall's, Holiday, Saturday Evening Post, Esquire.*

During 1965, beginning March, I plan to make a trip through the wine regions of Italy, France, Germany and Switzerland. I will be driving only short distances so I will touch all the principal centers. My primary purpose, however, is not to visit the wine country purely as such—this is also Romanésque Europe and I will be visiting all the great pre-Gothic churches from San Ambrogio and San Zeno to Aix la Chapelle as well as the museums.

Burgundy, the Dordogne, Provence, the Moselle, Piedmont—here Europe eats best. I will also be writing about food and the book will be larded with recipes. I have been a professional cook and know what I'm talking about. Ask anybody that knows me. I will provide my own illustrations.

Not to sound conceited and oversell myself, but imagine: The Chamberlain's FLAVOR OF FRANCE; the great classic, long out of print—WHAT TO EAT AND DRINK IN FRANCE by Austin de Croze; The Focillon ART OF THE WEST, volume 1, ROMANESQUE ART; Les Beaux Payś PROVENCE; and VILLAGE IN THE VAUCLUSE, stirred up together with comments on current affairs, people met, literary and historical connections, all in the form of a travel diary of an epicurean philosopher—or a Catholic skeptic—or a Montagnian or whatever it is I am. . . .

I see this thing as eminently readable and saleable to all kinds of people, a sort of *Lincoln's Doctor's Dog Abroad*. Would you be interested in serializing such a thing or taking selections? If so, please let me know at, as they say, your earliest convenience. I don't like to push, but I must get this thing all planned in the next month or so and it must be self-financing. No foundation will be paying for it, that's for sure.

This book will follow on my autobiography, now in production with Doubleday, the story of the first twenty-one years of my life, and will be almost totally different in tone, style and subject. . . .

Faithfully
KENNETH

/ · /

travel book: If completed, this book was never published.

121. TLS-1

September 25, 1964
[Norfolk]

DEAR KENNETH,

Thanks ever so much for your good letter of September 17th. I sure agree with you about the falling apart of civilization. I was watching the Beatles on TV the other night, and I said to myself, "It wasn't the latifundia that brought Rome down."

The next thing of yours that I would like to see us do would be those translations of [Pierre] Reverdy. It's just a shame that he isn't known over here more. Couldn't you put enough of them into good shape to make a small bilingual paperback?

I know what you mean about the problem of storing your books. We have it even at Norfolk, where there is a great deal of room. The upper hall is all stacked with cartons. I have gotten rid of some things by giving them to the library down at Choate, on an arrangement where they keep catalogue cards and I can borrow anything I need to work from, but of course, the boys down there are too young for a lot of my things. . . .

Best to all, as ever
JIM

122. TLS-2   16 April 1965
                                                [San Francisco]

DEAR JIM,

Your letter is the most insulting I have ever received from a publisher. It is not only insulting. It is fatuous, pusillanimous and stingy. These are the symptoms of senility, but they now have overwhelmed you. I have been expecting a letter from you with contracts for my complete collected poems, a new book of essays and my plays in paperback and an estimate on the cost of the complete poems. What I want now is a quit-claim on all books of mine that you publish. Since, with almost no exceptions, you have never bothered to copyright them, your claim is of the most tenuous nature. Anyway, I have had quite enough. There is no point in continuing to deal with an aged schoolboy slumming on Montparnasse in 1930.

You threw away Louis Zukofsky a generation ago because you believed that he is a Dadaist who writes nonsense. Today you do the same with Robert Creeley. On the other hand you are devoted to utterly meretricious frauds like Tennessee Williams and [Lawrence] Ferlinghetti. You have operated your publishing house all your life on one principle only: Your contempt for writers and artists. Long ago you shocked me by referring to your best writers as "the crazies." This is still your opinion but you can't even keep up to date with crazies. You are still busy editing *The Little Review* and on exactly the same principles as those employed by Margaret Anderson. . . . The boys you grew up with look on you as a hopeless anachronism who got stalled in his second year at Harvard and who has no connection whatsoever with the contemporary world.

There may be errors of meaning in my translations of [Pierre] Reverdy but they are few. That you should be unable to understand what my translation does with the French text only shows how ridiculous has always been your claim to be an avant-garde publisher. I certainly am utterly uninterested in the opinions of a "real French expert"—perhaps one of your pals? Wallace Fowlie? Enid Starkie? It would never be possible to give you even the most infinitesmal vestige of a suspicion that you have uttered under the New Directions imprint what are without doubt the most inept and misleading translations of French and German poetry and Italian. . . . Not only that but you know that I know that you have turned down dozens of excellent translations of Rilke, Supervielle, Rimbaud, Eluard, Cendrars, and so on and on. I am not likely to have forgotten the way in which you junked my translation of Rafael Alberti and gave it to [someone else] because you got government money and because you considered him socially presentable. Nor am I likely to forget how you refused to publish my anthology of American avant-garde poetry simply because the stuff seemed to be a collection of "the crazies" to your taste. It will never penetrate your mind that the day will come when such a collection would be outselling [Louis] Untermeyer and making money for your heirs. . . .

A man who is pathologically parsimonious is a dangerous man to do business with. By refusing to function as a businesslike publisher in your relations with me but as a contemptuous dilettante indulging one of his "crazies," you have cost me a small fortune. Please send a quit-claim to my books. This letter constitutes a finalization of our relationship.

Yours
KENNETH REXROTH

[note appended in JL's holograph: "(KR phoned 2 days later to apologize for this outburst)."]

/ · /

never bothered: According to JL, "this statement concerning copyrights is incorrect" (letter to the editor).

Margaret Anderson: American editor, founder of *The Little Review.* Between 1914 and 1929, the *LR* published Pound, Crane, Hemingway, Eliot, Joyce, Stevens, and myriad other High Modernists.

Wallace Fowlie: (1908–), American critic, translator. ND published his *Rimbaud* in 1946.

Enid Starkie: ND published Enid Starkie's biographies of Baudelaire in 1958 and Rimbaud in 1962.

Untermeyer: Louis Untermeyer (1885–1977), American poet, editor. Served as cultural editor for Decca Records, 1945–58. Untermeyer's popular anthologies *Modern American Poetry* and *Modern British Poetry* were published in 1942.

123. ALS-2

20 Sept [19]65
San Francisco

DEAR JIM—

Thanks for the extraordinary careful work on [Pierre] Reverdy. You caught several things I missed—but by & large you miss the point of what I am doing. I can conjugate French verbs—I have simplified tenses throughout. "Oh" I dont believe is American & I usually use "you." I certainly *dont* say "it is I." My god! Jim I'm ashamed of you. Moi is almost always *me.* "Me, I wait for you there." I, I—is an animal haunting crossword puzzles. So it goes. If you will read the poems in *The Art of Worldly Wisdom* contemporary c̄ Reverdy's more advanced poems you should see what I am doing. Particles,

prepositions, conjunctions, & many adverbial connections are eliminated. . . .

faithfully
KENNETH

124. Airletter. TLS

Dec 24 [19]66
Berlin

DEAR JIM

. . . It is so obvious that you live in mortal terror
that I might walk into somebody's office and say
"Laughlin sent me," and disgrace you. You know
that I know that you probably have more personal
friends in Japan and India than you do in New York.
. . . As I told you long ago, to you your authors are
"The Crazies." It doesn't occur to you that the years
have slipped away and I didn't turn out to be another
Dylan Thomas or Ezra Pound, but am considerably
more respectable and more a member of the latter
day establishment than James Laughlin IV. I can
assure you I won't offer to trade blow jobs or Communist Party cards with the professors of American
literature in Japan, India and Hawaii. . . .

I'm high up in radio-TV and I already am de facto
cultural minister of San Francisco. Also, I am noto-
riously well bred in social contacts. I am damn sure
I have never told beautiful ballerinas I was sleepy and
wanted to go home, or announced at a party in my
honor that a friend had insisted on giving the party
but that it bored me and I wanted to go to sleep. . . .

It is you who have friends like Gregory Corso and
Tennessee Williams, not me. . . .

faithfully
KENNETH

/ · /

Gregory Corso: (1930–), American poet. His work has appeared in *ND* 17, 18, 19, and 31; see note, letter 115. In *APTC*, KR writes: "In my opinion Gregory Corso is one of the best poets of his generation. He is completely a natural, like the painter *le douanier* Rousseau. You either like him or you don't." Corso's ND books were *The Happy Birthday of Death* (1960), *Long Live Man* (1962), *Elegiac Feelings American* (1970), and *Herald of the Autocthonic Spirit* (1981).

125. ALS-2

25 VII [19]67
[San Francisco]

DEAR JIM—

Tomorrow Mary [Rexroth] will be 17 years old! Remember her—small enough to walk under a horse. 17 years passed like a dream—like a white pony seen running past a gap in a fence! . . .

Why dont you publish [Charles] Bukowski? He is by far the best to come up in recent years, though he's near as old as you. I think he is great and would love to do an introduction.

I am almost through the finale for the Complete Collected Longer Poems. You'll like it. Very spiritual. Locale—Kyoto. How about printing it in the Annual? Let me know. It's years since I've been in it and I'd like to be again. . . .

Love and kisses
KENNETH

/ · /

Bukowski: Charles Bukowski (1920–), American poet. KR's opinion notwithstanding, ND has never published work by Bukowski.

the finale: Heart's Garden / The Garden's Heart.

126. ALS-4

18 Aug [19]67
[San Francisco]

DEAR JIM—

    . . . Did you see the piece [on Denise Levertov] in *The Sixties*—just out? It is true she is slowly reverting to the type of British writress encottaged in a nook of the Sussex downs—even personally—even physically. Oh well—better than becoming a female Gregory Corso. [Robert] Creeley too is running down. Psychoanalysis has made him square. He begins to look like Kay Boyle—a money writer whose clumsy apprenticeship was mistaken for avant-gardism. Too bad—this leaves [Lawrence] Ferlinghetti, Denise, [Gary] Snyder, and after knitting, nutting. Maybe [Philip] Whalen will overtake & surpass. . . .

KENNETH

/ · /

the piece: "Crunk's" "The Work of Denise Levertov" appeared in issue 9 of *The Sixties* (Spring 1967): Despite her "lack of vision," "sentimentality," "talkiness," and "Victorian mist," Levertov "is an absolutely genuine artist, in whose best poems words come alive by mysterious, almost occult means."

Snyder: Gary Snyder (1930–), Philip Whalen (1923–), American poets. ND has published a number of titles by Snyder, including *Regarding Wave* and *Turtle Island*. In *APTC,* KR writes of Snyder and Whalen: "Theirs is a kind of ecological esthetics. They are always aware that the poem is the nexus of the biota, they know of macrocosm and microcosm, a jewel in Shiva's necklace." According to Robert Duncan, "The person who is straight-line Rexroth is Gary Snyder. He had the same bookshelf. Both thought that Arthur Waley was a prime Chinese translator. Philip Whalen is more of a mixed thing, but Snyder is straight-line Rexroth" ("On Kenneth Rexroth," *Conjunctions,* 4). And Allen Ginsberg: "In San Francisco Kenneth Rexroth was 'at home' one day a week. I must have gone with Gary Snyder at one time or another, I went by myself once or twice, I went there once with Phil Whalen and Jack and Gary and Peter. Kenneth had a house with a large library and lots of copies of the *I Ching* and *Secret of the Golden Flower* and

Chinese Poetry, Japanese Poetry, and old English, German dictionaries—a great library. He knew Gary already. He connected me with Gary originally, and thus connected Gary with Kerouac" *(Jack's Book)*.

127. TLS-2   24 January 1969
                                               [Santa Barbara]

DEAR JIM:

. . . I was up to Ping Ferry's for dinner and they came down to our house for a party and then I was up to the Center for lunch and had a long talk of old times. . . . A couple of other people are still with it. Whatever their age, they are still this side of the generation gap and the Formers and the Exes don't communicate any more than they do with their barefooted grandchildren. Terribly funny, it's Formers like Jim [Pike] who wear the beads and peace symbols. He for instance revealed himself as having only the vaguest idea of whom Malcolm X was, and then he went on to say that before Muhammed the Arabs were an uncivilized people without a literature, city life or art, and that Muhammed got *The Koran* in Jerusalem from the Ebionites. However well we know Jim as of old, his silliness surprises us.

Santa Barbara is Nixonville with a vengeance and the English Department is completely dominated by avowed fascists like your deaf and dumb friend. How does it feel to be the son in law of a woman who is now ruling America from a medium's booth in the East Room? . . .

Love from all. Faithfully
KENNETH

/ · /

Ping Ferry: Wilbur H. Ferry (1910–1969), vice-president of the Center for Democratic Institutions at Santa Barbara, 1954–69. "Ping" Ferry had developed a close association over the previous decade with Thomas Merton, who had been introduced by their mutual friend JL.

Jim Pike: James Pike (1913–), American Episcopal bishop, lawyer, writer.

Malcolm X: Malcolm Little (1925–1965), Black American radical. His *Autobiography of Malcolm X* (co-written with Alex Haley) would appear in 1973. According to Leroi Jones (Amiri Baraka) in *Home* (New York, 1966): "Malcolm X's greatest contribution, other than to propose a path to internationalism and hence, the entrance of the American Black Man into a world-wide allegiance against the white man (in most recent times he proposed to do it using a certain kind of white liberal as a lever), was to preach Black Consciousness to the Black Man. As a minister for the Nation of Islam, Malcolm talked about a black consciousness that took its form from religion. In his last days he talked of another black consciousness that proposed politics as its moving energy."

128. ALS-2   7 Sept [19]69
                                                  Santa Barbara

DEAR JIM—

. . . I am responsible for starting the [Joseph] Alioto-Mafia investigation. Let's hope it all comes out. I could never publish what I know because I couldn't prove it & have no money to fight a suit. . . .

It is gratifying to see the Kennedy myth finally destroyed—first by the [Aristotle] Onassis marriage . . . and now by the replay of [James M. Cain's] *The Postman Always Rings Twice.* When I was a boy and read Suetonius I thought he was a deranged propagandist for the Senatorial party. Little did I think I would see him overtaken and surpassed.

Think of that "summer cottage" with a bunch of brutal drunken Irish politicians in their shirts, sox & shoes & nothing else, and those poor naked little stenos all wallowing around, bellowing, giggling and vomiting. The horrible thing is that the girls—due to their jobs—couldn't say no—an orgy c̄ slaves. . . . Or is that better than a computer in the J. Walter Thompson office baptized by Billy Graham?

Love and kisses to all
KENNETH

/ · /

Alioto: Joseph Alioto, Democratic Mayor of San Francisco, 1968–76. In September 1969, *Look* magazine published an article alleging that Alioto was "enmeshed in a web of alliances with at least six leaders of La Cosa Nostra." The mayor won a libel suit against *Look* in 1977.

the Onassis marriage: After the assassination of President John F. Kennedy (1917–1963), his widow married Aristotle Onassis, an extremely wealthy Greek shipping magnate.

Billy Graham: (1918–), American evangelical minister. Author of *The Secret of Happiness* and *Angels: God's Secret Agents.*

129. ALS-2

5 May [19]71
[Santa Barbara]

DEAR JIM—

. . . I have stayed c̄ you all these years because I honestly look on you as my best friend and for no other reason except your non-commercialism & total lack of "business"—what are considered your faults as a publisher. There is scarcely a major publisher in the past 25 years who has not tried to get me away from ND on a total exclusive basis. The only reason I deal c̄ H[erder] & H[erder] is that you simply can't handle all I write. . . .

I do hope you are in better health. You worry me very much. And I am sorry you couldn't get to

Santa Barbara to see us. Take care of yourself—you are one of humanity's valuable people.

Love to all
KENNETH

/ · /

H & H: In 1970, Herder and Herder published two volumes of KR's essays, *With Eye & Ear* and *The Alternative Society;* and in 1971, *American Poetry in the Twentieth Century.*

130. TLS-4   May 10, 1971
                                                         [Norfolk]

DEAR KENNETH:

. . . Do rest assured that there is no question of my "retiring" from New Directions. But my doctor did tell me to cut down on detailed work as much as I could, and you yourself should know, from the way I used to work when I was staying with you, what a compulsive worker I am, and how that has finally had its bad effect on my health. But it would be about as easy, psychologically, for me to "retire" from New Directions as it would be to chop off one of my legs. But it doesn't make sense, as I now understand, to keep up a degree of detailed work which might lead to a real physicial breakdown. Hence, the effort to delegate as much as possible, and to concentrate on policy matters, book selection, that sort of thing. And, of course, the correspondence with old friends, such as yourself. . . .

Needless to say I am greatly touched by the last line of your letter, and only wish it were true, and I do appreciate the way you have stuck to New Directions out of personal friendship, and am grateful for what your name on the list, and your sales, have done to help us. I wouldn't be honest with you if I didn't admit that sometimes I get annoyed with you, when you use harsh language on me, as you have done sometimes in the past, but these feelings of hurt usually don't last very long, and I remember all the good times we have had together, in San Francisco and the mountains and elsewhere, and think of you, too, as one of my oldest and best friends. . . .

Fortunately, I have had a lot of help on the editing of the [Thomas Merton] *Asian Journal* from Naomi Stone and Br. Patrick [Hart] down at the monastery, and also now from [Amiya] Chakravarty over at New Paltz, who has been wonderful about the spellings of religious terms, transliterations, and that sort of thing. Also a marvellous English Bikkhu [Khantipalo] in Bangkok who sent in five beautiful pages about "mindfulness" in Buddhism, which transformed Tom's notes, which were really gibberish, into an intelligent and beautiful essay. It's really a very touching book. Just think of it, there he was, Tom, locked up in that rather drab monastery for nearly 30 years, and then suddenly let loose, by the new Abbot, to see Asia and to fulfill his dreams of meeting the Asian contemplatives. He had wonderful conversations with the Dalai Lama, and a lot of other geshes and rimpoches, and also a good time with our old friend Raghavan in Madras, and various people whom he met in Ceylon. It's clear from the diary that he was greatly tempted to find himself a "master" in "Tantric Buddhism" to explore that fully, but then finally decided that Gethsemani was his home, and that he wanted to go back there. There are also very interesting paragraphs about Kanchenjunga. He became obsessed with the mountain, sort of fell in love with it, you might say, when he was making a little retreat in a cabin on a tea plantation near Darjeeling.

Best to all
JIM

/ · /

Asian Journal: The Asian Journal of Thomas Merton, edited from his note-books by Naomi Burton, Brother Patrick Hart, and JL (with Amiya Chakravarty serving as consulting editor), was published by ND in 1975. According to JL, "I did almost all the editing on the *AJ*. Spent the better part of two years on it. Tom Merton was mixed up about the religions and I had to research and correct" (letter to the editor). Appendix II in the *AJ* offers Bikkhu Khantipalo's brief essay "On Mindfulness." Naomi Burton and Patrick Hart were very close friends of Merton's, and Burton acted as his literary agent and editor. Dr. Amiya Chakravarty (Indian poet, philosopher) served as a delegate to UNESCO and counted among his acquaintances Gandhi, Jawaharlal Nehru, Albert Schweitzer, Boris Pasternak, and Albert Einstein, as well as Merton.

131. TLS-2   July 2, 1971
                                                                [Norfolk]

DEAR KENNETH:

I have now completed the reading of your *American Poetry in the Twentieth Century*—the fact is, once I got started with it, I couldn't put it down, and read far beyond my usual bedtime—and I certainly must congratulate you on a really extraordinary piece of work. How you have been able to remember all those poets, and what they were like, I simply cannot fathom, except that you must have a photographic memory. And the combination of the brilliant critical insights, and the relationship to social history of the various poetic movements, and the highlights of "intimate biography" make it quite unlike any other book on modern poetry that I have seen. . . .

About the only complaint I can make on the book is that you don't seem to have brought in Tom Merton, and I have felt that while his early religious poems were rather run-of-the-mill, the ones that he did toward the end of his life, "Cables to the Ace" and "Geography of Lograire" are a different story, really very interesting, and pointing toward new techniques and methods of exploiting the underconsciousness. Did we perchance omit to send you those volumes, or do you just not agree with my estimate of their interest and importance?

I am grateful also for the charity with which you have treated poor old Pound. He has at least, as you doubtless know, recanted on the anti-Semitism, the documentation on this being in that piece in *Evergreen Review* some years ago, by Michael Reck, telling of the lunch with [Allen] Ginsberg, where Ezra said that anti-Semitism was a "stupid suburban prejudice" and he was ashamed of it. . . .

As ever
JIM

/ · /

where Ezra said: "A Conversation Between Ezra Pound and Allen Ginsberg," *Evergreen Review* 55 (June 1968).

132. ALS-1   12 July [19]71
                                [Santa Barbara]

DEAR JIM—

. . . I am so glad you are pleased with the book. Like everything I do it gets alternately raving or savaging reviews. Of course it's designed to upset the Establishment, whether of John Crowe Ransom, Ezra Pound, Karl Shapiro, or Charles Olson. Do you realize that the Young Poets I once fought for are now grey haired and *established* with a vengeance? Even [Gary] Snyder is now getting into all the straight anthologies that ignore even [Allen] Ginsberg & [Lawrence] Ferlinghetti. As for Denise [Levertov]— she has become a latterday Lou[ise] Bogan.

Do you know the poetry of Charles Simic? Joseph Ceravolo? Jerome Rothenberg is the next guy in line. He is going to become a Power. He has all the answers the young want to learn. And he is good.

Love to all
KENNETH

/ · /

Charles Simic: (1938–), American poet, translator. A group of his poems was included in *ND* 3.

Joseph Ceravolo: (1937–), American poet, civil engineer. Ceravolo would win a National Endowment Award for Poetry in 1972.

Jerome Rothenberg: (1931–), American poet, translator, editor. ND would publish a number of books by Rothenberg, beginning with *Poland / 1931* in November 1974.

133. TLS-2   July 20, 1971
                                [Norfolk]

DEAR KENNETH:

. . . Yes, you certainly made very good suggestions and choices in the early days, Denise [Levertov], [Gary] Snyder, etc., and there were probably a number of others whom we got to doing because of your recommendations. Snyder sent me the other day one of the finest poems of his which I have ever seen, "Prayer for the Great Family," which was gotten up as a benefit broadside for some society that helps the Indians. If he didn't send you one, do ask for it, from him as it is a magnificent poem, and the kind of thing to put up on the wall. He is a big seller for us, not yet up to [Lawrence] Ferlinghetti, but drawing close.

Yes, I know Charles Simic, he came in with Vasko Popa, one day at the office, and [I] liked him, and also admire his work, but I believe he is already being published by somebody. [George] Braziller, I think, of all people.

Joseph Ceravolo I don't know much about, except as a name which you have mentioned before. I'll try to dig up some of his stuff, who publishes him?

Jerome Rothenberg I have known for a long time, but mostly as a translator, and as a collector of myths, and that sort of thing. But he seems like a good egg, and perhaps we should do something about him, I'll look into it.

Very best to you all, as ever
JIM

/ · /

Snyder sent me: Gary Snyder's "Prayer for the Great Family" was collected in *Turtle Island,* published by ND in 1974. The volume won the Pulitzer Prize for Poetry.

Vasko Popa: Yugoslav poet. Charles Simic's *Homage to the Lame Wolf: Vasko Popa—Selected Poems, 1956–75* was published as no. 2 in the *Field* Translation Series in 1979.

134. TLS-2   January 18, 1972
                                          [Norfolk]

DEAR KENNETH:

As you can imagine, I am feeling very sad about the death of poor old Kenneth Patchen, last Saturday, though, to be sure, it's a blessing that he doesn't have to endure any more of that intense suffering. I talked to Miriam [Patchen] on the telephone, and she sounded very composed and on top of the situation, and took the same view that it was good that his suffering was over. But somehow his death marks the end of a chapter for me, or seems to, we had been associated for so long, and goodness knows we have had our scraps, arguing over what should go into various books, and how they should be designed, but I never forgot his devotion when he was living down in the cottage here on the place, doing all the work of getting the books mailed out, while I went skiing or roamed around the country.

I suppose I should feel sad, too, about [John] Berryman—*nihil nisi bonum*—but I always found him absolutely impossible to get along with. I guess it was drink that did him in. . . .

                                          As ever
                                          JIM

/ · /

about Berryman: John Berryman had committed suicide on January 7; his first book, *Poems,* had been published by ND in 1942.

135. ALS-2

12 Ap[ril] [19]73
[Santa Barbara]

DEAR JIM—

Very sweet of you to have written Frank Gardiner. You do show your naivete however. Being liked by students and being "a truly outstanding teacher" is the kiss of death in academia. You should have said "His paper in *PMLA* on the relative incidence of the definite and indefinite articles in the works of Edmund Spenser and Herbert Spencer" is a landmark in modern scholarship. Believe it or not—they have told students that my article for the *Encyclopaedia Britannica* "Literature, Art of" is "just a hack job given to any journalist they can get." I am being forced to retire precisely *because* I am a popular teacher. You are good hearted, but unworldly.

Meanwhile I am trying to get a Fulbright or other government money—US or Japanese—to go to Japan. . . . If I can get to Japan I may stay the rest of my life. The USA has become a land of horror.

Love—

FROM KENNETH, CAROL

/ · /

Frank Gardiner: on March 22, 1973, Rexroth had written in a pc to JL, "They are trying to drop me from the English faculty here next year. You could write Frank Gardiner, Chairman, Dept. of English, UCSB."

my article: KR's "The Art of Literature" would appear in the *Encyclopaedia Britannica,* 15th edition, 1974.

Carol: Carol Tinker, American poet, translator. Tinker and KR married in 1974. See KR's "A Crystal Out of Time and Space: The Poet's Diary," edited by Tinker, in *Conjunctions* 8 (1985).

136. ALS-3

5 July [19]73
[Santa Barbara]

DEAR JIM—

. . . Yes I was reappointed for a year. . . . I think Meg [Randall]'s poetry is fair—her life absurd—her lover an archetype male chauvinist pig who thinks he's a feminist. Both were named long ago by Wyndham Lewis—"revolutionary simpletons."

Yes I will be glad to give you a blurb for Jerry [Rothenberg]'s book. He—[Nathaniel] Tarn—[David] Antin are the 3 of that age group you should take over in toto—they'll be the leaders of the next 10 years. . . .

I do hope you have set up ND so it goes on after you've retired or passed away. Do you realize what a social & historical responsibility your back list is? . . .

Love & kisses
KENNETH

/ · /

Meg: Margaret Randall (1936–), American poet, essayist, editor. ND published her *Part of the Solution: Portrait of a Revolutionary* in 1973.

Tarn: Nathaniel Tarn (1928–), American poet, translator; ND published Tarn's *Lyrics for the Bride of God* in 1975. Later, KR would write of Tarn that he "is one of the most outstanding poets of his generation, and as such very much a part of international modern literature—an excellent translator of several languages; a successful and imaginative editor; a scholar of a wide range and depth in literatures of both the past and the present." Tarn was general editor of Cape Editions in London and founding director of Cape Goliard Press.

Antin: David Antin (1932–), American poet; ND published his *Talking at the Boundaries* in 1976 and *Tuning* in 1987.

137. ALS-2

26 Dec [19]73
[Santa Barbara]

DEAR JIM—

Another Christmas—and another birthday—68. Very successful celebrations . . . I do hope you can come to Santa Barbara from Alta and spend some time with us. We scarcely saw you last time. Also— at 68—I want to discuss with you and plan the disposal of my estate, literary and otherwise. . . .

If you can get the rights to the Liveright H. D. *Collected Poems* and to the *book* (there was also a pamphlet) *Red Roses from Bronze,* the two largest collections, and all the other stuff, you are crazy not to do a *Complete Collected Poems of HD* as soon as you can get them to the printer. After all she is one of the Big Ten of classic American Modernism and of course very promotable now as a feminist & Lesbian. It is as bad, her being unobtainable as it would be if [W. C.] W[illia]ms or [Wallace] Stevens was. Also, it is a scandal. I dont care for her talky discursive verse of later years, but the imagist poems are amongst the finest ever by a woman in English— better far than Mina Loy, and for my taste than Marianne Moore, of her generation. Her novels are inordinately precious, but appeal to a certain audience. I guess *Hedylus* was the best. Bryher died last Fall, I believe.

I read Denise [Levertov]'s collection of prose. I was not much impressed. And as for her poetry— she has come to write far too much. Did you see Muriel [Rukeyser]'s new poems? Very good indeed. She is probably the best of those still alive from before War I.

Love, Happy New Year
KENNETH

/ · /

get the rights: ND would eventually publish H.D.'s *Collected Poems 1912–1944,* edited by Louis L. Martz, in 1983.

Marianne Moore: (1887–1972), American poet, essayist. Moore won both the Pulitzer Prize and the National Book Award for her *Collected Poems* in 1952.

Bryher: Winifred Ellerman, H.D.'s long-time patron and companion. Her *The Heart to Artemis: A Writer's Memoirs* appeared in 1962.

Denise's collection: Denise Levertov's first collection of essays, *The Poet in the World,* was published by ND in 1973.

Muriel's new poems: Muriel Rukeyser's *The Gates.*

138. TLS-4   December 16, 1974
                                                Norfolk

DEAR KENNETH:

. . . We drove up into the foothills of the Sierra to see Gary Snyder at his beautiful place. If you haven't been there you really ought to go sometime as it is extraordinary. A wooded ridge, with big trees, about a thousand feet above one of the branches of the Yuba River. His Japanese style house, which he built with local timbers, cut right on the place, is lovely, and so is Masa, his wife, a beautiful and highly intelligent girl. And the two little boys, who look more Japanese than American, are wonderful kids. They go by bus to a one-room schoolhouse there somewhere in the mountains, and don't want to learn any Japanese from their mother, they just want to be Americans like the other kids. [Allen] Ginsberg has a "meditation house" built at the other end of the meadow, which we saw, though he wasn't there, and there is also a little Japanese temple house which [Richard] Baker, the Roshi of the San Francisco Zen group, had brought over from Kyoto. No electricity, and no running water, but they seem to be thriving on the simple life, growing most of their own food, and keeping chickens. Masa cooked us a delicious dinner, and then we took the plane back East from Sacramento. But somehow San Francisco, too, just wasn't the same without you there. . . .

As ever

JIM

/ · /

without you there: KR was living during these months in Kyoto.

139. TLS-2   April 14, 1975
                                                                [Norfolk]

DEAR KENNETH:

. . . Ann [Laughlin] and I both went down to Washington for the ceremony on April 2nd, but I think you were lucky to avoid it, as it was terribly stuffy. Mostly a lot of very pompous people patting each other on the back for their good works, except for the poets. Charles Simic, who is a nice person, won the "middle-aged" prize, and a handsome young man from Colorado, who was dressed rather like a cowboy, and looked like a young blonde version of Gary Cooper, whose name I never did exactly catch, won the not-previously-published book prize.

The judges who actually decided on your prize, I learned, were [W. D.] Snodgrass, Donald Hall, and Anthony Hecht, of whom only Snodgrass was present, and who read your citation at the prize-giving. I was curious to know who swung the decision in your favor—I can't exactly see you as being Anthony Hecht's cup of tea—but thought it would be undiplomatic to ask Snodgrass, and the other two were not there. Probably it was Donald Hall, though perhaps Snodgrass. Or the two of them must have ganged up on Hecht. I did talk to Snodgrass a little, and he is pleasant enough, and interested chiefly now in Troubador music, trying to figure out how they actually sang it, and then perform it with various groups on ancient instruments. . . .

Mr. Copernicus (Edward J. Piszek) is a nice large, square man, who never cracks a smile. He is really Mrs. Paul's Kitchens. He has a national franchise chain that markets something called, I believe, Mrs. Paul's Frozen Fish Sticks. His public relations man, a Mr. Cuneo, who is an old-time Washington political lobbyist, had written a very touching little speech for him, Mr. Copernicus, to read at the ceremony, in which he explained, reading from the script completely without intonation, that he was just a poor boy from Poland who had made it in this country, and that this country had been very good to him, and therefore he wanted to do something for American artists and scientists. In handing me your check and diploma (which I had better keep here for the present as it is framed in glass and would probably get broken in the mail), he neglected to explain to the audience that I am not you. As a result, after the ceremony was over, a number of aged Washington ladies came up to me and wanted to tell me about their trips to the Sierras in the 1920s. . . .

> Very best to you both as ever
> JIM

/ · /

the ceremony: KR was awarded the 1975 Copernicus Award of $10,000 given to American poets over forty-five, honoring "the winner's life-time achievement and contribution to poetry as a cultural force," at a ceremony at the Folger Library. As KR was still in Kyoto, JL accepted the award and read from "Time Is the Mercy of Eternity" on his behalf.

young blonde: Reg Saner (1936–), American poet, who was awarded the first Walt Whitman Award.

Snodgrass: W. D. Snodgrass (1926–), American poet. Won the Pulitzer Prize for Poetry in 1960.

Donald Hall: (1928–), American poet, critic, editor. Served as Poetry Editor of the *Paris Review,* 1953–62.

Anthony Hecht: (1923–), American poet, critic, editor. Won the Pulitzer Prize for Poetry in 1968.

140. TLS-1

March 1, 1976
[Santa Barbara]

DEAR JIM:

Don't worry about my health. I have the best car-diologist in Santa Barbara who says there is nothing wrong with my heart, and my high blood pressure is controlled by a new medicine. The severe shock which I went into was a reaction from a new pill which almost killed me, but which was immediately discontinued.

I think it's great that you are publishing the [Kazuko] Shiraishi and I think it should be as suc-cessful as such things may be. To answer your ques-tions: 1) She can send you all sorts of photographs including those at the mike in the show clothes—but she wears clothes like that all the time. Two) Sure. I think she has written an autobiography already in Japanese but she can send you a brief bio and her opinions on life and letters. Don't forget that she is a passionate negrophile and as she says "hasn't had a white or yellow cock in her in fifteen years." Three)

It seems to me a publisher's job is to get blurbs. Don't forget that [Gary] Snyder and [Lawrence] Ferlinghetti are worse male chauvinists than you. . . . She knows a number of jazz musicians and is a good friend of the actress and singer Abby Lincoln, the wife of drummer Max Roach. She could get a blurb from her. I doubt if I could. I once turned down Abby's pussy because of her crazy violent husband, so she may be mad at me. Besides, in her eyes I'm a White Devil. . . .

> Take care. Love n kisses to all
> KENNETH

/ · /

the Shiraishi: Kazuko Shiraishi's *Seasons of Sacred Lust*, with an introduction by KR.

141. APCS   [October 27, 1976]
                               [Santa Barbara]

DEAR JIM—

Thanks so much for the [David] Antin. It is very impressive. There has really never been anyone like this. I read his work with great pleasure. It will sell enough to meet the breakeven point. I hope so.

Is Djuna [Barnes] still alive? This is the time to reprint *Ryder*. It is a feminist novel if ever there was one. I'd love to do an introduction for it. Remaindered, it now costs a small fortune.

PLEASE send me the new early Pound & Octavio [Paz]'s new book, [George] Oppen's, ND 33 & the [W. C.] W[illia]ms. . . .

> Love to all
> KENNETH

/ · /

the Antin: Talking at the Boundaries.

Djuna: Djuna Barnes died in 1982.

the new early Pound: Collected Early Poems of Ezra Pound, edited by Michael
King; Octavio Paz's *Eagle or Sun* (trans. by Eliot Weinberger); George
Oppen's *The Collected Poems;* William Carlos Williams's *Interviews with
William Carlos Williams: Speaking Straight Ahead* (ed. by Linda W. Wag-
ner); all published by ND.

142. TLS-1   12 / 17 / [19]81
                                                    [Norfolk]

DEAR KENNETH—

I'm glad that we came by to see you, even though
it was sad to see you so reduced. I remembered our
trips in the Sierras and our rock climbing when you
were in prime form. But I remembered what you
told me when Aunt Leila was ill, that I didn't understand the will to live, and I think you have got that,
and you will make it back to health. You've just got
to want to, and all of us are wishing for you to do
that. So keep working at it and get back to the speech
therapy when you can. You aren't any worse off than
Bill Williams was and he made it back.

The big excitement this past week was the party
at Gotham Book Mart for the festschrift. I was a bit
nervous about that, but you and Brad [Morrow]
carried it off. . . .

Your interview with Brad is the high spot. Really
great. You have understood better than anyone what
ND was all about. And I loved your talking about
the old days on Potrero Hill. They were so great,
the high points of my life. You educated me more
than Ezra [Pound] did, taught me more about literature and life. You were a great teacher, too. I apologize again for insulting your ballet dancer friend by

wanting to go home to bed. I guess I have never been very adventurous. . . .

With much love
JIM

/ · /

so reduced: KR had suffered a disabling stroke.

the festschrift: Conjunctions I (Winter 1981–82), edited by Bradford Morrow (KR's literary executor), was "A Festschrift in Honor of James Laughlin." Contributors included Creeley, Snyder, Everson, Levertov, Hawkes, Oppen, Omar Pound, and many others. KR contributed a long interview on his relationship with JL.

143. Cablegram   [June 6, 1982]
                                                [New York]

MR. JAMES LAUGHLIN:

REXROTH DIED PEACEFULLY SUNDAY NIGHT. CAROL DOING FINE. PER BRAD MORROW.

144. TLS-2   June 16, 1982
                                                San Francisco

DEAR MR. LAUGHLIN,

. . . I think that you should know a bit about Kenneth's final days, since you are the friend who deserves to know the circumstances surrounding these last days. They may serve to calm the feelings, and assure you of the unique beauty of Kenneth's passing.

When I arrived in Santa Barbara on Thursday June 1st I was expecting to see Kenneth very much in the same condition as in April. At that time Carol [Tinker-Rexroth] had determined with much encouragement to reduce all the drugs with the exception of those absolutely necessary. However, my feelings were that this might be difficult, since Kenneth was still in much pain. My visit to Kenneth on June 2nd was a complete surprise, and a complete turn of events. Kenneth was no longer on drugs, had surrendered the gastric tube, and was eating solid food, speaking clearly, and looking forward to longer days in the sun, with possible physical therapy beginning soon. He was very happy.

The sun in Santa Barbara was brilliant and his life cast a special glow. In spiritual terms I might say that he was experiencing "fervor caritatis"; that is, joy and tears from this good feeling. He no longer felt any pain, and was able to communicate easily. So easily in fact that it was obvious that he had come out of the darkness; was now living in the light and that we could all anticipate a speedy recovery. We even joked about his Mass and Communion. I promised him that I would say Mass for him on Saturday, June 5th at 11:00 A.M. It so happened that the Mass for that Sunday was that of the Holy Trinity. Because of this I decided to say Sunday Mass for him on Sat. morning. It was very simple. Carol was there, and we prayed together in thanksgiving for what was, indeed, a complete turn of events.

Afterwards I discussed with Kenneth the paradox of this change, and the fact that Trinity Sunday had to be one of the most intellectual religious solemnities in the Catholic liturgical calendar. I reminded him of how impressed I was when in Jan. of 1981 I had seen him reading from Plotinus' works. It was kind of a secret between us—he loved to read about how God related to himself in this Triune form. And as he had told me then, it was beautiful to read Plotinus' cosmic descriptions. We both laughed about this, since we both knew that Plotinus was no easy person to get through.

The next day, Sunday, I visited him after saying Mass in a local church. He looked good and was anticipating another hour in the sun, or watching another hummingbird play before him (as he had done on Sat.). Evidently his heart began to show signs of fluttering in the later p.m. An e.k.g. machine was ordered for an electrocardiogram. About 7:00 P.M. it arrived. He was hooked-up to it. Between 7:15–7:30 he began to experience a massive heart attack. Craig, the male nurse, attempted to revive him by pounding on his chest. Nothing happened. However, the electrocardiogram machine kept on registering peculiar signs, and eventually blew a fuse of sorts. To say the least, from these events Kenneth himself would have written a most interesting chapter of his autobiographical novel. I can just imagine how he would write it; and link it all to those early visions, and the subsequent religious experiences at Holy Cross on the Hudson, or the conversions of his own father and mother. He probably would say that the damn machine couldn't handle this spiritual overflow. All in keeping with the Rexroth way of life and death.

The rest you know from Carol and others who by now have briefed you on the funeral, and other details. I am including a series of clippings which appeared in various newspapers. With it goes a copy of the eulogy that I was asked to deliver at the 10:00 A.M. Mass of Christian Burial at Mount Carmel Catholic Church on June 11th. You will have received from Bradford Morrow a memorial card. If not I am sending you one.

Good friend of Kenneth and Carol, mission accomplished! May the Lord bless you for your comradeship, friendship, and love.

Sincerely yours
FR. ALBERTO HUERTA, S.J.

/ · /

you are the friend: During KR's last months, JL quietly supported the poet financially, covering over $40,000 in medical bills alone.

Plotinus: (205–270?), Roman philosopher, founder of Neoplatonism.

145. TLS-1

August 12, 1982
Norfolk

DEAR FATHER ALBERTO:

I can't begin to tell you how much your letter about Kenneth meant to me. I had been suffering for him so, and it was wonderful to know that toward the end he had some good days when he could sit out in the sun and be himself again. I never doubted, of course, when I saw him in one of his lowest moments, and he could not speak, but his eyes told me that his spirit was going very strong. But the pain that he had to endure was so awful.

I am happy that when he had to go it was calm and peaceful. Although he was deeply interested in Buddhism, I was always convinced, during our long friendship, that basically he was a Christian, and I am confident that Our Blessed Lord has taken him to Himself.

The service that you spoke for him is very beautiful.

And I am very glad to have the clippings about him, many of which I had not seen.

I only regret that Kenneth never knew my other great friend Thomas Merton. They had so much in common and they would have liked each other.

Sincerely yours
JAMES LAUGHLIN

SELECTED BIBLIOGRAPHY

Kenneth Rexroth

Books:

In What Hour. New York: Macmillan, 1940.
The Phoenix and the Tortoise. New York: New Directions, 1944.
The Art of Worldly Wisdom. Prairie City, Illinois: Decker, 1949.
The Signature of All Things. New York: New Directions, 1950.
Beyond the Mountains. New York: New Directions, 1951.
The Dragon and the Unicorn. Norfolk, Conn.: New Directions, 1952.
A Bestiary for My Daughters Mary and Katherine. San Francisco: Bern Porter, 1955.
Thou Shalt Not Kill. Sunnyvale, Calif.: Horace Schwartz, 1955.
In Defense of the Earth. New York: New Directions, 1956.
Bird in the Bush. New York: New Directions, 1959.
Assays. New York: New Directions, 1961.
The Homestead Called Damascus. New York: New Directions, 1963.
Natural Numbers. New York: New Directions, 1963.
An Autobiographical Novel. Garden City, N.Y.: Doubleday, 1966.
The Collected Shorter Poems. New York: New Directions, 1966.
Heart's Garden / The Garden's Heart. Cambridge: Pym Randall, 1967.
Classics Revisited. Chicago: Quadrangle, 1968.
The Collected Longer Poems. New York: New Directions, 1968.
The Alternative Society. New York: Herder and Herder, 1970.

With Eye & Ear. New York: Herder and Herder, 1970.

American Poetry in the Twentieth Century. New York: Herder and Herder, 1971.

Sky Sea Birds Trees Earth House Beast Flowers. Santa Barbara, Calif.: Unicorn, 1971.

The Elastic Retort. New York: Seabury, 1973.

Communalism: From Its Origins to the Twentieth Century. New York: Seabury, 1974.

New Poems. New York: New Directions, 1974.

The Morning Star. New York: New Directions, 1979.

Excerpts from a Life, ed. by Bradford Morrow. Santa Barbara, Calif.: A Conjunctions Book, 1981.

Selected Poems, ed. by Bradford Morrow. New York: New Directions, 1984.

World Outside the Window: The Selected Essays, ed. by Bradford Morrow. New York: New Directions, 1987.

Editions, Translations:

Selected Poems of D. H. Lawrence. New York: New Directions, 1947.

The New British Poets: An Anthology. New York: New Directions, 1949.

Fourteen Poems of O. V. de L. Milosz. San Francisco: Peregrine, 1952.

One Hundred Poems from the Japanese. New York: New Directions, 1955.

One Hundred French Poems. Highlands, N.C.: Jargon, 1955.

One Hundred Poems from the Chinese. New York: New Directions, 1956.

Thirty Spanish Poems of Love and Exile. San Francisco: City Lights, 1956.

Poems from the Greek Anthology. Ann Arbor, Mich.: University of Michigan Press, 1962.

Pierre Reverdy: Selected Poems. New York: New Directions, 1969.

Love in the Turning Year: One Hundred More Poems from the Chinese. New York: New Directions, 1970.

The Burning Heart: Women Poets of Japan (with Ikuko Atsumi). New York: Seabury, 1977.

The Buddhist Writings of Lafcadio Hearn. London: Wildwood, 1981.

The Orchid Boat: The Women Poets of China (with Ling Chung). New York: New Directions, 1982.

JAMES LAUGHLIN

Books:

The River. Norfolk, Conn.: New Directions, 1938.

Some Natural Things. New York: New Directions, 1945.

Skiing East and West. New York: Hastings House, 1946.

A Small Book of Poems. Milan and New York: Giovanni Scheiviller and New Directions, 1948.

The Wild Anemone. New York: New Directions, 1957.

Patent Pending. London: Gaberbocchus, 1958.

Confidential Report, and Other Poems. London: Gaberbocchus, 1959.

In Another Country. San Francisco: City Lights Books, 1978.

Stolen and Contaminated Poems. Santa Barbara, Calif.: Turkey Press, 1985.

Selected Poems, 1935–1985. San Francisco: City Lights Books, 1986.

The Master of Those Who Know: Pound the Teacher. San Francisco: City Lights Books, 1986.

The Owl of Minerva. Port Townsend, Wash.: Copper Canyon Press, 1987.

Pound as Wuz: Essays and Lectures on Ezra Pound. St. Paul: Graywolf Press, 1987.

This Is My Blood. Covelo, Calif.: Yolla Bolly Press, 1989.

The Bird of Endless Time. Port Townsend, Wash.: Copper Canyon Press, 1989.

Random Essays. Mt. Kisco, N.Y.: Moyer Bell, 1989.

William Carlos Williams and James Laughlin: Selected Letters, ed. by Hugh Witemeyer. New York: Norton, 1989.

Random Stanzas. Mt. Kisco, N.Y.: Moyer Bell, 1990.

Editions, Translations:

New Directions in Prose and Poetry. Norfolk, Conn., and New York: New Directions, 1936–.

Poems from the Greenberg Manuscripts: A Selection from the Work of Samuel B. Greenberg. Norfolk, Va.: New Directions, 1939.

The Fourth Eclogue of Virgil. Muscatine, Iowa: Prairie Press, 1947.

Spearhead: Ten Years' Experimental Writing in America. New York: New Directions, 1947.

Perspectives. New York: Intercultural Publications, 1952–56.

Perspective of Burma (with U Myat Kyaw). New York: Intercultural Publications, 1958.

A New Directions Reader (with Hayden Carruth). New York: New Directions, 1964.

The Asian Journal of Thomas Merton (with Naomi Burton, Brother Patrick Hart, and Amiya Chakravarty). New York: New Directions, 1975.

SECONDARY SOURCES:

Aaron, Daniel. *Writers on the Left*. New York: Harcourt, Brace & World, 1961.

Anderson, Elliott, and Mary Kinzie. *The Little Magazine in America: A Modern Documentary History*. Yonkers, N.Y.: The Pushcart Press, 1978.

Bartlett, Lee. *Kenneth Rexroth*. Boise, Idaho: Boise State University, 1988.

————. *The Sun Is But a Morning Star: Studies in West Coast Poetry and Poetics*. Albuquerque, N.M.: University of New Mexico Press, 1989.

————. *William Everson: The Life of Brother Antoninus*. New York: New Directions, 1988.

Biner, Pierre. *The Living Theatre*. New York: Horizon Press, 1972.

Carruth, Hayden, and James Laughlin. *A New Directions Reader*. New York: New Directions, 1964.

Cherkovski, Neeli. *Ferlinghetti: A Biography*. Garden City, N.Y.: Doubleday, 1979.

Cox, Shelley. *A Personal Name Index to New Directions*. Troy, N.Y.: Whitson, 1980.

Davidson, Michael. *The San Francisco Renaissance: Poetics and Community at Mid-Century*. Cambridge: Cambridge University Press, 1989.

Duberman, Martin. *Black Mountain: An Experiment in Community*. New York: Dutton, 1972.

Duncan, Robert. "On Kenneth Rexroth," *Conjunctions* 4 (1983), 85–95.

Ehrlich, J. W. *Howl of the Censor*. San Carlos, Calif.: Nourse, 1961.

Faas, Ekbert. *Towards a New American Poetics: Essays and Interviews*. Santa Barbara, Calif.: Black Sparrow Press, 1978.

———. *Young Robert Duncan: Portrait of the Poet as Homosexual in Society*. Santa Barbara, Calif.: Black Sparrow Press, 1983.

Ford, Hugh. *Published in Paris*. Yonkers, N.Y.: The Pushcart Press, 1975.

Gardner, Geoffrey, ed. *For Rexroth* (*The Ark,* 14), 1980.

Gibson, Morgan. *Kenneth Rexroth*. New York: Twayne, 1972.

———. *Revolutionary Rexroth: Poet of East-West Wisdom*. Hamden, Conn.: Archon, 1986.

Gifford, Barry, and Lawrence Lee. *Jack's Book: An Oral Biography of Jack Kerouac*. New York: St. Martin's Press, 1978.

Guttierrez, Donald. "Natural Supernaturalism: The Nature Poetry of Kenneth Rexroth," *Literary Review,* 26 (1983), 405–22.

Hamalian, Linda. "On Rexroth: An Interview with William Everson," *Literary Review,* 26 (1983), 423–26.

———. "Robert Duncan on Kenneth Rexroth [interview]," *Conjunctions,* 4 (1983), 85–95.

———. *A Life of Kenneth Rexroth*. New York: Norton, 1991.

Hatlen, Burton, ed. *Sagetrieb,* 2,3 (Kenneth Rexroth Issue, 1983).

Laughlin, James. "For the Record: On New Directions and Others," *American Poetry,* 1,3 (1984), 47–61.

———. "The Art of Publishing: James Laughlin (with Richard Ziegfeld)," *Paris Review,* 89, 90 (1983), 155–93, 112–51.

Levin, Harry. *Memories of the Moderns*. New York: New Directions, 1980.

Lipton, Lawrence. *The Holy Barbarians*. New York: Julian Messner, 1959.

———. "Notes Toward an Understanding of Kenneth Rexroth," *Quarterly Review of Literature,* 9,2 (1957), 37–46.

Malina, Judith. *The Diaries, 1947–1957*. New York: Grove Press, 1984.

Mariani, Paul. *William Carlos Williams: A New World Naked.* New York: McGraw-Hill, 1981.

Meltzer, David, ed. *The San Francisco Poets.* New York: Ballantine Books, 1971.

Miller, Brown, and Ann Charters, "Kenneth Rexroth," *Dictionary of Literary Biography: The Beats, Literary Bohemians in Post-War America.* Vol. 16, part 2. Detroit: Gale, 1983.

Morrow, Bradford. "An Interview with Kenneth Rexroth," *Conjunctions,* 1 (Winter 1981–82), 48–67.

Parkinson, Thomas. *A Casebook on the Beats.* New York: Crowell, 1961.

———. *Poets, Poems, Movements.* Ann Arbor, Mich.: UMI Research Press, 1987.

Perkins, David. *A History of Modern Poetry: Modernism and After.* Cambridge: Belknap / Harvard, 1987.

Smith, Larry. *Lawrence Ferlinghetti: Poet-at-Large.* Carbondale, Ill.: Southern Illinois University Press, 1983.

———. "The Poetry-and-Jazz Movement in the United States," *Itinerary,* 7 (Fall 1977), 89–104.

Tytell, John. *Naked Angels: The Lives & Literature of the Beat Generation.* New York: McGraw-Hill, 1976.

Weinberger, Eliot. *Works on Paper.* New York: New Directions, 1986.

INDEX

Page numbers in *italics* refer to notes.